STANDING ON
HOLY
GROUND

Sandra E. Johnson

STANDING ON
HOLY
GROUND

A Triumph Over
Hate Crime in the Deep South

St. Martin's Press ◙ New York

www.stmartins.com

Design by Kathryn Parise

"I Ain't Noways Tired," written by Curtis Burrell and published by Savgos Music, Inc. © 1978. International copyright secured. Used by permission.
"Neighbors in Dixiana" © CBS Inc. All rights reserved. Originally broadcast on CBS SUNDAY MORNING over the CBS Television Network on November 3, 1985.

LIBRARY OF CONGRESS CATALOGING-IN-PUBLICATION DATA

Johnson, Sandra E.
    Standing on holy ground : a triumph over hate crime in the Deep South / Sandra E. Johnson—1st ed.
        p. cm
    ISBN 0-312-26928-5
    1. Southern States—Race relations. 2. African American churches—Fires and fire prevention—Southern States—History—20th century. 3. Arson—Southern States—History—20th century. 4. African Americans—Crimes against—Southern States—History—20th century. 5. Hate crimes—Southern States—History—20th century. 6. Church maintenance and repair—Southern States—Citizen participation—History—20th century. 7. Southern States—Biography. I. Title.

E185.92 .J64 2002
975'.043—dc21
                                                                2001058852

First Edition: May 2002

10 9 8 7 6 5 4 3 2 1

For Ammie and Barbara

Now Moses was tending the flock of Jethro his father-in-law, the priest of Midian, and he led the flock to the far side of the desert and came to Horeb, the mountain of God. There the angel of the Lord appeared to him in flames of fire from within a bush. Moses saw that though the bush was on fire it did not burn up. So Moses thought, I will go over and see this strange sight—why the bush does not burn up.

When the Lord saw that he had gone over to look, God called to him from within the bush, "Moses! Moses!" And Moses said, "Here I am."

"Do not come any closer," God said, "Take off your sandals, for the place where you are standing is holy ground."

EXODUS 3:1–5 (NIV)

CONTENTS

INTRODUCTION

I sat with Ammie Murray outside of St. John Baptist Church in Dixiana, South Carolina, on an unusually warm Tuesday afternoon in late January 1999. On the surface, we were complete opposites. Ammie was white. I was black. She was a sixty-six-year-old grandmother. At thirty-seven, I was young enough to be her daughter.

The African-American house of worship was almost literally in the middle of the woods, and the area was so remote that I couldn't hear much except for soft winds stirring the trees, birdsong, and cicadas. Despite having spent most of my life in Columbia, I had not realized such a secluded area existed so close to the capital. The land surrounding us bore little evidence of modern times. I felt as if I had stepped back into another century.

Ammie agreed to meet me there after I had called her concerning my interest in writing about St. John and how she and others had risked their lives to save it. I had offered to come to her house, but she suggested we meet at the church. "I feel so much at peace there, and that helps me to remember all of the details of what has gone on over these fourteen years."

While I was talking to her on the phone, her words struck me as strange because I knew the church was where someone had tried to kill her, where vandals had committed unspeakable acts of hatred and depravity, where years of her and others' hard work had gone up in flames. How could she feel at peace there?

I learned the answer as we sat talking beneath tall longleaf pines. Newly freed slaves had cut down pine trees to construct the original St. John Baptist Church. It replaced a Lutheran church, where slaves used to worship with their masters before Emancipation. Completed in the late 1860s, St. John Baptist was only five hundred to six hundred square feet, but for its small congregation, it was a spiritual refuge from a society that refused to recognize their humanity, that they were children of God. I could almost feel their presence, shining down on us like rays from the January sun.

But I had other unanswered questions: How had Ammie marshaled together a veritable army of volunteers who were as racially, politically, and socially diverse as imaginable to rebuild St. John—not once, but twice? What had kept them from giving up despite relentless threats? What had kept the church's congregation from disbanding after enduring decades of attacks from perpetrators of hate crime?

The answers to these questions uncovered concentrically layered stories that spoke of the infinite possibilities and power of faith, perseverance, justice, forgiveness, reconciliation, and, most important of all, love. The answers were as simple as the friendship between two women and as complex as the epidemic of racial intolerance that swept across America and provoked millions of people, including the nation's president, to battle against it. They were centuries old and yet current as today's news.

The four hours Ammie and I spent on that warm winter's day would be the first of countless conversations we would have as this book came into being, and a deep bond formed between us. But we had met once before, on November 8, 1998. I came to the church that day to attend a rededication ceremony marking the completion of the most recent rebuilding effort with my parents, George and Mary Johnson.

Dad had gotten my mom and me involved with St. John as volunteers, along with fellow members of the Columbia Travelers RV Club, a group of people who owned recreational vehicles and enjoyed camping trips together. The club was mainly composed of ex-military African-American families like ours, and each year they did a community service project. After Dad spoke of St. John needing volunteers, the club decided to do all of the painting at the church.

He carried on so much about what a great time they were having and how wonderful all the other volunteers were—especially a lady named Ammie Murray—that I figured I was missing out. In October of 1998, I went down and helped with the painting. Although there had been some media coverage about St. John, prior to meeting Ammie, the only thing I remembered about it was that it had been burned down by someone.

I returned to the church when Dad invited me to go with him and Mom to the rededication on November 8. What I saw there was still a fairly rare sight in this country—a church filled with an equal number of blacks and whites; people attired in Sunday finery chatting with those wearing threadbare jeans, plaid shirts, and cowboy boots; prominent business owners, attorneys, and politicians among blue-collar folks. Regardless of their backgrounds, all of them expressed their love for St. John, its congregation, and Ammie.

To loud applause, Ammie made her way to the podium. Her brilliant smile belied the discomfort she had to be feeling—she had broken her left arm a few days before and wore a cast that appeared to weigh as much as she did. Her left hand was slightly swollen and blotchy with bruises.

But the story she began to tell from the podium made me forget about her arm and everything else. She told of the years of racist vandalism that culminated in the church's total destruction on New Year's Eve, 1984. She spoke of how she had gotten involved with helping to rebuild it as a result of her friendship with one of its members; how others responded to her calls for help; and how they and the congregation had twice accomplished the impossible. I was swept up in the story, but was saddened when she broke down crying about the recent death of a cherished family member. It took several minutes for her to compose herself enough to continue on. And from what she recounted, I also sensed the absence of another person important to her, someone who had played an essential role with her at St. John.

She received a standing ovation after speaking, and we had a hard time making our way through the crowd that gathered around her. Once we did, she and my parents exchanged hugs, and Dad introduced me to her.

"Darlin', thank you for helping us out down here," she told me as she embraced me.

A half-day painting walls paled in comparison to what she and others had done, but I told her that I had enjoyed doing it and stepped aside so some other people waiting to speak to her could do so.

As I discovered later, the compelling saga I heard that afternoon had not been fully told, despite a segment on *CBS Sunday Morning*, articles in the *New York Times* and *Los Angeles Times*, and coverage by various other news organizations. The more I thought about it, the more I thought it would make an important subject to write about, so I called Ammie, and we met that beautiful winter day in the churchyard where she shared more of the story with me.

As the afternoon neared its end, we walked about the grounds, including the cemetery with a grave and an old stump that held special significance for her. She had collapsed on the stump after first seeing the church's 1984 New Year's Eve desecration. In the following years, it continued to be a place of rest and solace. The cemetery ended at the edge of thick woods, and through the trees, we heard the hum of cicadas, the calls of mourning doves, and sounds of other wildlife resonating from the Congaree River, which flowed nearby. I delighted in our discovery of fresh deer tracks.

We had almost made a full circle around the churchyard when she stopped at a massive oak tree. Leaning against it, she looked up at the church that was outlined by a clear sky as blue as a robin's egg. As if talking more to herself than to me, she said, "Anybody who comes here can see that this is a place of worship. This is sacred, holy ground."

As if in agreement, a breeze blowing in from the river rustled the pines.

BOOK ONE

ONE

Silent Tongue

The morning of January 2, 1985, started out ordinarily enough for Ammie as she maneuvered her Topaz sedan into its customary parking space behind the small office building where she worked. Winter's chill made the air crisp and glittered the ground with frost. She looked forward to getting into the office and finding out how her close friend and coworker, Barbara Simmons, had enjoyed the holidays.

Gathering her purse and briefcase, she thought back to the day seven years earlier when she first met Barbara. The shy, full-figured African-American woman had come into Ammie's office looking for a job. With large, golden hoop earrings that swayed in cadence with her words, Barbara said, "Joanne Helms is a friend, and she told me you may need some help over here."

Indeed, Ammie had mentioned to their common acquaintance, who ran a store and restaurant where Barbara worked part-time, that work was running her ragged. In a man's world of labor-union organizing, she was the business manager for a laborers' union and office manager for an ironworkers' union. She loved working for the two unions, which shared an office across the bridge from downtown Columbia. However, between her career, a recent marriage, raising two teenage daughters from her first marriage, maintaining a home, and being active in Democratic Party events, she was barely keeping up.

Ammie explained to Barbara that Charles Murray, who headed the union, needed to be consulted before any hiring decisions were made. As they continued to talk, Ammie guessed that Barbara, at best, only had a high school education, but there was something about her easy smile, warm openness, and shy but determined manner that Ammie liked. She hired her on the spot, doubting that Charles would take issue with her spontaneous decision. After all, in addition to being president of the union, he was also her husband.

Barbara came in each Monday, Wednesday, and Friday. In the beginning, she mainly cleaned the offices, but as time passed, Ammie taught her how to type, file, and help out with other clerical tasks.

The two women often had the place to themselves, and it was during those quiet periods that they opened up to each other about their lives. A strong friendship soon replaced what had been only a business relationship—though Barbara insisted on calling her Miss Ammie, no matter how many times Ammie asked her to drop the "Miss." As far as she was concerned, she and Barbara were equals, regardless of the differences in their racial, educational, and economic backgrounds.

They shared an admiration for Mary Modjeska Monteith Simkins, an African-American octogenarian who had been a local civil rights leader for decades. They looked up to Ms. Simkins because of how she had broken away from the conventional roles that black women of her generation were normally relegated to, and she became a trailblazing advocate for minorities, the poor, and the disenfranchised. No one was too lowly for her aid and no one too high for her sharp, witty criticism. Even at her advanced age, she still spoke occasionally at various functions around the state, and whenever she did, Ammie, Barbara, and Barbara's husband, Willie, went together to see her.

As one of the few female union officials in the country, Ammie particularly identified with the difficulty of adopting an untraditional role. She also had a high profile in the state Democratic Party. All of this resulted in her being under constant pressure, and Barbara continually looked for ways to cheer her up. Like many Southern women, Barbara often showed her affection through cooking. Ammie would frequently come into the office to discover that Barbara had placed a plate of hot, deliciously fried fish on her desk or had fixed her a ham and buttermilk biscuit made from scratch. Other times Barbara would put a few pieces of candy or a little card on the desk—never anything expensive, but always from the heart. Sometimes the small gifts bordered on being gags. Once, Barbara found a little plastic pig, put it in a jar, and poured some dry pinto beans around it. The gift went on Ammie's desk with a small hand-lettered sign—PORK AND BEANS.

Both women were overjoyed when Barbara and Willie discovered they were going to have another child. They already had two sons—Willie Lee and Jonathan—along with Barbara's teenage daughter, Robin.

Ammie couldn't stop herself from worrying about the pregnancy; Barbara was in her late thirties and nearly fourteen years had passed since her last pregnancy. Although she wasn't much older than Barbara, both joked that she was acting like a mother hen because of how she nagged Barbara to take her vitamins and get plenty of rest.

When Willie called to tell Ammie that Barbara had given

birth to a baby boy they named Michael, she couldn't wait to get to the hospital to see them. A nurse blocked her as she stepped out of the elevator at the hospital's maternity ward. "Visitation is for family only," she said.

"I am family," Ammie told her.

Eyeing her blond hair and blue eyes skeptically, the nurse asked, "What relation?"

"Grandmother to the baby," she answered, sailing past without a backward glance.

Barbara got a big laugh out of the escapade and added, "We're salt and pepper, Miss Ammie. We season each other."

After getting out of the car, Ammie walked to the rear entrance of the office and wondered what surprise Barbara would have on her desk that morning. It hadn't been long since Barbara had returned to work from maternity leave, and Ammie hoped that the Simmonses had enjoyed Michael's first Christmas.

She opened the door. The office was strangely quiet and devoid of the aromas of Barbara's good cooking and freshly brewed coffee.

"Barbara?" she called out.

No answer.

"Are you here?"

Looking around, she saw that the empty room appeared exactly as it had before they closed it for the holidays.

Walking in the next room, she called her friend's name louder. Again, silence greeted her.

Growing worried, she searched another room and another, until she ended up in the conference area. She found her there.

Barbara sat slumped over in one of the fold-out metal chairs, her face buried in her arms which she gripped tightly as if in great pain.

Ammie dropped to her knees to face her. "Barbara! What's wrong?"

Slowly, with obvious effort, Barbara raised her head, tears

streaming down her dark face. She was so distraught, she couldn't speak. Ammie knew something horrible had happened.

"Is it Mikey?" she asked, using her nickname for Michael.

She shook her head, tears steadily flowing.

Ammie asked about the other three children and Willie. Barbara shook her head after each name, and Ammie was nearly in tears herself trying to figure out what had happened. In all the years they had been friends, she had never seen Barbara so upset.

"It's the church," Barbara was finally able to say.

"St. John?" Ammie asked. She had heard Barbara frequently speak of her small Baptist church out in the country. Ammie had never seen the church but had helped her make flyers or programs whenever any special events were held there.

Nodding, Barbara said, "Somebody's hurt the church real bad."

Barbara agreed to take Ammie down to St. John. They went later that afternoon, allowing time for Barbara to pick up Robin and Michael.

As Ammie followed her to the church, she realized she had driven past the turnoff to the dirt road leading toward St. John probably hundreds of times. Her mother's people had lived a few miles away since colonial times. During her frequent visits to them, she had never noticed the turnoff because it was nearly hidden by pine and scrub trees, and it bore no street sign, only a black-and-white numerical county marker.

After less than one hundred yards, the blacktop disintegrated into a hard-packed dirt road that was so brutal, the entire Topaz shook and barely held together as she followed the cloud of dust rising behind Barbara's car. She felt like she was driving over endless rows of railroad tracks.

The denseness of the trees and brush choked out even the sounds of traffic from nearby Interstate 26, and the tops of the trees intertwined to create live canopy. Had she freed her imag-

ination, she could picture herself in another time, before the
frenetic pace of modern living.

They arrived at the church, a simple whitewashed cinder-
block building set in a clearing beneath spiraling longleaf pines.
The first thing she noticed as she got out of her car was that all
the bulbs on the light poles had been shot out. Looking around,
she saw that every single window of the church and the adjoining Sunday school building was shattered. The ground was covered with bullet casings, crumpled beer cans, and cheap liquor
bottles. "KKK" had been carved in huge letters across the
wooden front doors that were chopped up and barely hanging
by the hinges.

Taking a deep breath, Ammie stepped inside. Still shaken,
Barbara remained inside her car with her two children.

More bullet casings crunched beneath her feet. Whoever had
done this had shot bullets into the pews, tearing them to pieces
and then knocking them over. What they hadn't shot, they took
an ax to. An old woodstove in the corner lay smashed to bits, as
did the water cooler in the vestibule. Her heart ached more
when she saw what they had done to the piano. As she was a
former music teacher, pianos were precious to her. Someone
had chopped it up, breaking it apart and even chopping the
strings inside. It was destroyed so badly, she couldn't tell whether
or not it had been an upright.

The vandals had chopped the chairs on the pulpit, including
the pastor's. They got hold of the crucifix, chopped at the figure
of Christ, and left his arms to dangle from the nails. They threw
what was left of his body on the floor before the altar amid
condoms—used ones. She struggled to keep her composure and
hold down the nausea rising in her throat.

Barbara summoned the courage to get out of her car and
followed Ammie at a distance along with the kids. They trailed
her into the Sunday school building.

Ammie felt acutely nauseated when she saw what the vandals
had done to the Communion cloth. She remembered Barbara
speaking of how the ladies of the church had raised funds to

order it and dressed in their finest to drive up to Columbia and buy it from Tapp's, an upscale department store. The Communion cloth had been removed from its storage area, spread on the floor, and defecated on.

Not able to take it anymore, Ammie turned to Barbara and the children. "Let me walk out in the cemetery for a while, you know, kind of give me a few minutes to myself."

It only got worse. One of the church members had died recently. The vandals had driven onto his grave and spun their tires through the freshly dug soil until his vault showed through and bore tread marks. Ammie ran to the edge of the cemetery and vomited.

She sat on a stump near the border of the cemetery, trying to gather enough strength to stand, and wondered what kind of people could do something so monstrous. More important, what could she do about it?

Steadying herself, she forced herself up. Though still weak from nausea, she managed to find Barbara, who had taken the kids back to the car and sat waiting for her. Ammie looked down into the frightened face of her friend. "I don't know what I'm going to do, but I'm going to do something. I'll call you later on tonight."

As Barbara drove home, she realized she had broken what fellow congregation members called the "silent tongue," the agreement not to speak to anyone outside of St. John about the mounting vandalism that had now culminated in the complete destruction of the church. They had pleaded with her not to tell for fear of what the church's attackers would do in retaliation. She understood their fear. Out of the forty-six counties in South Carolina, the Klan was strongest in Lexington County, where the majority of the congregation lived and where the church was located. When the KKK, formed in Tennessee by six ex-Confederate soldiers, first entered the state in 1868, it gained a foothold in the upstate, where fewer African Americans lived and could mount an armed resistance. For example, in York County, which bordered North Carolina, nearly 80 percent of all white males were Klansmen by 1870. As decades passed, its strength spread, and even public officials such as Gov. Coleman Blease (1911–1915) openly advocated the lynching of African Americans as "necessary and good." Elderly members of St. John had vivid memories of the "Invisible Empire" attacking and murdering blacks with impunity.

At its height in the mid-1920s, between four and five million Americans belonged to the Klan. Despite the hate organization losing strength and splintering into various factions, it still remained a dangerous force within the state, particularly in areas like Lexington County, historically sparsely populated by blacks. Indeed, blacks only composed about 12 percent of the county. Just two other counties—Pickens and Oconee, both in the upstate—counted lower percentages of African-American residents. Of the two Klan factions remaining active in the state, one of them, the Christian Knights of the Ku Klux Klan, was based in Lexington. The other was the Keystone Klan, centered in the upstate county of Laurens. It was difficult for law enforcement officials to pinpoint accurately how many members belonged to either cell, but it appeared that the Christian Knights was the more dominant of the two. Even as recent as the late 1970s, they drew two to three hundred people to their rallies.

Before their Grand Dragon, Horace King, helped start the Christian Knights in the state, he belonged to the United Klans of America. Based in Tuscaloosa, Alabama, the UKA was the most violent of the more than one hundred Klan factions scattered across the country. Its members were responsible for the 1961 attacks against the Freedom Riders, the 1963 bombing of Birmingham's Sixteenth Street Baptist Church—in which four young black girls died—and the 1965 murder of Viola Liuzzo as she drove Selma civil rights marchers. King found Lexington County to be fertile ground for recruiting poor whites looking for someone to blame for their troubles. The fact that he lived only about a fifteen-minute drive from St. John and held Klan meetings within a few miles of church was more than unnerving to the isolated congregation.

But while Barbara recognized the reasons for keeping the "silent tongue," it had not been making things better through the years, only worse. She had no choice but to break it and hope the others would understand. She hoped they would realize she would do whatever she could to protect them and St. John.

She had fallen in love with the church and its people the first time Willie took her there. It had been his maternal grandparents' place of worship, and he had attended it since childhood along with his brothers and sisters. He told her how he grew up watching his granddaddy, who was the senior deacon, open the church up every Sunday and prepare for services. In the winter, that meant chopping and toting wood to feed the potbellied stove so that the place would be nice and warm. In the summer, he opened the windows and made sure there were enough paper fans from a local funeral home for people to cool themselves with. When he died, a fellow named Roscoe Sulton took over his church duties and also became a surrogate grandparent to Willie and his siblings.

St. John's congregation had always been small. On a good Sunday, a few dozen people came. Most of them were frail and bent with age—children or grandchildren of the slaves who lay in the cemetery that formed a semicircle around the sides and rear of the cinder-block building. Keeping with old ways brought from West Africa, some of the graves were still decorated with plates, silverware, clocks, and other favorite personal objects of the dead below, things that helped them journey from this world to the next in peace. The items were purposely broken to free the person's spirit of the need to return. Breaking the things or punching holes in them also severed death's chain, preventing other family members from immediately following the deceased. Because West Africans viewed the world of the dead as being a watery, upside-down one beneath that of the living, it was important that graves be located near water—in St. John's case,

near the Congaree River—and that the deceased's broken pos-
sessions be turned upside down. Clocks, set to the time of death,
symbolized that while alive, blacks were bound to the oppressive
schedules of whites, but through dying, were finally free.

To Barbara, sometimes it seemed as if time had forgotten
about the tiny house of worship located in the middle of what
had once been a large plantation that stretched to the banks of
the Congaree, which flowed about one mile behind the cemetery. After talking to Willie, Deacon Sulton, and others about
recent changes, she wished that time had indeed left St. John
alone. The recent years had been cruel.

St. John had enjoyed a serene existence for generations until
Carolina Eastman, a large chemical plant, came in 1962 and
bought up 2,300 acres just beyond St. John's 1.5 acres. In an
effort to lure the plant to Lexington, state government agreed
to reroute Old State Road, the road that used to run in front
of the church. They dead-ended the road right in front of the
churchyard. Traffic that used to run down it was siphoned off
to Old Pine Plain Road to the north. The change left St. John
isolated and vulnerable. Trouble started not long after.

It hadn't been so bad in the beginning. The vandalism
seemed the work of mischievous kids with too much time on
their hands rather than that of anyone malicious. Church members would make their way to services—held the second and
fourth Sunday of each month—to find the grounds littered with
empty soda and beer cans, cigarette butts, and food wrappers.
More of the same was found inside along with crudely spray-
painted images on the walls of things like stick figures, a school
bus, an umbrella.

They started locking the place up at the end of services. The
break-ins continued. They put stronger padlocks on the doors
only to find them broken and pried open. Rosa Bell Eleazar,
who grew up attending St. John and lived next door, spoke to
Barbara and the others of lying in bed at night and hearing
the sounds of cars driving up to the church at all hours of the
night—and of doors slamming, laughter, and talking and the

church bell ringing when it wasn't supposed to. She saw lights flashing, too.

She would lie in bed, nearly too terrified to breathe. Like most of the rest of the congregation, she was up in years. She had to think about not only her own safety, but that of her small grandsons who lived with her, as well. Yes, there was the police, but what would happen when they weren't around or couldn't respond quickly enough? And what would they care about a handful of poor black folks out in the middle of the woods? She lay in bed waiting for dawn and did the only thing she knew to do—keep the "silent tongue."

There was no order to the pattern of the trouble. Sometimes incidents happened in quick succession. Other times, uneventful months went by. But there was always a next time, and it would always be when no one was around to discover who was doing it or why. Then, things started getting smashed and stolen. The windows were favorite targets for attacks, and the church's only source of water—an outdoor water pump—was the favorite of thieves. Vandals also assaulted the cemetery with what looked like four-wheelers or dirt bikes to rip up the grass, knock over and shatter tombstones, and destroy mementos and flowers laid on graves.

When she joined St. John and learned of what had been going on, Barbara was conflicted about what to do. While she thought telling the authorities would help, what if it didn't and someone got hurt or killed because of her advice? On the other hand, keeping silent appeared to be increasing the danger, too. The only other way out was for everyone to abandon the church, but she knew that was not an option. That church meant everything to the few who clung to it. They would rather die and be buried along with their slave ancestors than leave it. Right or wrong, they wanted to keep the silent tongue, and she felt she had to respect their wishes. Being a newcomer, she believed it wasn't her place to go against them.

Willie was optimistic about the trouble nearing its end, and his optimism encouraged her. The husband of one of the members knew how to install water pumps, and he promised to fix the broken one. Once he did that, Willie planned to build a small cinder-block enclosure over the pump to protect it from any more attacks. He would also use more of the cinder block to build a Sunday school building. That would pick everybody's spirits up and maybe help convince some former members, who had left because of the vandalism, to return. Meanwhile, he would replace the broken glass. Pretty soon, the church would be as good as new, and before long, whoever was bothering them would lose interest and move on.

He desperately wanted to believe that, and so did Barbara. She helped him clear away the glass and clean up. She threw herself into teaching Sunday school, serving on the usher board, being the church's secretary, and doing anything else they needed her to do. Because she and Willie were one of the few couples in the congregation with cars, they picked up many of the members before church and took them back home after the services.

As he promised, Robert Clybourn installed a new water pump. He was a member of another church, but his wife, Bessie, had been attending St. John for years. She came down before services on Fridays with her children to give the place a good cleaning although she worked two, sometimes three jobs and had her own home to keep up.

After putting in a full day at his job as a crane operator at a steel mill and grabbing some of Barbara's cooking, Willie came over during the evenings and worked on the water pump house and Sunday school building. One evening, he discovered the water pump smashed again. Someone had even stolen some of the cinder blocks.

He got more and had Mr. Clybourn return and repair the pump again. Once he finished construction, Willie gave both structures a dazzling coat of whitewash. After putting a sturdy padlock on the Sunday school building, he put one on the pump house, feeling sure that now the church's water supply was secured.

A small stream called Tom's Creek fed St. John's well. They used it to fill the outdoor baptismal pool that Willie had also built. Before they had a water pump, members used to tote water from the creek in buckets to the baptismal pool. It was some of the best, purest water Barbara had ever tasted. It was so good that people from other churches asked to be baptized there. Rosa Bell Eleazar got baptized in it twice.

The attacks worsened as the months passed. During one Sunday service, Barbara sat in church listening to elderly Rev. John Shepherd deliver his sermon. Even though he stood only a few feet in front of the congregation, his voice had faded so badly as he aged that they pooled together some money for a microphone and amplifier for him to use in order to hear him. As he clutched the mike and weakly preached into it, Barbara heard an unmistakable sound—a gunshot. She looked around and could tell by the faces of the others that they had heard it, too.

She knew the area was popular with hunters. Because of the surrounding woods and nearness to the Congaree, the area was chock-full of deer, rabbit, duck, and other game. During hunting season, it wasn't uncommon to hear distant shots, but this didn't sound like that. It sounded like somebody aiming at St. John.

It had gotten to the point that some of the assailants grew bold enough to come out during the day—mainly white, pimply-faced teenage boys who looked like they got their bravado from six-packs of beer. Mrs. Eleazar had been out chopping wood in her front yard when a carload of them raced past her, hurling obscenities and raising a cloud of dust from the dirt road.

Bessie Clybourn was getting to where she was afraid to come down Fridays to clean and prepare the church for Sunday services. While cleaning, she could hear gunfire, and later, she, Barbara, Willie, Deacon Sulton, and others discovered bullet holes in the entrance doors and pews.

Toward the close of one service, Barbara's sister-in-law, Pat Lowman, heard odd noises coming from outside that didn't sound like the deer or other animals that occasionally strayed onto the property. Sliding off the pew, she tried not to disrupt

Reverend Shepherd's sermon as she tiptoed to the front doors.

Opening the doors and stepping out into a cold drizzle, Pat felt her heart leap up into her throat. She found herself facing a small gang of white teens unloading dirt bikes from the back of a pickup. The boys looked hardened beyond their years. Cigarettes dangled from the corners of their mouths. They had bandanas tied around their heads, and their faces bore angry, sullen expressions. Some girls had come with them. Ignoring the freezing, wet weather, they wore nothing but skimpy tube tops and too-short cutoffs.

In an instant, thoughts flashed through Pat's mind. Should she confront them alone or call for help? These kids could be strung out on drugs or have weapons. If she called out, she could be placing the others inside in danger.

She stepped out onto the porch, forcing herself to smile while quickly praying, "Good Lord, what am I walking into?"

"Hey!" she greeted them. "What are y'all doing here? Don't you know services are going on?" She was so frightened that even the hairs on her legs felt like they were standing on end.

"Y'all got church going on?" one of the boys asked, a note of skepticism in his voice.

"Yeah. Didn't you see our cars parked out front?"

Shrugging, another said, "We thought y'all had just come out to have some fun, like us."

"No, no. We're here having church. We've got a preacher, people, kids—we're having services." Feeling a little more confident, she tried taking a humorous, motherly approach. She turned to the girls. "My goodness, y'all must be freezing. You're going to catch pneumonia without a sweater or something." She took off her coat and wrapped it around one of the girls, who started giggling.

"Don't you know she needs something on, as cold as it is out here?" Pat asked a boy standing next to them. Then she said, "Listen, I don't want any of you kids to get in trouble. You'd better go before someone else comes out here."

With relief, she watched them grudgingly load the bikes back onto the truck as the girl returned her coat. The kids piled into the truck and drove away just before the service ended.

Neither her relief nor anyone else's lasted long.

Dusk was setting in during a late afternoon service. The congregation heard a car roar by. The crash of glass followed as a bullet smashed through one of the windows, whizzed right above their heads, and then thumped into the wall behind the pulpit.

That was the last straw for Bessie Clybourn. She told Barbara, "I'm not coming back here to get my head shot off. You ought to get yourself and your kids up out of here and leave, too, before you get killed."

Some others left, also. Occasionally, visitors came, but once they saw the vandalism or heard the gunfire, they never returned. A part of Barbara thought Bessie was right; but she also wanted to hold out hope that somehow things would get better.

It appeared to her that Deacon Sulton was taking it harder than anybody. Like the other members—especially Willie—she had grown close to the old man who had become the spiritual pillar of the besieged house of worship and had used his savings and Social Security pension to buy the church its piano. He arrived before everyone else to open the building and was often the first to discover evidence of the latest attack. Barbara hated to see tears fill his eyes after each assault. She watched him lead them in song as the tears streamed down his dark, timeworn face. Out in the cemetery, he often walked from one desecrated grave to the next, sobbing.

With Bessie Clybourn gone, Barbara took over cleaning the church and getting it ready for the two Sunday services each month. She usually went down on Saturdays. As the vandalism escalated, she never knew what to expect. Some days, she would come and see only minor damage, like the Communion candles broken in half, paper fans torn apart, or the offering plates thrown out in the churchyard along with empty beer cans, cheap liquor bottles, remnants of fast-food meals, and other trash.

Other times, urine and feces soiled the entrance porch. Inside, she discovered used condoms on the carpet and tried to force from her mind what kinds of disgusting acts had taken place before the pulpit and the reasons why anyone would choose a church as the place to perform them.

What she often saw made her suspect that Satanists were among the church's many assailants. She would find mutilated animals or parts of them strewn throughout the church or floating amidst rotten leaves in the outdoor baptismal pool. It looked like someone had dipped a finger in blood to write on the walls "Kill," "Death," and "XXX." Blood was smeared on the carpet, too. Whether it was from a human or an animal, Barbara couldn't be sure, though she guessed it was from some type of bird because feathers were frequently around. Sometimes, the carpet was powdered with what looked to her to be flour or cornmeal, and pages were ripped from the church's big Bible.

While cleaning, she was careful not to let the condoms, blood, or dead animals come in contact with her skin. She always wore rubber gloves and used sheets of plastic or old newspaper to remove the filth. Because the water pump had been stolen again, she had to bring water in plastic jugs from her home. Sometimes she brought her older kids and they scrubbed, shampooed, swept, vacuumed, polished, and dusted as fast as they could, hoping each time to finish before carloads of toughs started making their rounds. There wasn't much variation in the things they would spew before speeding away in souped-up cars: "Niggers!" "Go home, niggers!" "We hate niggers!" "We're going to blow your church up, niggers!"

Quickly going to her old sedan, Barbara thought it no wonder the congregation was petrified with fear. This couldn't go on much longer. Her children didn't even want to come to St. John anymore. The windows were being broken out so frequently that Willie kept a supply of glass panes at the house. Some of the keys on the precious piano that Deacon Sulton had sacrificed to buy were so damaged, the piano couldn't be played anymore. They had to sing all the hymns a cappella. Hardly a month passed that they didn't discover new slugs studding the pews, walls, or pulpit. It was only a matter of time before a bullet hit and killed a member or one of the attackers made good on the threat to dynamite the place, maybe with all of them inside.

Even given the present situation, Deacon Sulton was already dying from pure heartache. Barbara didn't know how much more the eighty-four-year-old could take. As Thanksgiving of 1984 approached, he told Willie, "Son, sometimes you've got to stand and stand alone, but God will be with you. Whatever you do, keep the doors of St. John open."

Willie gave him his word that he would. Barbara did the same.

She arrived at the church early with her kids the next Sunday service, noticing that Deacon Sulton and his wife, Mary, apparently had gotten there moments earlier and were walking toward the building. Gathering up the new Sunday school books she needed to distribute, her purse, and a pitcher of water so that she and others would have something to drink despite the inoperable water pump, she shooed the kids toward the entrance. She had barely made it past the doors before she heard Deacon Sulton's screams from inside the church. In her rush to get to him, she nearly toppled over him. He had fallen to his knees amidst the shattered glass blanketing the floor. Barbara looked up, seeing the latest destruction that had rendered the old man incoherent. Nearly every window of the place was shattered; pews had been knocked over, the pastor's chair slit apart. She noticed that the front doors had almost been busted from their frames.

"Just look!" Deacon Sulton cried out. "Just look! Why do they keep doing this? Why, Lord? Why? This isn't right!"

His screams and crying caused others, pulling up in their cars, to race inside. Hyperventilating, Mary Sulton collapsed onto the floor beside her husband. Barbara tried to help pull the elderly couple from the floor. The broken shards of glass had cut through their clothes, imbedding into their flesh and drawing blood. Oblivious of his wounds, Deacon Sulton sobbed in anguish, his entire body shaking.

Barbara and others carried the two outside and got them into a car. Continuing to sob as he was being driven away, Deacon Sulton cried that he didn't want to leave his church.

Those who remained gathered outside under the trees in a loosely formed circle. Many of them eyed Barbara anxiously, imploring her not to break the silent tongue. They would fix everything that had been broken. The Lord wouldn't allow "the badness" to keep on much longer, surely. Barbara wondered if they were trying to convince her or themselves.

She could make no promises about remaining silent. Her kids—Robin, Willie Lee, and Jonathan—asked her why no one spoke out about what was going on. When she was only able to give them vague excuses, they responded to her, "Mom, maybe you need to do something."

Willie and a couple of men quickly patched the church back up, but her children's words lodged in her mind.

On November 24, 1985, a few days after the attack, Deacon Sulton died. A heart attack was listed as the cause of death, but Barbara knew what had really killed him. They buried him in the cemetery where he had spent so many hours weeping as he walked amidst sacrilege, asking God when it would stop.

Vandals struck again on New Year's Eve, leaving the church in utter desecration. As if it were a personal assault, they drove onto Deacon Sulton's grave, spinning their tires through the mounded earth until they seared his casket with tread marks.

Upon discovering the grave, Barbara stood in the churchyard along with the others. At first she was too shocked to cry, but as she took in the scene of depravity, the tears came and, once unleashed, overwhelmed her. As she wept and tried to console the other grieving church members, wind stirred the pine tree boughs, and from somewhere she heard a voice as clear as her own—"Now is the time to open your mouth." She had to speak out. She wasn't sure whom to approach, but she knew she had to tell someone—and soon. She could keep the silent tongue no longer.

The next day, she forced herself to go into the office but

could only make it as far as the conference room before col-lapsing onto one of the metal folding chairs. The mounting grief she had been holding in check for so long was too unbearable now. She was vaguely aware of Ammie calling her name from the back entrance but couldn't pull herself together enough to answer. All she could do was cry.

Ammie finally got her to open up and take her to see the destruction for herself. Now, as she drove home with Robin and infant son, Michael, her grief eased a little. Perhaps there wasn't anything Ammie could do to help, but Barbara knew she would try everything possible. It gave her hope that at least St. John wasn't alone anymore.

TWO

Lifted Hands, Open Hearts

As Ammie drove away from the desecrated site, she couldn't believe what she had just seen. The more she thought about it, the angrier she got. What kind of sick, perverted, disgusting excuses for human beings had done such a thing? Even though she didn't tip the scales past one hundred pounds, had she gotten her hands on whoever had done it, she could have torn them apart.

Once she got home, she slammed the door shut behind her and snatched up the phone. She called the first person who came to her mind—Rev. Robert Sims, her pastor at Ebenezer Lutheran. Located in downtown Columbia, it was one of the oldest and largest Lutheran churches in the state.

Before he could barely say hello, Ammie erupted, raging at

what she had witnessed that afternoon. "The statehouse is only twenty minutes away from that church! How can something like this be going on?" Not letting him get a word in edgewise, she told him about how assailants had even fired into the church during services.

When she paused long enough to let him say something, he asked her simply, "So, what are you going to do about it?"

"I don't know, damn it!"

"Okay, what's first?"

His question forced her to think clearly through her fury.

"Well, first things first. We've got to keep the rain and the other elements out. They've got no windows, no doors."

"Who do you know that might want to help?"

Only one week ago, she had ended a two-year service on Lexington County's grand jury. Through that experience, she had gotten to know important law enforcement officials, including the sheriff, detectives, judges, and others. And then there were people she knew through the labor union and the Democratic Party. Surely, some of them would be willing to help.

Before contacting anyone, she called Barbara and asked when the next church service was. She wondered if she could visit to get the congregation's permission for her to solicit help. Getting their approval was critical. They had been through enough without having her or a bunch of other outsiders bulldozing over them in misguided, though well-meaning, efforts to lend a hand.

Barbara told her the date. "You're welcome to come, Miss Ammie. We'd appreciate anything you can do."

"I'll be there."

After attending Ebenezer Lutheran, Ammie made her way to St. John. On her way to the service, she went over in her mind what she wanted to say. She wondered how the congregation would react to her. Would they think she was just some white, condescending do-gooder in search of a charity case? She could only do her best, speak from her heart and pray that they recognized her genuine compassion and desire to help.

Had it not been for the few cars parked outside, the church would have appeared long abandoned. She eased her Topaz behind one of the cars and cut off the motor.

While gathering up her things, she heard a woman's voice from inside the church pierce the morning's quiet. The woman sang a cappella with such power and beauty that she moved Ammie to tears. When the singer finished, Ammie grabbed some tissue and wiped away her tears.

Barbara, who was an usher, met Ammie at the door, and they threw their arms around each other, whispering so as not to interrupt the service that was already under way. She led Ammie to a seat before taking her place again near the door with the other usher. Ammie sat on one of the metal chairs from the office that Barbara had borrowed because many of the church's wooden pews were too damaged to sit on. Willie smiled a greeting from his seat near the other deacons. Michael tottered over to Ammie and climbed onto her lap.

The service took her back to her childhood when she and her sister, Emmala, occasionally attended church with their family's black housekeeper. Ammie loved everything about it, especially the music. The songs like "Hand Me Down My Silver Trumpet, Gabriel," "Swing Low, Sweet Chariot," and "Jacob's Ladder" captivated her.

After she had married and had her first daughter, Ammie was hired as a children's music director for a prominent white church. She taught the children the spirituals she had heard. She felt the children deserved to know the richness and historical significance of gospel songs. Some in the church protested, saying the kids had no business learning "colored" music. Ammie went toe-to-toe with them. They backed down.

Now, holding little Michael, she saw something amazing. Barbara and the other ushers took up a special collection. Barbara explained to her that at each service, people donated whatever they could spare to help elderly shut-ins or residents of a local nursing home. It didn't matter their color; they received whatever little treat Barbara could find at a flea market or discount store using money from the collection. Amidst the destruction, St. John's first concern was for others.

They had returned to the church, cleared away as much debris as they could, and set upright the few pews still salvageable. Someone had tried to glue the arms back to the figure of Christ, but the glue failed to hold, leaving the arms dangling from the nails once again. Despite it all, they praised God. Ammie wondered if other churches could show the same resoluteness in the face of such tragedy.

Toward the end of services, Willie introduced her and said, "Miss Ammie has something she would like to say."

Placing Michael down on the chair, Ammie walked to the front. "I see what has happened. It's terrible. I wanted to ask your permission to get some people together, maybe a committee or something to see what we can do, starting with getting some doors and windows. I don't know what we can do, but I want to help, I—" Her voice broke as she started crying.

Softly, the woman Ammie heard as she drove up, Katherine Brown, began to sing "Amazing Grace." Reverend Shepherd joined in, then someone else, then another until all the congregation was singing. When Ammie found her voice, she joined in, too. Tears streamed down everyone's cheeks, and no one, not even the men, showed any embarrassment about them. As Ammie looked at their faces, she sensed that while many were still afraid, their fear was matched with renewed determination.

When they finished, Deacon Wallace "Wally" Smith, who was senior deacon and went about things with military precision, said, "All right, all right, now. Sister Murray is here. This is God's way of helping us. Let's assist her in any way that we can on our part because this is something that the Lord is doing. C'mon, c'mon, we got to get a vote. Let's get a vote." Everyone quickly voted to give Ammie permission to help and to contact anyone she thought could be of assistance.

They formed a circle and held hands. Katherine Brown, who

pronounced her first name Kathereen, led them in "Blessed Be the Ties That Bind." As they sang, they slowly swung their arms to the hymn's rhythm, lifting their clasped hands as they reached the higher notes.

After the song, the congregation engulfed Ammie in loving embraces. She tried to remember when she had had a more moving experience and could think only of the births of her children.

It would be a fight to protect the church and bring its defilers to justice, but it was a fight that she was willing to take on. She took courage in knowing that no matter what she had battled throughout her life, she always got in the last punch.

THREE

Who the Hell Is Ammie Murray?

Through serving on Lexington County's grand jury, Ammie had gotten to know most of the area's law enforcement officers. She knew which ones were good and which ones weren't. The best detectives in the county were Derrell "Bulldog" Yarborough and James "Stick" Harris.

Yarborough was white, and had earned his nickname because of his drive to solve cases. Harris was a black man who supervised Yarborough and several other detectives. As a kid, he had earned his nickname because he had been so skinny. The nickname stuck despite the fact that he filled out soundly as a grown man.

Desperate to get the case assigned to the two men, Ammie called the sheriff's department and asked to speak to Sheriff James "Jimmy" Metts.

"He's out of town," Louis McCarty, Metts's assistant, told her.

Unable to disguise her urgency, she told him of what happened at St. John and demanded that Bulldog and Stick be assigned to investigate it. She carried on so long that McCarty gave in.

When he informed Yarborough of the change in assignments, Bulldog replied, "Man, I'm working a homicide."

"Well," McCarty said, "that man's not getting any deader, and this woman's driving me crazy!"

"Ammie Murray," Bulldog repeated the name that sounded familiar. "Who the hell is Ammie Murray?"

"You're going to find out."

She had been born March 30, 1933, in Spartanburg. At the time, Spartanburg was a small city in upstate South Carolina and its main industry was textile manufacturing. Her father's family had lived in the area for generations and were landed gentry, including her great-grandfather who served in the Confederate Army and was a congressional representative during Reconstruction. Her father worked as a cotton buyer for Clifton Manufacturing Company, a textile mill run by the uncle he was named after, Jefferson Choice Evins.

Ammie's early childhood was the stuff of fantasies. She and Emmala, her younger sister, were doted on by their parents and extended family. The two girls whiled away hot summer days in the dim coolness of the downtown movie theater or visiting with their great-aunt Mamie at her vacation home in Myrtle Beach. They also enjoyed trips to visit some of their mother's relatives in Sandy Run, an area in Lexington County.

One of Ammie's favorite relatives was "Uncle Choice," her father's employer and uncle. Apparently, she was his favorite, too. Recognizing her love for music, he bought her first piano when she was four years old. He had the grand piano shipped from England and brought to his house, where she came over and played by ear until she started taking music lessons. The piano was only one of many reasons she loved to come over to the huge house. His collection of carved ivory figurines mesmerized her, as did his long, ornate dining table that was wired with electric buttons under its edges to summon house servants.

He would often take her out to lunch, sending his chauffeur over to pick her up in a limousine. Her short legs dangled from the leather-upholstered seat as she looked out the window at the textile town. They ate wherever she preferred, usually at Silver's or Walgreen's drugstores.

His generosity extended to others as well and highlighted the value he placed on education. In addition to setting aside money for Ammie and Emmala's future college tuition, he also covered the costs, usually anonymously, for numerous other young people to attend college regardless of whether they were related to him or even knew him well. Through this and other kind acts, he showed Ammie that true success was not what a person had, but what he did to help others.

Ammie's idyllic world came crashing down when her dad died in 1946. Though close to her mom, she had always been a daddy's girl, and his unexpected death when she was thirteen left her numb. Her beloved Uncle Choice had died a year before, and another favorite relative—her dad's brother, Robert "Bobby" Evins—had been killed in World War II when his naval plane crashed at sea. Grief-stricken, her grandfather, John Evins, died shortly afterward, and before Ammie knew it, nearly all her father's family was dead.

With her husband dead and most of his family gone, Ammie's mother decided to move with her two young children to Lexington County, where some of her mother's family lived. She found an administrative clerical position with the Veterans Administration hospital in Columbia. At first, they lived out in the country, down in Sandy Run, where she let Ammie have a pet cow. A few months later, they moved to Cayce, a small city across the bridge from Columbia.

Ammie found solace from her grief by throwing herself into schoolwork and extracurricular activities in high school, excelling in everything she did. She made the honor roll, became a cheerleader, played timpani with the marching band, participated in girls' sports, and continued her piano studies. Consequently, she won a scholarship to Coker College in Hartsville, South Carolina.

Though her classes were strenuous, Coker struck Ammie as being as much a finishing school as a college. It appeared to her that the main thing they were being educated for was how to land a rich husband. They wore evening gowns to lectures and were required to take etiquette classes during their freshman year. They were even graded on table manners during each meal, including how daintily they used silverware to eat fried chicken.

While a junior, she married a young man she had dated since high school and within a few short years, her life was transformed from that of a college debutante to that of a young wife and mother of two daughters, Elizabeth "Betsy" and Christina "Christy."

The births of her girls proved to be among the few things that she did not later regret from the marriage which ended in divorce in the mid-1960s. Afterward, Ammie wondered how she could make a living in an era where few jobs existed for her gender that offered adequate pay and benefits. She took a job teaching music. It didn't pay much, but it was better than nothing. An acquaintance mentioned to her one day that he needed help in his office and asked if she wanted the job.

Sensing that it was nothing more than a typist position, Ammie said, "I don't know anything about typing. I'm a music teacher."

Charles Murray responded that she wouldn't have to do much typing. Since he had to spend so much time on the road in his job as manager for the Ironworkers' Union, what he needed was someone who could run the office in his absence,

including talking to contractors and dealing with the ironworkers.

Ammie had known Charles for years on a casual basis, but
she didn't know the first thing about working for a union and
told him so. Assured that she would catch on easily, she agreed
to give him a hand until he could find someone permanent.

Despite her saying that she would only work for a short while,
she couldn't stop herself from approaching the job the way she
did everything else—wholeheartedly and with a determination
to do her best. The first thing she did was to learn as much as
she could about the union. She discovered that its members
worked in some of the most perilous conditions imaginable.
These were people who usually labored high up in the air with
dangerous, heavy machinery and little to protect them from
plunging to their deaths.

What started out as a temporary position turned into a permanent one as Ammie found that she enjoyed the work. She
liked the idea that what she did made a difference, that through
her job, she helped union members and their families. She also
appreciated that the position offered enough income and benefits to get by on.

With the wide latitude Charles gave her, she was able to dem-
onstrate the leadership skills that had laid dormant for years.
People in the construction industry and union organizations
soon took notice of the petite blonde who showed up at high-
powered meetings, participated in negotiations, and represented
union members. Though she always presented herself as a lady—
even wearing dress suits, fashionable pumps, and pearls to construction sites along with a hard hat—she made it clear she
meant business and could play hardball with the best of them.

Charles let another union, one for laborers, use one of the
extra rooms in the office to start a new local. Ammie gave the
new union local a hand, too, helping to set up their office and
get it organized. The laborers' union was so pleased with the
quality of her work that the members made her their business
manager while she also worked for the Ironworkers' Union.

Some men didn't know what to make of her. Many of the business meetings she attended began with introductions around the table, and she got a laugh at how jaws dropped when she introduced herself as a union business manager and not just someone's secretary.

"Excuse me?" one of them would say.

"Ammie Murray," she repeated. "Business manager for the Laborers International Union of North American AFL-CIO local 1293."

It was challenging enough that she was a female in a male-dominated environment. Added to that was the reality of South Carolina being one of the most anti-union states in the country. From trying to unionize industrial sites like the Mack Truck plant in Winnsboro, South Carolina—where she stood in the bed of a pickup singing "We Shall Overcome" with Rev. Joseph Lowery and national union leader Cass Stevens—to negotiating contracts, she met resistance at nearly every turn.

Sometimes the work got downright dangerous. One day in 1975, she was in the office alone when a young man came in. As soon as she looked at him, she realized he was strung out on drugs.

"I just got in from Florida, and I'm looking for work," he said, his eyes dancing crazily.

After he told her the type of job he was looking for, she said, "We don't have a call in for that right now, but if you can give me your name and a phone number where I can get in touch with you, I'll call you as soon as something comes in."

Sitting at her desk, she searched over it for a pad and pencil, but the sound of a metallic click made her head jerk back up.

He gripped a switchblade, its steel blade gleaming in the fluorescent light. "I ain't got time to wait, lady. I need money now."

Paralyzed with terror, Ammie tried to absorb the mind-numbing concept that her life could end within moments. She sat with her back facing the wall and only her desk separated them. From where he stood, he blocked her closest escape route, out the back door to the parking lot.

Realizing that her only hope of survival lay in diverting his attention, she struggled to think of something to do or say. She blurted out the first thing that came to her. "Have you registered to vote?"

"What?" he asked loudly, screwing up his face in shocked confusion.

"If you haven't, you'd better register right away so you can vote for Jimmy Carter," she babbled on while trying to think of her next move. Waving absently toward the window, she went on, "There's a voter's registration van right down the street. You ought to go over there and get registered."

He stared at her, apparently wondering if she were crazier than he was.

Seeing that she had thrown him off balance, she said, "Oh, I hear those cars coming."

"What cars?"

"You don't hear them? The ironworkers are coming back."

He stepped out of her office to see if there was anyone pulling up. When he did, she bolted out of the building.

She never saw him again. He evaded capture by the police even after the following week when a woman in a nearby office building was found stabbed to death.

Her ability to maneuver her way through tough situations impressed Charles. During the days he was in the office, she filled him in on her progress, and he brought her up to date on his, along with what was happening on a regional and national level.

He also introduced her into the area political scene. Like Ammie, he was a staunch Democrat and had been active in the party for years. He encouraged her to accompany him to many of the party functions—from black tie dinners to cookouts and pool parties. At such events, Ammie met members of the established Democratic old guard as well as up-and-coming young leaders. Becoming friends with them renewed a passion for political activism that she had not felt since the days of John F. Kennedy's presidential campaign.

The keen interest she and Charles discovered that they shared led them into campaigning for people such as Tom Turnipseed, who won a position in the state senate, and Richard "Dick" Riley, who twice won the gubernatorial seat before going on to be President Clinton's secretary of education.

Whether because of union business or political activities, Ammie found herself spending more and more time with Charles. In a low-key sort of way, he began courting her. At first, she couldn't imagine a romance between them—he was thirteen years older than she was, and for years she had looked upon him only as a friend, but she enjoyed his dry wit, their common interests, and, more important, how kind he was to Betsy and Christy.

They married in 1977. The first years were blissful. They bought a place on Lake Murray, an enormous lake at the northern tip of the county. Ammie especially loved the weekends there. She and Charles spent them relaxing on their pontoon boat with family and friends or lounging on the deck of their home that overlooked the water.

They formed a zany Southern rat pack with Tom Turnipseed, his wife, Judy, and other young Democrats. Dubbing themselves the Donkey Serenaders, they often got together at parties to perform skits and songs that lampooned themselves and Republicans, especially Congressman Floyd Spence, who was parodied as Pretty Boy Floyd, with a roving eye for the ladies.

Ammie finessed her way amidst political circles as easily as she had within those of the unions and was quickly elected to party leadership positions such as presidency of the Democratic Women's Council. Her rise in stature was matched by Charles's increasing resentment that she had begun to overshadow him. He grew possessive, never wanting to let her out of his sight to the point of maneuvering his way into an honorary membership with the Democratic Women's Council so that he could attend meetings with her.

By 1982, their marriage crumbled. Barbara, who had been working in the office for about six years by then, was amazed that the two were still able to work together though they no longer lived together. In fact, they worked together another two years until his retirement.

Upon leaving the lake house that she had so enjoyed, she bought a home out in the country. After Betsy and Christy graduated from college with honors, they went on to establish their own professional careers and families, but remained close to their mom and saw her frequently.

Ammie settled into her little home off a dirt road with her two dogs, Honey Bear and Max. The place wasn't much, but she made do. She had faced harder challenges before. She didn't realize that her involvement with St. John would be one of the toughest—and most dangerous—challenges she would ever face.

FOUR

Whatcha' Helping That Nigger Church For?

Ammie couldn't quit thinking about St. John. Images of what she had witnessed during her two visits there kept washing over her like waves rhythmically breaking onto shore—the arms chopped from the figure of Christ's body, the bullet holes, the broken glass, the used condoms, Deacon Sulton's grave, Barbara's anguish, the embraces from people who risked their lives for the church.

The longer she thought about it, the more determined she was to get help for them, no matter what. She would contact everyone she knew and those she didn't to form a committee to help the church recover from the brutal attack. She had to get people to help her save St. John. That thought triggered the appropriate name for the new committee to pop into her mind. She grabbed a notepad and scribbled, "Save St. John Baptist Church Committee." If only she could get people to see the destruction with their own eyes, they would want to help, they would want to do something. But first, she had to get them to see.

Detective Yarborough was one of the first who did. The attack on St. John was one of the sickest things he had ever seen, and he wondered how the assailants carried it out without fearing God would strike them dead in the act.

After getting her address from Louis McCarty, he stopped by Ammie's home, and as soon as she opened the door, he recognized her. He had seen her countless times on the grand jury. He, McCarty, and Stick Harris had discussed the St. John case, and the decision was made for him to lead the investigation. Ammie responded, "I've watched you for two years with the grand jury, and if anybody can catch who did this, it's you."

He was used to getting the most difficult and controversial cases. He tackled each one of them with a vengeance, freely admitting he was a workaholic. In the years since he joined the Lexington Sheriff's Department following retirement from the navy, he had developed a network of informants that provided a steady stream of reliable tips. He figured whoever attacked St. John wouldn't be the type to keep their mouths shut about it. The crime was too outrageous not to tell someone else, if no one other than a close friend, and that could give him the break he needed.

Hitting the streets, he told his informants, "I want whoever did this and I want them now. Not later—now."

Within a few days, he received a tip that led him to two white eighteen-year-old boys. Tracking them down, Bulldog interrogated them separately. Years of detective work had taught him the psychological techniques of how to get suspects to crack and, if cohorts existed, to implicate them, too. He got right in the boys' faces, his eyes masked behind dark glasses as he tore apart their flimsy protestations of innocence and weak alibis. Then he posed this question to each of them: "Pretend you're a judge and you have to decide between two defendants. Both of them are guilty, but one is cooperative while the other one is trying to act tough. Who would you go easier on?"

Playing one against the other, he planted seeds of doubt in their minds that the other had agreed to turn state's witness in exchange for a lighter sentence. "C'mon," he said to each of them, "whoever gets to the trough first gets the first drink."

The tactic worked. Although they maintained their innocence, their combined statements implicated not only themselves, but two other white teens. One of them was another eighteen-year-old young man. The other was a younger girl who, judging by the used condoms strewn in front of the altar, had had sex with one or more of the boys during the attack.

Although Bulldog couldn't find any clear evidence that they were active in the Klan that met so near the church, they certainly exhibited the same kind of racist intolerance the hate group espoused and carried it out through their attack on St. John.

He arrested all four of them.

Stick Harris and Sheriff Metts both visited St. John and couldn't have been more pleased with Bulldog's lightning-quick work. However, after being informed that the New Year's assault had only been the worst of a long series of many, they vowed to make protecting the little church one of the department's priorities. Four of St. John's assailants were in custody, but God only knew how many were out there walking the streets, free to return.

For the life of him, Stick couldn't understand why anyone would want to hurt St. John. It wasn't like it had controversial leadership or took aggressive stances on political issues like a few of the other churches in the Midlands area. It simply was a tiny house of worship in the middle of the woods with a handful of members who wanted to do nothing but serve God. He wondered not only why St. John had been attacked, but also how anyone could do it with such hatred and viciousness.

The same questions troubled Sheriff Jimmy Metts. In all the years he had been sheriff, he knew of no other churches that had been assailed by vandals. The idea of a small country church minding its own business being struck like that made him livid. Not only did he order tight patrolling of the area, but he also agreed to serve on the Save St. John Baptist Church Committee.

He realized he would take some heat for it—Lexington County had seldom won acclaim for its race relations. More than a few would lambaste his efforts to help the African-American congregation. He didn't care. After all the years and everything he had done, he was used to it.

Ever since he had been elected sheriff in 1972 at the age of twenty-five—making him at that time the nation's youngest county sheriff—he had been shaking up the county's status quo. He was the first sheriff in the state to hire an African-American deputy. It created a firestorm when black deputies responded to calls made to the department.

His phone rang off the hook. "You sent a nigger out here," "We're not used to having niggers come. We don't want you to do that."

Metts responded, "You called the Lexington County Sheriff's Department wanting a deputy, didn't you?"

"Yeah."

"Well, you got a deputy, and that's what you're going to get from now on."

That Lexington was the base for the state's strongest Klan faction added to the challenges of his job. In the early years of his law enforcement career, he worked as an undercover agent, attending Klan rallies and listening to Horace King's diatribes against the black race and assertions that God had made whites superior. At one point, Metts saw hundreds of Klansmen and supporters attending the rallies. In more recent years, the numbers had dropped dramatically to the point that there were often more undercover agents than Klan members. Still, the group

remained active. Though Bulldog had not uncovered evidence
that the teens who had attacked St. John were members, the
Klan's influence pervaded the area. It was not only among poor
whites in search of scapegoats for their misfortunes, but among
the more affluent who viewed the gains made by blacks through
civil rights legislation as a threat to whites' political and economic domination. In its isolation, St. John had made an easy
target.

In addition to Sheriff Metts, a few dozen others agreed to serve
on the nascent Save St. John Baptist Church Committee. Among
them was Lowell "Butch" Spires. He hadn't known Ammie personally until she asked him to be on the committee. Her name
was familiar, however, due to his being active in local politics,
too—he was a longtime Republican representative on the Lexington County Council. In fact, St. John was in his district. He
had grown up in the area, and all the lazy summer days he had
spent as a boy swimming and fishing in Tom's Creek made him
familiar with the church's location.

Hearing what had happened, he surveyed the damage even
before Ammie contacted him. Like Ammie, he had a visceral
reaction to the desecration, nearly vomiting at the sight of it.
He took note of the "KKK" carved onto the doors. He had had
a run-in with that sorry bunch years ago. While he chaired a
committee for the county recreation commission in the early
sixties, the Klan started holding their meetings in the recreation
building on the grounds of the public ballpark complex. The
ballparks were popular, frequented during the warm months by
area softball and baseball teams.

The Klan locked the doors of the building during their meetings, forcing those playing on the fields—most of them young
mothers with their children—into using nearby bushes to relieve
themselves, since the bathrooms were inside the building. To
make matters worse, Butch discovered one of the Klansmen

served on the same recreation committee that he chaired and had been sabotaging the commission's efforts to keep the Klan out.

Butch kicked the guy out of his position, and the next time the Klan met, Butch packed his truck with every firearm he had and drove out to confront them. "Y'all can't use that building anymore," he told them. "If it was the NAACP locking themselves up here in this building, you'd be screaming and hollering. The ball fields are for everyone's use, and here y'all have got women and children having to go into the woods. It's not fair, and I'm not going to allow it."

One of the men replied, "You're not home all the time, and we know your wife and children are there."

"Look," Butch said, "I know some of y'all, and I know your names. If anything happens to my wife and or my children, you're dead."

Seeing that they weren't getting what they wanted through threats, the Klansmen said they would sue the commission.

"Go ahead," Butch replied.

They actually did get an attorney, but when Butch told the lawyer that he would publicize the fact that he was representing the Klan, the lawyer backed out of the case, and the entire matter ended.

Standing amidst what was left of the church near a creek that had been the site of so many pleasant boyhood memories, Butch burned with anger, and when Ammie called him shortly afterward, he immediately agreed to join the committee—she was going to need all the help she could get.

John O'Leary and his wife, Mary Ellen, had found it impossible to say no to Ammie when she called. They could tell simply from how she spoke that the matter was urgent. They first became friends with her after she and Mary Ellen served on the county grand jury together. The three of them often found their paths crossing at Democratic events as well. John fondly joked that they were the only three Democrats in arch-conservative, Republican-dominated Lexington County.

While Mary Ellen was a math professor at the University of South Carolina, John directed the state's Criminal Justice Academy, the agency responsible for training every law enforcement officer in South Carolina, from city cops to county probation agents to highway patrolmen.

Despite Ammie's description and the fact that some of the desecration had been cleared away by the time of their visit, neither John nor Mary Ellen was prepared when they first saw St. John. They were struck not only by the destruction, but also by the church's isolation. It seemed cut off from the rest of the world—trapped in its solitude.

In all of his years in law enforcement—and there had been many—John had never seen anything approaching what lay before him. A native New Yorker, he assumed he had already seen the worst intolerance in the South when, as a cadet at the Citadel in Charleston, he saw his fellow cadets cheer when the news spread that John F. Kennedy had been assassinated. Scanning the desecration, he realized that assumption was wrong.

He also realized the damages to the church were far beyond what general volunteers could tackle. What St. John needed were skilled craftspeople with extensive experience in construction—people like some of his own employees who worked in the agency's capital improvement division.

Lorenza "Matt" Mathews and his supervisor, Russell Long, were two of the people at the Criminal Justice Academy who John approached about joining the committee. Neither needed any arm-twisting.

Matt was a middle-aged African American originally from a poor farming community in Alabama. One of fourteen children, he had decided that the military offered a way for a better life, and he took it. He had seen more than his share of destruction during his career in the army that stretched across three decades. He had seen it during a tour in the Korean War and saw more of it while stationed in West Germany during the early fifties, when much of that country still lay in rubble. He witnessed even more during two tours in the Vietnam War. Still, what he saw at St. John shocked him.

Russell had some idea of how the church's congregation felt. A few weeks earlier, shortly after he and his wife got their kids off to school and left for work, he received a call telling him that his house had caught fire and was burning to the ground. They lost everything. Fire department investigators couldn't determine what caused it. Russell searched his memory for anything that was awry before leaving the house, but everything had appeared fine. His home had been destroyed as the congregation of St. John's had—without provocation or warning. He understood the pain that came from that. In whatever way he could help, he would.

When Ammie's friends Tom and Judy Turnipseed saw St. John, they were also stunned by its vulnerability and the cruelty of the assault. Without hesitation, they joined the committee she was putting together.

Probably more than anyone else who was joining it, Tom and Judy had insight as to why the white teens struck the church. When they were much younger, they had borne a racism that was as destructive as the kind the four teenagers apparently harbored. Now, even more than the law firm that Tom headed, their main focus was to fight against the bigotry that they had once cherished and built their lives around.

Disregarding the years that have passed, many people, even close family members, had a hard time grasping Tom and Judy's complete transformation in the early 1970s. They remembered how Judy, a direct descendant of Jefferson Davis, participated in the cheers at her Alabama high school when federal officials were trying to integrate it: "Two, four, six, eight! We ain't going to integrate!"

They recalled how Tom didn't consider African Americans as

being really human beings, but instead some sort of subspecies. How he had garnered wide recognition as Gov. George Wallace's race-baiting national campaign director during the 1972 presidential election. How he used his political savvy and organizational skills to help Wallace spread his message of hatred across the country under the guise of populism.

Their journey out of racism was a painful one, one they freely shared with others in hopes that they, too, could make the same journey.

They both were from Alabama but met at the University of North Carolina at Chapel Hill, where they were students. Judy had been raised to believe in "white privilege," that certain things were due her by virtue of her skin color. Within the cocoon of racism, it never dawned on her that blacks should enjoy the same rights she did. Their purpose was to serve whites. Tom had had a similar upbringing that included learning to revere his paternal grandfather known as "Big Daddy," a Klansman who had murdered a young black boy.

The murder occurred after he accused the fourteen-year-old youth of stealing something from his store, explaining that "all niggers steal." Apparently the child relayed the incident to his father because the next day his dad refused to return Big Daddy's greeting when they passed each other in a pasture. Enraged, Big Daddy said, "You'd better speak to me, nigger."

But the man walked on to his home in silence. Big Daddy showed up at the man's home brandishing a shotgun. When the boy tried to defend his father with a hoe, Big Daddy shot and killed him.

In what was exceptional given the time and place—rural, Klan-controlled Alabama during the Depression—Tom's grandfather was convicted of the crime by an all-white jury. He escaped years of imprisonment only because of a pardon from the governor.

Nevertheless, Tom's dad thought the world of his father. Matching Big Daddy's violent hatred toward blacks was his loving attentiveness to his son. Out of loyalty and deference to Big

Daddy, Tom's father looked kindly upon the Klan. Tom recalled his father speaking of the KKK—"Well, son, there's a lot of trash in it now, but there used to be a lot of good people in it, like Big Daddy. They did a lot of good."

Tom carried that belief with him through college, as did Judy. After graduation from college, they settled in Barnwell, South Carolina, where one of Tom's brothers had moved. The young couple started going to a Methodist church, but left when some of the church's literature portrayed white and black children holding hands. Tom became a lay minister at a small rural church where he preached the righteousness of segregation.

His and Judy's racial intolerance propelled Tom to head the South Carolina Independent Schools Association, an organization that founded thirty-five academies throughout the state. Judy supported her husband fully and taught English at one of the newly created schools. On the surface, the reason for the academies' creations was to provide more intensive educational environments, but everyone knew their real purpose was to preserve school segregation.

During his commencement address at one of the academies, George Wallace's older brother Jack took note of Tom and reflected on how his brother needed someone to run his third-party campaign, including the critical need of getting on ballots across the country. He told Tom, "You know George is going to run for president, and you're a real good organizer. You helped organize this school association. Would you help us do this ballot initiative? We're a third party, and we've got to go to all of these different states because the laws are different."

Thrilled by the opportunity, Tom jumped at it, successfully getting Wallace on the ballot in all fifty states. Judy shared his zeal, and she was proud of Tom's prominent position. She worked for the campaign also, organizing and managing the supply office.

But after a short while, the Wallace supporters they met made them begin to look at themselves and recoil at what they saw. During one rally, a fellow from Massachusetts approached Tom.

"Is it true that once Wallace wins, he's going to round up all the blacks and shoot them?"

"Heck, no!" Tom responded.

"Well." The man turned away in disappointment. "Then I don't know whether I'm for him or not."

Incidents like that forced Tom and Judy to question if what they were a part of was right. Increasingly, the answer they arrived at was no. A growing sense of shame ate at them like a toxic chemical. Finally, in 1971, they left the campaign. Upon returning to South Carolina, a meeting with Ralph Nader introduced them to consumer activism, and they discovered that South Carolina utility companies were overcharging low-income residents, a disproportionate number of whom were African Americans. Through involvement in grassroots efforts at rate reform, for the first time in their lives, Tom and Judy worked with blacks as equals toward a common goal. They were both astonished and chastened at how they were welcomed in black communities, how people readily forgave them for their well-known efforts to keep schools segregated and get George Wallace elected president. That blacks were even willing to speak to them surprised Judy. She knew many whites—ingrained from birth to be suspicious and fearful of others—could never respond with such forgiveness.

After attending an NAACP meeting where they heard Harold Boulware, South Carolina's first black family judge, recount how he had to spirit a black defendant out of town in the trunk of his car to avoid a white lynch mob, neither Tom nor Judy could contain the emotion that had been welling inside. Listening to the African American heightened their awareness of how racist they had been and the kind of pain it wreaked. They both began crying on the drive back home. "I can't believe what we've done," Tom said to his wife. "I can see my own responsibility in it."

"Me, too," Judy said through her tears.

"Look, if we don't do anything else, I want us to fight for racial justice."

That's what they did. They never looked back—not when they forced the giant utility companies to slash their rates for the poor, not when they became life members of the NAACP and became civil rights activists, and not when they joined the Save St. John Baptist Church Committee.

Jerry Bellune had seen a lot in his three decades as a journalist. He was editor of the weekly *Dispatch-News.* Before that, he had worked for several other newspapers. He had covered the Pentagon, interviewed presidents, reported from the Middle East and the civil rights battlegrounds in America, but when a stranger named Ammie Murray called him and took him to St. John, he told her that for the first time in his life, his faith in humanity was shaken. He opened his editorial the following week by writing

> Ammie Murray is a petite, attractive woman who carries her years better than I do. She makes up for her size with fierce determination. When she called the other day, I thought she was just another reader ready to bite my head off. There are a few of them that way, and editors develop a sixth sense about them when they snarl at us.
>
> But I was wrong about Ammie. Her tone simply reflected her disgust with a few fellow members of the human family. But she wasn't calling to cuss me out. She was calling to put me to work.

Indeed, she did, quickly adding his name to the roster of committee members, which had grown to sixty in number. Jerry, Ammie, and those already involved were buoyed by the news of the arrests and that the solicitor for the area, Donnie Myers, promised to prosecute the St. John cases in such a way as to put the fear of God—and the law—into the four arrested. Myers, who also volunteered to be on the committee, had unquestionably earned his reputation of being one of the fiercest solicitors in the Southeast and had won so many capital cases that his nickname became Death Penalty Donnie.

The arriving donations offered hope, as well. A thousand-dollar check from the Lexington County Law Enforcement Association matched the thousand that various individuals had cumulatively sent in. A lady by the name of Patricia Quinn gave her piano to replace the one from Deacon Sulton and three gospel groups announced plans for a benefit concert.

On February 15, Ammie, Barbara, and about a dozen other committee members held a press conference announcing that the Save St. John Baptist Church effort had officially begun and that Saturday, February 23, would be the first workday at the church. Anyone wishing to volunteer was welcome to come.

Early that Saturday morning, Barbara bustled around in her kitchen. She had taken on the responsibility of feeding all of the volunteers during workday lunch breaks and making sure there were enough cold soft drinks and iced tea. For much of the night, she had been up frying chicken and cooking other foods. She didn't know if she had prepared too much or too little because no one knew exactly how many would show up. If she erred, she hoped it would be on the side of excess because she couldn't stand the thought of someone going hungry after hours of hard volunteer work.

She wrapped the fried chicken snugly with some aluminum foil. Who would come? Ammie of course, but what about all of the others who said they wanted to help? It was one thing to go to committee meetings to talk and plan, but it was another to put words into real action. The people she met seemed sincere and caring, but would they really come through for a poor, small, black church out in the middle of nowhere? And why? Neither she nor anyone in the congregation had little except heartfelt gratitude to offer in return. She stacked the foil-wrapped food on the table to take out to the car. Her questions would be answered soon enough.

———

The air was crisp and the sky bright as Barbara, Willie, and their kids arrived at the church early, eager to set up and get started with the work. Soon, they were joined by members of the congregation who were physically able to work, which weren't many, but among them were Rosa Bell Eleazar and Magnolia "Miss Mag" Bristow, the oldest member of St. John. She was in her eighties, but that didn't stop her from sweeping out broken glass along with the other ladies. Katherine Brown, the soloist whose singing had so moved Ammie, came, too, although she wasn't a member. Many assumed she was because she often attended and helped out so much, but in actuality, she was a member of St. Paul African Methodist Episcopal, located on nearby Old Wire Road.

As they set to work clearing away glass, Barbara paused, shielded her eyes against the morning sun, and caught sight of Ammie's little Topaz bumping its way down the dirt road toward the church. A smile broke across Barbara's face. Her friend had come just as she promised. But her smile grew wider when she looked beyond Ammie's car. A string of vehicles followed Ammie's representing nearly every make and model of autos from pickup trucks to Mercedes sedans. They had come—just as they had promised. They did care.

The churchyard swarmed with activity as people started with a massive cleanup effort. Dozens of people including Ammie, Barbara, Butch Spires, Russell Long, Mary Ellen O'Leary, and Tom and Judy Turnipseed fanned out across the grounds with chain saws, rakes, axes, and pruning shears to remove some of the trees and overgrowth that nearly hid the church from view. The growth's density had made it hard for patrolling sheriff's deputies to see St. John from the road. Ammie occasionally broke away to make quick spot checks to make sure that the overall campaign was progressing smoothly, and Barbara divided her time between helping to clear off the grounds and getting lunch set up.

While they worked on the grounds, Willie, Deacon Wally Smith, Sheriff Metts, and a number of the other men emptied the inside of the building. They moved all of the furniture and other items outside and piled everything that was damaged beyond repair in a heap to be hauled off while stacking what little was salvageable together and securing it under tarp.

Jerry Bellune seemed to be everywhere at once with his camera and notepad. When he snapped a picture of Butch cutting down a sapling, Butch groused, "Don't do that to me." He was there to work, not to win any public recognition.

John O'Leary and Matt Mathews rumbled up in the dump truck that would be used to haul away debris. A high pile already awaited them. The old truck belonged to the Criminal Justice Academy. To avert criticism from his numerous political opponents that he was using state property to help a private church, John had retrieved it from his department's junkyard where they stored vehicles and equipment too decrepit for official use anymore.

Ammie waved at them, wondering why John drove with one arm hanging out and gripping the driver's side door. She understood why after he hopped down from behind the wheel. The door fell off, clattering to the ground.

"What in the world?" one of the volunteers asked.

"It fell off when we stopped to gas up, too," John said sheepishly as he repositioned it.

"John, you've got to get another truck for us to use," Matt said, laughing as he came around from the passenger side. "This one is a piece of junk."

"Yeah, yeah, I know."

John and Matt put on their work gloves, and Matt quickly surveyed the progress. Ammie and the rest of the committee had taken note of the way Matt knew every facet of construction, including who were some of the best craftsmen they could tap for volunteer labor and where were the best suppliers for building material at the lowest costs. He had already managed to pull a few strings to get donations of some material.

All of that in addition to his gentle yet self-assured manner made him their natural choice for the general construction manager. The same attributes had contributed to his success in a similar, though paid, position with the Criminal Justice Academy. Indeed, he was one of the highest-ranking African Americans in the agency. John knew that this fact rankled some of his white subordinates, but if Matt picked up on their resentment, he didn't let on.

The two of them loaded the dump truck, and Ammie went inside the church to see how it was coming along. With it completely empty, it was easier to assess not only the surface damage, such as the broken windows, but the more serious structural damage—and there was a lot of it. Many of the structural problems existed before the most recent attacks. The congregation was poor and hadn't been able to keep up maintenance. From new plumbing and wiring to wall paneling to a new roof, the church literally needed rebuilding from the ground up.

She realized it was going to take many more workdays, perhaps hundreds to finish it. She also realized they needed much more money. When she had managed to get two thousand in donations, she had been overjoyed, but assessing the extent of the damage in the cold daylight, she knew that the money was just a drop in the bucket.

But they would take one day at a time, and the present one was pretty good, Ammie thought as she looked over the working crowd. It was pretty damned good.

She and Jerry made another visit to St. John for Sunday services to give an update. To the beaming smiles of the congregation, Ammie told them, "About sixty of your friends were out here yesterday, and they're coming back the next Saturday."

Though the workday had been both mentally and physically exhausting, Barbara felt energized as she looked at her friend who had brought so many to help. They had a long way to go, but they had made a good start. She was also relieved that the four assailants had been arrested and with such speed.

Willie, Reverend Shepherd, and the rest of the congregation shared her relief. They were pleasantly astonished at the intense response by the police, and it helped ease their fear of repercussions. Mainly, they felt a great deal of compassion for the four youths and had mixed feelings about the possibility of them ending up in prison. Yes, what they did was horrific, but they were young, and a prison record could ruin their lives forever. They prayed for the vandals. Maybe the kids deserved a second chance.

It was all Ammie and Barbara could do to stay on top of the work for the union while they made plans for the next Saturday workday. They called committee members and other volunteers, solicited donations from businesses, rounded up supplies, typed public service announcements, and arranged for the next press conference to try to recruit more volunteers and raise funds.

Press interviews were something that took Barbara some getting used to. By nature, she was quiet and reserved, but she found that a quick prayer for guidance and speaking from her heart gave her all the confidence she needed. She spoke about her church in a way that let people witness what she had seen and imagine how they would feel if it were their church that had been destroyed. It didn't matter that she didn't use big fancy words or perfectly correct sentence syntax like some University of South Carolina graduate, she spoke with a power that made such things unnecessary.

During the time that she and Ammie discussed doing an interview on a popular local radio program, Ammie received a call from Bill Joyner, an elderly white fellow who was a retired maintenance supervisor. He had sent Ammie ten dollars and called to apologize that he couldn't send more.

"Oh, no," Ammie told him. "We appreciate your donation. Every dollar helps."

"I used to be able to do carpentry work, but I'm too old, and I've got arthritis real bad," he went on. "I can't do much."

"We could use your advice."

"Well," he said, his voice growing more upbeat, "I had me three Poland China hogs. It's the best kind of hogs."

Wondering where this was going, Ammie let him continue.

"Now, I done sold two of my hogs, but I got one more named Red."

"Red?"

"Yeah, he weighs five hundred pounds. Red's been fed nothing but ground corn and soybeans. I don't feed my hogs slop. If the members of St. John would like to have him, I'll give him to 'em. They can eat him or sell him, but he'll be theirs to have."

After hanging up, Ammie cajoled two of the county's animal control officers to pick up the hog. Mr. Joyner, dressed in overalls and a baseball cap advertising farm equipment, led the officers to him. Jerry Bellune came out, too, and got a picture of the proud owner with his prized hog. Giving Red an affectionate pat, Mr. Joyner told Jerry, "I don't feed him no slop. This hog will make some of the best sausage you ever put in your mouth."

Apparently, Red picked up more of the conversation than any of them bargained for because he refused to get on the truck. In fact, he wouldn't budge from the stall. The men pushed, pulled, tugged, and yanked, but he didn't give an inch. The guys called it a day but came back the next. Same results. Another day yielded the same. Finally, on the fourth try with two additional animal control officers, they got him on the truck.

A local butcher bought him from St. John. Through the donation of Red, who very grudgingly made the ultimate sacrifice, Mr. Joyner ended up contributing $350.

Other donations continued to arrive, too, some for only a few dollars, others for more, including in-kind donations such as lumber and other supplies. It built Ammie and Barbara's already growing excitement about the upcoming Saturday. They hoped to finish clearing off all the overgrowth if as many volunteers came as had before. Six of the newest volunteers were teenagers in the county's Pre-Trial Intervention program, where they did community service in exchange for having minor crimes removed from their records.

As they worked, Ammie and Barbara discussed the feelings among the congregation that the pretrial program in combination with a fine might be a good alternative for the teens who had attacked the church. Their trials were scheduled for later in the spring.

Ammie spoke with Sheriff Metts, Donnie Myers, and several others with the county's criminal justice system about having weekend offenders come, too, and work off their sentences. Weekend offenders were folks who had mainly been picked up for failure to pay child support, DUIs, pot possession, or bounced checks. They were allowed to remain home and work from Monday through Friday afternoon, and then do their time in jail on the weekends.

The volunteer effort needed anyone available. After consulting with Matt, Ammie mentally reviewed what they had to tackle over the next few weekends—they needed somebody to start rewiring the place. And with some of the brush removed, they uncovered what appeared to be additional graves that had become lost through the passage of time. Ammie called a local surveying firm, Palmetto Surveyors, who agreed to provide a free intensive survey and mark any graves they found. No doubt there were several more besides the thirty or so that were visible and many of those needed to be filled in again because the soil had sunk so low.

She had also organized a history committee headed up by Clayton Kleckley, who was the director of a nearby museum. Although everyone knew the church was old—the cornerstone said it was founded in 1857—its history had never been researched or recorded. In fact, Clayton told Ammie that he doubted that it was built by its congregation in 1857 because that was before Emancipation—a time when most African Americans in the area were still enslaved and legally prohibited from owning property. Prior to the Emancipation Proclamation, most slaves in the Congaree area worshiped either in the churches of their masters or beneath trees in secluded areas of plantations.

After going over plans for Saturday with Barbara, Ammie glanced at her watch. "All right, Barbara, it's long past time for us to call it quits."

"I guess you're right." Barbara looped her purse strap over her shoulder. "Night, Miss Ammie."

Ammie smiled to herself. Was she ever going to get Barbara to quit calling her that?

She ran a few errands, then went home. The hectic stress of the day melted at the sight of her two dogs, Honey Bear and Max, running to greet her as she slowed the Topaz at the mailbox before turning up the dirt drive to her home. They were from the same litter—Honey Bear was female and Max male—and it was hard to tell what mixture of breeds had gone into the making of them. Yet if they had had the finest pedigrees, she couldn't love them any more. With Betsy and Christy off on their own, the animals gave her warm companionship, and she loved cuddling them in her lap. Without fail, no matter what the weather, they always ran to her car as she stopped to check for mail and then trotted alongside until she parked near the house.

"You two are so silly." She petted them and laughed at how they jumped on each other trying to get closer to her. Shifting the weight of her purse, briefcase, and mail, she made her way to the door and opened it, the dogs bounding in before her.

Hitting the button on her answering machine, she listened to the messages from Matt and Butch, who had called to firm up arrangements for Saturday. A few other people she didn't know left messages, as well. They wanted to either volunteer or donate supplies. Since she was chairwoman of the Save St. John Baptist Church Committee, her phone number was listed with any media contacts, including Jerry Bellune's *Dispatch-News*.

As soon as she got something to eat, she'd return the calls. She was looking in the refrigerator when the phone rang.

"Hello?" she said, scanning the refrigerator's contents.

"You nigger-loving bitch," a man growled. "Whatcha' doing helping that nigger church for?"

"What?" Ammie nearly dropped the phone from shock.

"That nigger church, St. John."

"Who is this?"

The line went dead.

FIVE

From the Past

For a moment, she listened to the eerie flat silence before hanging up. "Nigger-loving bitch." She kept hearing the words as if they came from a tape recorder that she couldn't turn off. "Nigger-loving bitch." Who had it been? Did he know where she lived? "Nigger-loving bitch." Had he seen her on TV? Read about her in the *Dispatch-News*?

She tried to steer her attention back to preparing dinner. St. John had been under racial attacks for years, and she had launched a huge campaign to rebuild it, so of course, she would get a crank call or two. And that's all there was to it, she told herself, just a crank phone call from some jerk with too much time on his hands. She felt her pulse slowing back to normal. It had taken her by surprise, but if that stupid caller thought she would quit just because of that, he had better think again.

The memory of the call was soon shuffled behind all the other things she had to keep track of for St. John. Preparations for the Saturday workdays took every spare moment of her time and Barbara's, too. They did what they needed to do for the union, but after that they spent hours coordinating with Matt, Butch, John, Russell, and the rest of the committee, visiting the church and doing every TV, radio, and newspaper interview possible to raise awareness of what was going on.

Jerry was almost a one-man press corps. He wrote about the church in each issue of the *Dispatch-News*, and as a result, South Carolina's largest newspaper, *The State*, also picked up coverage, as well as the local news programs. He appeared with Ammie on a one-hour radio interview and call-in show with WSCQ's Bill Benton, one of the area's most popular radio personalities.

Benton cued his listeners as to how to say Ammie's often mispronounced first name. "It's Ammie, as in *Miami*," he told them.

"I'm just thinking out loud," he said later, "but what if you made the young people who were arrested responsible for the security at the church? If anything else happens, they know they'll go to prison. You can bet they'd pass the word to their friends to leave those folks alone." His words brought smiles to Ammie and Jerry's faces, although his question was merely rhetorical.

After noting how remarkable the outpouring of help from whites was, Benton opened up the phone lines. One of the callers was Barbara. "I don't see their color," she said of the volunteers. "I look at their hearts."

Ammie wished all of her callers were as kind. She had received a number of harassing calls since the first one a couple of weeks ago. They sounded as if more than one person was making them, but all the calls started out the same, "You nigger-loving bitch . . ."

Not wanting to spread alarm, she discussed it only with close committee members. Butch and Russell mentioned they had gotten a few similar calls and while not using the word *nigger-lover* directly, one person had the nerve to actually walk up to Butch and ask, "Why are you out helping that black church? There's plenty white churches that need help. Why ain't you doing anything for them?"

Butch chose to ignore the remark, chalking it up to thick-headed ignorance.

Barbara was getting them, too, and none of them could figure out how; her number was unlisted. Whites phoned, heavily peppering their verbal attacks with the word *nigger,* saying things like, "Nigger, go back to Africa!" Unexpectedly, she had gotten a few anonymous hateful calls from blacks, also. "You think just because you're on TV that you're Miss High and Mighty now, huh?" Another snapped, "Just because you're on the news with that white woman, don't go thinking that you're white now."

Ammie wondered what the world was coming to when even Barbara was coming under attack by other blacks for soliciting aid for a black church—her own church, but she expressed hope that the calls would slacken off as the weeks passed.

"Yeah, Miss Ammie," Barbara agreed. "Maybe it will just wear off after a while."

The progress they made at the church helped them to remain focused. By the third week, they had cleared trees and brush away from the church and were making headway inside the building, as well. Nearly two hundred people had come—whites, blacks, Hispanics, Asians. State senators and business executives labored side by side with truckers and assembly-line workers. The common uniform of jeans and sweatshirts made it impossible to tell one person from another.

Some of the volunteers, like Tom and Judy, as well as John and Mary Ellen brought their children to help, too. Barbara and Willie's teenage children always came, especially Willie Joe and Jonathan, who assisted the men with the heavier work. Yet still, there were so many young people there from Pre-Trial Intervention that unless he knew them, Jonathan assumed that any young person was there working off PTI time. Ann Davidson, the director of the PTI program, began working beside him. He glanced up at her. She looked like a cover girl for *Seventeen* magazine. "So what did you get charged with to end up down here?" he asked out of curiosity.

With the grounds cleared, Palmetto Surveying came. They discovered that in addition to the thirty or so graves that were visible, 250 others existed, some dating back to the colonial era. That information dovetailed with what Clayton Kleckley had uncovered through researching court records and county archives. "Well, we were right," he told Ammie.

"About what?"

"The date on the church—1857. I didn't think it was right."

"What is it, then?"

"It was founded back in the 1700s."

"What?" Ammie said, amazed. "Lord, get me a chair!"

Ironically, St. John started as a place of worship for white Swiss-German immigrants who had been attracted to the Congaree region during the early 1700s because of the offer from South Carolina's colonial governors to provide free land and money. The governors wanted to increase the number of whites to create settlements within the interior and western border of the

colony to buffer against the still strong Cherokee and other native peoples, as well as to offset the population of African slaves,
whose numbers were increasing exponentially. By 1720, for
every white South Carolinian, there were two blacks.

The numerical superiority of African Americans was not lost
on whites, who grew more fearful of slave insurrections. Gov.
Robert Gibbes wrote on May 15, 1711:

> [T]he great quantities of Negroes that are dayly brought into
> this Government and the small number of Whites that comes
> amongst us, and how many are Lately Dead and gon off. How
> insolent and mischievous the negroes have become . . . for the
> better increasing our Number . . . it might be highly necessary
> if an act did provide for the Transportation of them who are
> not able to Transport themselves.

Whites' anxieties were heightened further after the Primus
Plot of 1720, when a slave named Primus nearly launched a
revolt before being betrayed by a fellow slave. Publicly hanging
the insurrectionist did little to dampen fears. The results culminated in European settlers receiving fifty acres of land for
each person they brought with them to the new territories, including family members, servants, and slaves. In addition to
land, the Common House of Assemble gave settlers money for
food, tools, and supplies along with waiving the fees to the royal
government for the first ten years.

The land close to the Congaree River was such a popular
point of migration for Germans and German-speaking Swiss that
it was originally called Saxe-Gotha before being renamed Lexington County. Among the settlers was a minister named Christian Theus, who immigrated from Chur, Switzerland, in 1735.
The exact year he started St. John was lost in time, but a biog-
raphy of Theus by his great-grandson indicated that it was constructed between 1739 and 1741. Its original name was St. John
Helvetic Reformed Church of the Walloon. *Walloon* meant "val-

ley," and Helvetic Reformed eventually evolved into the Lutheran denomination. The settlers attended the services led by Theus and allowed their slaves to sit in the church's gallery.

St. John's story took another twist in 1761, when, had it not been for a "kind-hearted Negro boat man," Theus would have been killed by a bizarre religious cult led by a fellow Swiss immigrant named Jacob Weber.

Weber teamed up with another settler, Schmidt Peter (also known as Smith Peter and Peter Smith) and an African-American man, remembered only as a "godless colored preacher." The three went around calling themselves the Holy Trinity with Weber as God, Peter as Jesus, and the African American as the Holy Spirit.

They ran around naked "practicing extreme wantonness," and they terrorized anyone who refused to join their growing band of supporters. When Theus confronted them, they captured him and argued with each other on how best to kill him— by hanging him or drowning him in the Congaree. He escaped by jumping in the river and being rescued by a slave who happened by on canoe.

When the Revolutionary War erupted, although some members of his congregation supported England, Theus sided with the rebelling colonists. He provided rations to Revolutionary troops, and his sons fought in the Continental Army. British troops swept through the area confiscating estates, burning buildings, and exiling, jailing, or executing patriot sympathizers. In 1781, they got revenge on Christian Theus for helping the Revolutionaries. They burned St. John to the ground.

He and the rest of the settlers decided not to rebuild. There were several other churches nearby that he had founded, so they began attending those, but the slaves left on the plantation had nowhere to go, and they legally couldn't build a church of their own. So instead, some of the men climbed up in the trees and tied branches together to create a brush arbor. They worshiped beneath the trees until after Emancipation when a former slave owner gave them a small plot of land close to where the church had been.

They constructed St. John Baptist Church in 1867. Like many new small black churches emerging during Reconstruction, services there were usually informal, collectively led by members as they felt moved by the spirit. "Ring shouts" were common to the area, and in the course of them church members gathered in a large circle within the sanctuary and moved together in a counterclockwise fashion to an intricate rhythm of singing, shouting, and clapping. True to West and Central African customs, worshippers were careful never to cross their ankles, which bordered on sacrilegious dancing. Some people even considered it sinful to fully lift one's feet off the floor instead of shuffling one foot in front of the other. Those wanting salvation were led, swathed in whitelike apparitions, to Tom's Branch Creek for their sins to be washed away. Life began anew as they rose from the baptismal stream to choruses of songs like "Take Me to the Water." St. John stood until April 30, 1924, when a tornado crashed down on it, flinging part of it into the Congaree and the rest of it across the river over into Richland County.

A single pine board was the only thing left of it. Someone saved it. Nearly penniless, the congregation turned to their only constant, the trees, and once again they created a brush arbor, sitting underneath on rough-hewn benches.

Pooling their money together, they came up with five dollars and used it to buy a bit of adjoining land. In total, St. John's property amounted to an acre. The congregation chopped down the biggest pines on the land to build a simple church made in the shape of a shoebox, and really not much bigger than one. As a crowning touch, they nailed on the single board saved from the original church.

Willie remembered attending the "old board church" as a kid—it lasted for thirty years. Seeing that it was no longer structurally sound, the new pastor, Rev. Lionel Ashford, decided to replace it in 1957 with a more sturdy structure of cinder block.

He saved the single pine board that survived the tornado to use in building the new church that was constructed a bit farther back on the property.

It was that church and its congregation that Barbara had fallen in love with and subsequently Ammie, too.

It was astonishing how far back St. John's history stretched. Even people who had attended all their lives had not been fully aware. A team of archeologists from the University of South Carolina traced St. John's history even further back into the past—when for thousands of years the site was a frequent resting place for Native Americans traveling on what became known as the Cherokee Trail. Native people called it the Broad Path or the Broad Way and used it as a trading route. The hard-packed dirt footpath extended from the Smokies down to Charleston and linked coastal tribes with those in the mountains. The section of the trail that ran in front of St. John became known as Old State Road.

Ammie walked along with one of the archeologists as he found Indian artifacts. "Look, there's another one," he said, coming to a stop and motioning to something on the ground.

"What do you mean?" Ammie asked, looking at what he pointed to. "That's a filtered cigarette butt."

"No, it's not. Pick it up."

When she did, she realized she was wrong, but she didn't have a clue what she held between her fingers.

"That's part of a peace pipe," he explained. "It's a long bone with a hole through it. When they passed it around, they would take a puff off it, break the tip that touched their lips, then pass it to the next person. They were very sanitary." He took a step away from her excitedly, "Look, here's another one."

The land that St. John was built on was an archeological treasure trove. Barbara's sister-in-law, Patricia, said in wonder, "This is incredible. We used to play around here as kids and toss this stuff around, pick it up and throw it back in the dirt like it wasn't anything. And here it turns out they're really ancient artifacts!"

Researchers combed through county records and came across the surnames of several of the Swiss-German families who had been land and slave owners in the area. Two of the names hit Ammie like stones: the Geigers and Keiglers. Her mother's ancestors. Her ancestors. Indeed, it was likely that they had owned some of the slaves who used to worship at St. John and now lay buried in its cemetery.

She sat on the old stump on the edge of the cemetery, trying to absorb the news. For much of her adult life, she had worked for social justice, only to discover that people from whom she had descended denied their fellow human beings the most basic of rights simply because of their skin color. Though slavery had ended, it left a bitter, lingering legacy that manifested itself through continued poverty, inadequate education, lack of health care, and other social problems that disproportionately affected African Americans. What hurt Ammie the most was the effect it had on the children. She had been active in educational issues for years and saw too many African-American kids stripped of self-esteem and aspirations for the future. Her ancestors had played a role in that. They were a part of her and she, them.

A breeze whispered through the trees, and she could hear the cicadas hum in rhythm as the sun began its descent. She wished there was some way to go back and change the past, but she knew the futility of such a wish. But she could do everything in her power to make a difference, and helping St. John was one of the best ways of achieving that. With the church rebuilt, African-American boys and girls could look to it as a beacon of resilient hope. She stood up from the stump. She had work to do.

With Easter approaching, Ammie divided her attention between repairs on the building and getting the churchyard in decent enough shape for the congregation and the committee to hold an Easter sunrise service there. When the overgrowth had been cut down, the clearing revealed the graves that had sunken in. Butch arranged for the trucking company he worked with, Aggregate Trucking, to bring in loads of sand and topsoil. Filling in the graves and laying down some grass seed created more work for the volunteers to do.

Ammie got Seaboard Railroad, which owned some of the land directly behind the church, to run an inch-thick cable around the rear of the churchyard to deter vandals from driving trucks and four-wheelers in from the back of the cemetery and desecrating graves. The railroad company also donated a strip of land adjoining the rear of the churchyard. Art Carter of Red Jacket Pump Company donated a water pump, and Willie Sox dug a well, and for the first time in ages, St. John had water again. Two electrical installation companies—Sistrunk Electric and Shealy Electric—came in and did all the wiring.

At the end of one of the workdays, Ammie kneaded her lower back to massage a kink out of it before heading home. Between the union and St. John, she often put in fourteen- to sixteen-hour days. She was exhausted but encouraged by what she saw. They still had a long way to go—they wouldn't be able to start on the interior until they finished major structural things like getting new roofs on the church and adjacent Sunday school building, but still, she could see how far they had come.

As Matt, Willie, and Butch locked away equipment, she looked around. It would be so beautiful once they finished. Even the sight of it now made her heart swell. That was one of the reasons she visited every day, although they only had major workdays on Saturdays. Sometimes she came two and three times a day. There was something about the church that kept drawing her in—drawing so many of them in.

She knew St. John had worked its way into a soft spot in Butch's heart, too, despite his tough exterior. He was forever working his many contacts to raise money for them or to get donations of supplies, completely disregarding a schedule that was already jam-packed with a full-time job, a seat on county council, and family responsibilities. But like a parent looking in on a child he had just tucked into bed, Butch came by nearly every evening on his way home to check in on it.

And while John didn't make a big deal of it, Ammie realized that his commitment to the church was placing him under political fire. The commonly held view that he was a Northern outsider who never played along with the bureaucratic "good old boy" system had garnered him enough ill will, but when rumor spread that he was allowing his Criminal Justice Academy employees to use state equipment to rebuild a black church, the daggers really came out. The fact that any state equipment that they used—which was mainly the old dump truck—had been gathering rust, sitting unused in a junkyard didn't register. Nor did the fact that they spent their own money to buy gas whenever they used the truck.

Nevertheless, two anonymous tips were made about him to the state's watchdog agency that investigated him for "abuse of state property." The backlash resulting from helping the church confounded John. He asked, "How in the hell can someone possibly oppose something like this?" and told his supervisor, "Look, if this is abuse, then I'm guilty, but I don't think it is."

The image of him saying that to his boss made Ammie smile. That was the effect St. John had on some of them, especially the core volunteers. They would go to the extent of risking their jobs to stand up for it.

She wondered if Matt risked not only his job, but his own safety, as well. Matt often worked at the church alone. He probably put more hours in than anyone else, going there directly from the academy and staying past nightfall. Ammie understood why he did it. From time to time, she enjoyed getting there before any of the rest of them arrived to enjoy the quiet of the place all to herself. The old stump was her favorite place to think and make mental notes of what she needed to accomplish. For some reason, she never felt fearful while she was alone, only filled with peace.

Still, it remained a good idea for none of the volunteers to be there by themselves. Barbara often accompanied Ammie or met up with her. Ammie couldn't understand how Barbara was able to do everything she did. Not only was she working as hard at the church as the rest of them, but she had four children to look after, as well. At least in her case, Betsy and Christy were grown and out on their own. She didn't know if she could devote as much time to St. John if she had two children to raise, much less four.

Naturally, Willie's devotion to the church was stronger than nearly anyone's. He came every weekend and occasionally during weeknights, too, but his job as a crane operator at a steel plant demanded his presence anywhere from sixty to eighty hours each week. He frequently didn't get off work until around nine or ten at night. That left Barbara with the responsibility of seeing to the day-to-day running of their home and working with Ammie, Matt, John, Butch, Russell, and the rest of the core group to coordinate the rebuilding effort.

Ammie's spirits got more of a lift when Jerry told her that he had contacted a former colleague about doing a story on St. John and that the correspondent expressed interest in it. They used to work together as reporters for the *Charlotte News*, a North Carolina paper that had gone out of business years ago. While Jerry eventually made his way to the *Dispatch-News*, his friend had made it to *CBS News*. His former coworker was none other than Charles Kuralt. He thought the interracial effort to rebuild the black church might make a good story for *CBS Sunday Morning*, which he hosted.

When he called Jerry from New York to follow up, Jerry's office manager asked excitedly, "Was that really Charles Kuralt on the phone?"

Ammie could hardly believe it, either. The idea of CBS doing a feature on them amazed her. She couldn't wait for Kuralt to let Jerry know whether they wanted to do the segment.

The volunteers spent the better part of the next Saturday work-day mounding all the uncovered graves. Though fewer people were able to come, they finished the work by nightfall, in time for Easter sunrise services the next morning. They put silk flow-ers on every one of the 280 graves, probably the first time most of them had been adorned in over a century.

"I am the resurrection, and the life: he that believeth in me, though he were dead, yet shall he live." Christ's words had spe-cial meaning to the fifty people gathered in the early chill of Easter morning as sunlight edged over the tall pines. Like their savior, St. John was being resurrected, given life anew.

As Katherine Brown sang "A Stranger in the City," her voice transfixed everyone, making them forget the cold and the grow-ing numbness in their feet and hands. It was fitting that birdsong and a soft breeze off the river accompanied her.

They all joined in singing "The Old Rugged Cross." It seemed each stanza was written for St. John, chronicling how despite adversity, it remained. After Willie and Deacon Smith led a de-votional, Rev. Julius Felder preached on the power of the res-urrection. A slight, elderly man, Felder had been a powerhouse as an NAACP leader for decades. Tom followed him with a med-itation; then Ammie spoke on the progress of the rebuilding. "Come back in a few weeks," she said, "and you'll see new roofs on the church and Sunday school. Come back a few weeks later, you'll see new doors and windows. After several weeks, come back again. You'll see new stucco on the outside walls. Come back—and see what faith and love can do."

A day that they had awaited for several months occurred the following Friday—the court hearing for the arrested teens. Only the three boys would stand trial. Charges against the younger girl had been dropped. St. John's congregation had prayed about what was the best thing to do. They were entitled to justice, and yet they felt the three eighteen-year-olds deserved mercy. They reached a consensus to ask that the judge not sentence the trio to prison.

Their decision didn't sit well with Bulldog Yarborough when he first heard it. He wondered if the church was sending a mixed message to future assailants that could lead to more trouble. Still, he admired not only how the church members talked about being Christians, but that they also put their words into action, especially after what they had been through.

Jerry shared Bulldog's reservations but joined Ammie, Barbara, Willie, and Deacon Wally Smith for the hearing that was scheduled on a Friday morning. They arrived early to meet with Solicitor Myers and Bob Rightsell, who worked under Myers as a victims' advocate. In addition to his job with the Eleventh Circuit solicitor's office, Bob also volunteered on St. John's committee and helped with press releases and other PR activities. He was such a big help that Ammie nicknamed him Right Arm Rightsell.

They all met to confirm the church's decision and then took seats in the courtroom. Judge Anthony Harris presided and ordered the three boys to stand and enter their pleas. Accompanied by their mothers, each of the teens stood up, looking uncomfortable in dark polyester suits and ties with hair in various stages of combed neatness. Avoiding looking toward St. John's representatives, they either stared down at the carpet or nervously peered up at the judge.

"How do you plead?" Judge Harris asked each of them by name.

"Guilty."

"Guilty."

"Guilty."

Only one of them offered a statement, mumbling something about how they had thought the church was abandoned.

"Why didn't you go in one Sunday morning to services and they'd have told you all about it?" Judge Harris retorted. Then he asked Donnie Myers, "Is five years the maximum I can give them on these charges?"

Myers stood. "Yes, Your Honor. That's the maximum because the crimes took place in an unoccupied dwelling, although breaking into someone's home carries a ten-year maximum sentence."

"This is God's home, isn't it?" the judge snapped back, referring to St. John. Ammie and Barbara stole glances at each other. This judge seemed ready to pounce on raw meat. Both women wondered if he would disregard the church's appeal for leniency. The youths bore expressions like deer caught in the high beams of headlights.

Myers spoke of the church's wishes for mercy and their preference for restitution and community service work as opposed to prison sentences. "They want these men punished, but at the same time, to put their futures into their own hands. The vandalism has stopped because these boys were arrested and because of the publicity. The word has gone out not to mess with this church."

With the judge's permission, Willie stood and briefly added, "We want them to learn their lesson, but we don't want them punished severely."

Although Judge Harris still looked as if he could bite nails into bits, and then spit them out, his demeanor softened a tad. He called a short recess, and when he reconvened court, he grudgingly set a sentence for each of them to three years of probation and individual payments of a thousand dollars in restitution.

Turning to the teens' lawyers, he asked them if their clients had jobs. "I want to make sure each one is working and making payments with their own money," he said. "I don't want their mothers and fathers paying it for them."

The lawyers assured him that the teens would pay the money back on their own.

Glaring down from his bench, Harris told the three defendants, "If it were not for the good hearts of these people whose church you tore up, I'd send you to the penitentiary right now. It's easy to see that these people put their faith into practice."

He rapped his gavel so hard that it sounded like a crack of thunder. "Court adjourned."

By the time Ammie made it home that night, she was so worn out, she could hardly stand. The court hearing ate up all of the morning, and after it ended, she and Barbara put in a full day at the office and then swung by the church to squeeze in a little bit of work. She was hopeful that the right decision had been reached that morning. As they filed out of the courtroom, she had nodded when Deacon Smith said, "I don't believe a prison sentence would have helped. These are young men. Maybe this will help get them off to a good start." The boys were also to do community service work at St. John. Maybe having to repair what they had done would bring about a change in them.

"Maybe so," she thought aloud, slumping into a chair at her kitchen table, but she had to get up again when she heard the phone ring.

She hesitated a moment before picking up the receiver. It had gotten to where her stomach lurched whenever it rang. Please, this time let it be one of her daughters or her sister or Barbara or Matt or Butch. Anybody but—

"You nigger-loving bitch," a venomous voice sneered.

Not again. Ammie didn't know if she actually spoke the words or not.

"That grandson of yours, Scott, sure is a cute young 'un."

"What did you say?" Her blood froze. Scott was Betsy's four-year-old son, Ammie's first grandchild. She loved him and his younger sister, Shannon, with everything in her being.

"Scott, yeah," the voice drawled. "Be a shame if anything was to happen to that thar boy, wouldn't it?"

The next thing she heard was a dead silence.

"Oh, God." Ammie dropped her face down into her trembling hands. Her grandson. They even knew about him. How? Who were they?

The kids had wanted to come over that weekend, but Ammie gave them and Betsy vague excuses about why they couldn't. Though she desperately wanted to see them, she had to figure out a way to do it that didn't put them in jeopardy. Not only them, but Betsy, Christy, and the rest of her family, including her mother, who, despite being up in years, often pitched in at St. John. Ammie was willing to risk her own life, but not theirs.

She decided to talk it over with Bulldog and Stick. Though she was still shaken up, she was determined not to quit. She'd only be giving her tormentors what they wanted. They would win. She'd be damned before she let that happen.

One of the first things the detectives advised her to do was to move from her home. "It's too far out in the country," Bulldog argued. "You're too isolated. We'll do what we can to provide protection, but we can't be out there twenty-four hours a day. You need to move into town, closer to the police station."

"Give up my home?" She loved where she lived, and the thought of having to leave because of some cowardly creeps infuriated her. She wouldn't do it. She would not.

Although she didn't agree to their advice, she did allow them to train her on safety measures and other techniques, like how to detect if someone was tailing her and how to shake them if they were. Once she finished the training, she felt confident that she could visit her family without jeopardizing them—she couldn't let them come over anymore, though. Without going into much detail, she would arrange it so that she met them somewhere else.

Knowing that they would worry themselves sick about her kept her from revealing to them what was going on. She could shoulder the stress of it alone as long as she was assured of their safety. Their safety was paramount, especially that of her precious grandchildren.

The weekend approached. When she and Charles lived on the lake, she used to savor weekends. They were days of relaxing on Lake Murray in the pontoon boat or grilling out on the deck, enjoying the company of family and friends. Now, she almost dreaded the end of the workweek. She noticed the frequency of the calls picked up then, especially on Friday and Saturday nights. Though it sounded like one person called more than anyone else, the calls came from numerous people, nearly all of them men. One Saturday night, it seemed like about a dozen guys piled into a room and took turns calling her. She didn't want to miss any calls from family, friends, or potential donors to St. John, but she finally had to turn off the phone.

Who were they? That question kept eating away at her. Had she seen them? Driven by them? Were they watching her now?

They seemed to know everything about her. They spoke of her separation from Charles and knew that he lived with a girlfriend at the lake house and that she was alone. They mentioned not only Scott's name, but Shannon's, too. Betsy and Christy's, as well. They even spoke about her two dogs. "Nigger-loving bitch." She had heard those words so many times, they echoed through her nightmares.

Standing up in her kitchen, she dimmed the lights and peered through her miniblinds into the yard. Nothing. Not one thing appeared out of the ordinary. Moonlight shone high overhead, illuminating her neat three-acre lot and the lonely stretch of dirt road that ran in front of it. There was only a smattering of trailers and small houses on the road, and few traveled down it unless they lived there or had relatives on it.

Who were they? Who were they?

She nearly jumped when the phone rang, but she picked it up with a surge of determination. Whoever they were, she wouldn't let them make her afraid in her own home.

"Hello?"

"You nigger-loving—"

She slammed it down. When would this end?

SIX

Honey Bear and Max

She and Barbara talked about the increasing danger. Barbara worried that Willie had started carrying a gun, and she feared that it would escalate an already tense situation. Before she had even spoken with Ammie about it, she decided to opt for the same solution that Ammie had—she would do whatever it took to protect her kids, but she wanted to shield them as much as possible from what was happening. It was bad enough that she was going through this, she didn't want them burdened with it, too.

In her own low-key way, Barbara had enacted safety precautions with them, not letting them out of her sight or that of close relatives. When the kids questioned the tighter supervision, she vaguely spoke of needing them around to help out more since she was so tied up with her job and the rebuilding effort.

She did confide in her parents however. They were scared to death for her, especially since Willie worked until late in the evening, leaving her and the kids home alone much of the time. They lived near the church—in the heart of Klan country. Her mom sounded much like Bulldog when he spoke to Ammie. "Barbara," she said, "you need to get out of there. Come up here where we are. We can keep a better eye on you."

In fact, Barbara's parents made it obvious that they wouldn't have minded if she quit St. John altogether. It wasn't that they didn't feel empathy for it—they did—but if a choice had to be made between their daughter's safety and the church getting rebuilt, there would be no question which they would choose.

Barbara couldn't consider abandoning St. John. She loved it as she would a family member. Besides, it was because of her that Ammie had become involved. Ammie was getting treated worse than she was, yet she wasn't backing down, and St. John wasn't even her church. And if Ammie was willing to stick with it when there were plenty of reasons not to do so, then she certainly could.

The arrival of warm spring days offered hope. Fed by spring rains, the effusion of azaleas, daffodils, and dogwoods in bloom lifted their beleaguered spirits. It was on one rainy day in late April that Ammie had a building trades meeting. Because the meeting extended into the late afternoon, she went home directly afterward.

Like always, she slowed the car at her mailbox to retrieve her mail. Rain drummed against the car as a wave of panic hit her. She looked through the streaked window. Something was wrong. Something was terribly wrong. Where were her dogs? She couldn't remember a day that they hadn't come dashing to the mailbox to greet her and trot alongside until she parked and let them into the house. They came no matter how bad the weather. Where were they?

Turning up the drive, she saw them lying in a heap near the house. "Oh, God." Her hand flew up to her mouth.

Getting out of the car, she found Max stretched across his sister's body. At the sight of her, he stood up. Honey Bear's blood darkened his silky coat. Ammie's heart stopped when she looked at Honey Bear. Someone had cleaved her head in two.

A man's voice reverberated in her mind. "Nigger-loving bitch, sure would be a shame if something was to happen to one of them thar dogs, now, wouldn't it?"

Still in her business suit and pumps, Ammie knelt and stroked the lifeless form. Hot tears stung her eyes and mixed with the rain pelting her face. She forced herself to stand and search for the things needed for burial. After finding a shovel and something to wrap the dog, she buried it in her backyard as the rain poured down, soaking her to the bone.

She managed to get most of Honey Bear's blood off Max and carried him into the house. Holding him tight, she fell into a rocking chair. That's where they stayed the rest of the night, both of them crying.

The next day, she returned by herself to the one place that gave her the most solace—the old stump in the cemetery. The spot had a peace about it that she couldn't quite put into words. Perhaps it emanated from the surrounding trees that had offered shelter down through the centuries to the people of St. John. Maybe it came from the serene but sure Congaree or from all of the wildlife and other living things that drew sustenance from it. Ammie didn't know. The only thing she understood was that sitting there made her feel a little more centered, a little less afraid, a little more sure that she could keep going.

———————

Jerry brought good news. CBS definitely wanted to do a segment on St. John for *CBS Sunday Morning*. Charles Kuralt had shared the story idea with acclaimed commentator Bill Moyers, who thought it was such a good one that he asked to be assigned to it. He and a film crew were to arrive in a little over a month, on June 18.

Ammie, Barbara, and everyone on the committee and in the church were ecstatic. "Bill Moyers! Can you believe it?" Ammie said to several people. "I watched him for years. He's one of the absolute best!"

They wanted to get as much done as possible before his arrival. The need for roofs on the sanctuary and Sunday school remained the most pressing problem. More welcome news came when C. P. Moorer of Columbia Wholesale and Royce Waites of Commercial Roofing announced that their companies would respectively donate supplies and labor for the new roofs. The roofs were completed within a couple of days.

A local R&B radio station, WWDM, contacted Ammie. Each month they held a fund-raiser for a different charity, and for June, they wanted to help St. John. Naturally, Ammie responded with ecstatic gratitude, and the station raised over one thousand dollars, bringing the total cash contributions past the six-thousand-dollar mark.

Ammie and Matt did a quick assessment of the progress. The dream of rebuilding the church appeared more a reality with each week. Though they hadn't been able to focus much attention on the Sunday school yet, the sanctuary approached the halfway point of completion.

Barbara and Willie's spirits were further buoyed when some of the people who had quit attending services returned. One Sunday, one week before Mother's Day, thirty-five people came, a huge crowd compared to what had been coming. Disregarding the scaffolding, drop sheets, and other signs of the ongoing renovation, they worshiped, filling nearly every seat in the small church.

The next Saturday, seventy people came out to work. They

were stunned by what greeted them. Sometime the night before, the church was vandalized once again. Disgusted, Ammie and Barbara stared at the words spray-painted in two-foot-tall bright yellow letters on the outside of a white cinder-block wall at the rear of the building. "Satan." "Devil."

Whoever did it also took the heavy metal lid of the water meter and one of the headstones from the cemetery and dumped them alongside the road. A sheriff's deputy happened to spot them while driving in his patrol car. Another gravestone inscribed with "Mother" in large lettering was knocked over and had fallen forward into the dirt. As an extra affront, someone threw a pair of bloodied panties on top of it. They had dug around another grave, too.

"This just kind of makes you sick to your stomach," Ammie said, shaking her head. But at least the damage was superficial. She was determined to take it in stride, and Barbara shared her determination.

Jerry scribbled a few quotes for the next edition of the *Dispatch-News.*

"We're disappointed, but not discouraged," Ammie told him. "They can't frighten us off. More and more people had been scared away, but now they're coming back. They've begun to realize the type of punks who do this stuff, and they're not scared anymore. Last Sunday, the church was absolutely full. That's the real blessing from all of this."

"We're not going to give up." Barbara's jaw was set firm. "We'll keep on."

Sheriff Metts was livid. He held a press conference a couple of days later announcing that he had gotten the nonprofit Crime Stoppers organization to offer a thousand-dollar reward, one that he would match should any information come in leading to the arrest of anyone caught harming St. John.

Ammie and Barbara rallied everyone to stay strong, which wasn't easy considering the private hell both of them were enduring.

Confiding in each other about what they were dealing with helped them to cope. Barbara channeled some of her energy into nurturing others, not only her family, Ammie, and other close friends, but also all of the other volunteers. She usually stayed up the entire night before major workdays frying chicken and preparing other food to ensure that every volunteer had a hearty meal.

Ammie found some distraction in throwing herself all the more into her work at the church and in the office. In his own way, Max helped, too, although his efforts left Ammie with bittersweet emotions. It was obvious to her that he was trying to comfort her by taking his sister's place through imitation. He went as far as to imitate her higher-pitched bark.

Four days after discovering that St. John had been vandalized again, Ammie returned home. When Max didn't bolt to her car, she knew instantly what happened. Even before she found him lying in a pool of blood in the exact same spot as his sister, a sick, sinking feeling hit Ammie in the pit of her stomach.

His head was cleaved open just as Honey Bear's had—two weeks to the day after she was murdered. Crying, Ammie buried him next to his sister. She went into the house and had just gotten out of the shower when the phone rang. "I know you're going to miss them thar dogs—"

She hung up before he could say anything more.

Seeing no other alternative, she told Stick and Bulldog about the dogs. Stick made an effort to temper his alarm with sympathy but Bulldog was blunt. "Woman, get the hell out of there. Those people mean business. Next time, it's going to be you."

This time, she couldn't afford to ignore the advice from the two detectives. To do so could cost her her life.

An acquaintance sold real estate, and Ammie feigned casual interest when mentioning that she was looking to move closer to town.

"There's a little house coming up on the market next week," the agent replied.

"Where is it?"

He said the name of the street.

Thinking aloud, she said, "That's near the police station."

"Yeah, two blocks."

They arranged to meet at the house the next day. It was in a neighborhood that doggedly clung to its middle-class status and resisted decay as an increasing number of elderly home-owners died and their homes were converted to inexpensive rental property. He started giving Ammie a tour of the small World War II–era brick home, but she gave it only a cursory walk through. "Hmm, the electricity works, so does the plumbing. The roof looks solid, the doors, windows—I'll take it."

"What?" He gaped at her.

"Yeah, I'll take it." It could have been a lean-to, for all she cared. It was just two blocks away from the police station, close to help. That's all that mattered.

"Gosh, this is the easiest sale I've ever made!" the real estate agent exclaimed.

The sudden move struck her family as odd, and Betsy and Christy noticed that Ammie never spoke of the dogs anymore.

"Where are they?"

"Oh." Ammie looked away evasively. "They got run over."

"Huh?" Both their faces screwed up in confusion at the information and the way their mom delivered it. Something about it all didn't ring true. Honey Bear and Max weren't the kind of dogs that chased cars or roamed around; in fact, they seldom, if ever, ventured off the three-acre lot. How on earth could both of them have gotten hit by cars?

Quickly changing the subject, Ammie steered the conversation onto the subject of her grandchildren and the general goings-on within the family.

Ammie's diversionary techniques weren't quite as effective on her mother. With worry etched on her face, she kept asking, "Ammie Jean, are you okay?" "Is everything all right?" "Is there something I need to know about?"

Using every acting skill she remembered from high school drama classes, Ammie assured her that everything was fine. She was just spread thin between the union, church, political activities, and other things. That was all.

Her sister's husband didn't buy any of it, but he knew her well enough to realize that once she sank her teeth into something, she didn't let go, and any efforts to try to get her to quit would only made her more determined not to do so. However, he couldn't hold back from warning her, "AJ, you're going to get yourself killed."

Though she didn't say it, she wondered if time would prove him right.

Even before she had a chance to move in all her furniture, she began spending nights in her new home. She brought over enough blankets and pillows to make a pallet on the floor, where she slept, feeling safe for the first time in months. If she could hold out a while longer, soon this nightmare would be over.

For the next several days, until she was able to have everything loaded onto a moving truck, she brought small items from the old house and slept on the floor at night. After she had all her belongings brought over, she had phone service connected.

She was unpacking boxes when she received her first call.

"Nigger-loving—"

She slammed the phone down. How had they found her?

The threats and harassment got worse. The weekends continued to be the worst, probably because the tormentors added generous helpings of alcohol to fuel their hatred. Ammie wondered if the day would ever come when she could stop dreading the ringing of the phone, or that she could quit checking her mail before opening it, or searching for someone following her as she drove. Unless someone called to tell her that they were coming over, she never answered the door. Never. It could be her mom or one of her daughters popping by to pay an unannounced visit—they would finally give up ringing the doorbell and leave, assuming she had ridden with a friend somewhere, since her car was still in the driveway.

In addition to the training from the detectives, she had picked up other tips to make her home more secure. She bought a police scanner and often let it play hoping the constant stream of men's voices would throw off any intruders.

Butch and some of the other men she had confided in suggested that she lower her profile with the media to deflect some of the harassment toward them, but she wouldn't go along with it. She wasn't going to back down, not even an inch.

Searching for humor in the face of danger, Barbara weakly joked that she had been called "nigger bitch" so many times, she thought it was a part of her name now. She was still getting harassment from what she called, "both barrels"—racist whites and mean-spirited blacks who despised her for socializing with whites.

Others working at the church felt it challenging to keep their spirits buoyed, too, especially when arriving and discovering that equipment, tools, and supplies had been either stolen or smashed out of pure and obvious meanness. Worse yet were the satanic symbols. On any given day, volunteers or church members arrived to find hexagons spray-painted on the side of the building or the numbers *666* etched into the dirt drive. Bloody chicken parts were thrown about the ground or in the open-air baptismal pool. Sometimes the animals tossed into the pool were so butchered, no one could tell what kind of animals they had been. On one occasion, volunteers found six mutilated possums lined in a perfectly straight row in front of the church doors.

Matt had been working at the church by himself when a gang of whites sped past. "Nigger!" one of them shouted. "Go back to Africa, nigger!" yelled another.

John commented that the men in the car were lucky to have gotten away. A decorated Vietnam veteran, Matt could have done a lot of damage to them despite being alone. But at the Criminal Justice Academy, the same people who had tried to get John sacked for helping St. John were now after Matt. Reports streamed in that he was working at the church while on state time, that he was using all sorts of state equipment there. John used his position to provide him cover against the unsubstantiated charges.

Tom Turnipseed had been under attack from racists for so many years that he wasn't the least bit fazed when he encountered hostility. He came to work one morning to find that someone had pasted a Ku Klux Klan flyer against his office window. The flyer advertised an upcoming rally.

Butch starting carrying one of his guns.

Spring gave way to the start of summer. By the first Saturday in June, nearly everyone working on the church had cast aside heavy work clothes for T-shirts, shorts, and lightweight jeans. As she worked and buzzed around, coordinating, Ammie noticed a tall, white, lanky teenager talking to a couple of other white volunteers. Indeed, while everyone else was working, this guy seemed to be doing more talking than anything else. She remembered him. He was Charles "Tony" Allen, one of the three eighteen-year-olds who had been sentenced for destroying the church and who was there working off some of his community service time. Well, he was supposed to be working.

In a casual manner, she moved close enough to be within earshot of what he was saying.

"Why y'all here helping these niggers for?" he asked the two young fellows near him. "Whites ain't got no business around niggers."

Storming at him, Ammie reached up and grabbed him by the collar. Even though he was at least a foot taller than her five-feet-two-inch frame, she yanked him up until he was nearly off the ground.

"Listen here, you sorry, no-good son of a bitch," she said between clenched teeth.

The teen stared at her, color draining from his face.

"You turn your sorry ass around, get on that road over there, and you start walking. You keep walking, and you'd better not ever set foot on this property again!"

He did just that.

Within two weeks he was behind bars again, not because of the church, but because he tried to extort money from the police. Shari Smith, a high school beauty queen and daughter of a prominent Lexington family, had been recently kidnapped from her home, as had a nine-year-old girl named Debra May Helmick in neighboring Richland County. The kidnappings had the entire Midlands region in a state of alarm, and the media covered every potential lead.

On June 19, Allen called the Lexington County Sheriff's Department and told them that for five hundred dollars, he would take them to the house where Shari Smith's body was and lead them to three men who he claimed had killed her. He wanted the money to get back the car he had posted as bond for the charges related to St. John.

As it ended up, Allen knew neither where Smith's body was nor anything about who killed her. He tied up a precious twelve hours of investigators' time by leading them on a wild goose chase before his story finally fell to pieces. He pled guilty to obstructing justice.

His public defender was at a loss to explain his behavior. "He needs psychological counseling," he offered lamely before ask-

ing that his client be allowed into a program for youthful offenders.

"Then he may be released in six months," Judge Hubert
Long said, "No, he'll be sentenced as an adult." He gave him
four years. "The good people of that church showed you mercy,
then you turn around and do something like this."

Allen had nothing to say.

Before June ended, St. John was hit again with vandalism. During his patrol of it, sheriff's deputy Donald Davis discovered that
someone had kicked out the bottom panel of one of the doors
to the Sunday school. Another door had been kicked wide open.
Davis measured the scuff marks on the white doors—a size nine
or ten shoe. He wished the timing of his patrol had matched
the appearance of the culprits.

Though the building housed much of the donated building
supplies, none of it appeared missing or tampered with. A window had also been opened in the church, but again, it didn't
look as if anyone had done anything inside.

Still, despite the damage being light, it made everybody sick
that it kept occurring.

They received word that Bill Moyers had to postpone his visit
until September, although a film crew came down to do some
preliminary shooting. With everything that had been going on,
the camera crew arrived before Ammie, Matt, or anyone had
been able to paint over the words "Satan" and "Devil" on the
back wall. The words were filmed shining brightly in the summer sun.

SEVEN

Under Attack

After leaving the union office, Ammie headed for St. John. Butch had arranged for the church to be featured in an upcoming segment of a local news program. The two of them were to meet later that evening at the church, along with the program's producer.

Glancing at her watch, she realized she would arrive more than an hour before the scheduled meeting, but it would be time she could use to gather the pictures left inside the church that the producer wanted. They agreed that the pictures would help raise people's level of concern, and they hoped that would translate into more donations, which they desperately needed.

As she almost always did, she chose Old State Road to get to St. John instead of Interstate 26, which had a doglegged exit about one mile away from the church. Willie constantly got on her for traveling down the isolated dirt road that cut a narrow path through heavy forests. "It would be way safer to stay on the highway," he urged, "especially riding by yourself."

But she loved driving with the woods so close on either side that they seemed to embrace her. The boughs of the moss-covered trees intertwined above to form a thick canopy, and sunlight fell through the greenness in dappled speckles. The road probably looked just as it had when President George Washington used it to travel from Columbia to Charleston. Letting her mind wander, she imagined herself living back in the colonial era—what she would do, how different her life would be.

The front of a burgundy sedan poking out through the trees shook her from her reverie.

Wondering why a car would be parked like that on the isolated dirt road, Ammie drove past it. The condition of the road had deteriorated badly since its last grading, and her little Topaz shook with each jarring bump.

The sedan slid out of the trees behind her. She slowed down to keep control of her car as she approached a washout. If she could coast over it, she could make it back onto firmer ground and continue the next five to six miles to St. John.

She had nearly gotten to the washout when she heard a tremendous crash—metal crumpling into metal. Slammed from behind, she was hurled against the dash. Turning to the rearview mirror, she saw five men in the sedan behind her. The look in the driver's eyes was one of pure hatred like she had never seen before.

Stomping on the accelerator, she knew her life depended on getting away. The car barely stayed intact as it flew down the rough road.

The sedan lurched forward once more, smashing into her again. Because she had picked up speed, the impact wasn't as horrible as the first time.

She gripped the wheel, fighting to keep control of the car,

which nearly skidded off the road. The interstate lay one mile past the church. If she could make it onto it, maybe there would be a chance of outrunning them or flagging down help. The sedan surged behind her, aiming for a third strike. She prayed for her car to go faster even with the windows rattling violently, threatening to shatter.

The eternity that was only seconds passed; she could see St. John in the distance. The interstate was just beyond.

For reasons that she didn't understand, Ammie yanked the steering wheel to the left, skidding toward the church. She knew that she would be alone, defenseless, and that they would kill her.

She flew into the parking lot with the sedan in close pursuit, and, to her amazement, she saw Butch's car and Willie's truck. Her two friends stood in the cemetery talking. At the sight of the men, the burgundy sedan screeched to a stop, jerked into reverse, and sped off in a jumble of dust.

Afraid that her legs would buckle under her if she immediately tried to get out of the car, Ammie sat for several minutes to rein in her nerves. By the time she managed to climb out of the car and tell her friends what had happened, the burgundy sedan was long gone.

Divine intervention. That's what had saved her. Ammie came to that conclusion over breakfast the next morning. Nothing else could have led Butch to arrive more than an hour earlier than planned or for Willie to have had a day off and decide to spend it there. A workhorse of a man, Willie got a day off once every blue moon. And yet, there he had been, he and Butch, exactly when she had needed them most. She tried to block from her mind what would have happened had they not been there.

If she could only hold on. They were more than halfway finished. She couldn't let them drive her away now. She could not. She would not.

Stirring her coffee, she mentally went over plans for a press conference scheduled for the next week. She and Barbara had mailed out press releases to all the major media outlets, and they anticipated extensive coverage. The majority of the congregation and committee indicated they would be there, as well. Together, they would bear witness to everyone about the small miracle occurring at St. John—that a diverse group could cross racial, economic, political, and religious boundaries to come together and right a horrible wrong.

In many ways, the church was like a supernatural beam of light. Once people walked through it, it changed them forever. She saw it nearly every workday. She thought back to a crusty old white man who came sporting a dingy cap with a Confederate flag on it. No one said anything to him about it, instead offering him a warm welcome and gratitude for his time. He fell into working beside Joe Wilson, a black middle school principal. Between racing around, helping to keep things organized, Ammie noticed how the two men began talking and laughing about various things. The elderly man kept showing up and working alongside Wilson, but one day he came and the cap was gone. He never wore it again.

That was one of the beauties of St. John; it helped people get to know others not as white, or black, or Republican, or Jew, but as fellow human beings. Of course, there were a handful of exceptions, Tony Allen being the most painful. It saddened Ammie that he had turned his back on the forgiving love St. John offered, but that could not diminish the effect the church had on others, and that would be apparent during the news conference.

The event would also let the public see the progress they were making, in addition to helping each person working at the church take stock of what they had accomplished so far. In the midst of the continuous workdays, it was easy to lose sight of that. On a more practical note, she hoped the continued media exposure would generate additional donations. They were running low on funds but still had a great deal left to do, especially on the Sunday school building, since they had devoted most of the initial efforts to the sanctuary.

Ammie savored her growing excitement about the event. It would be a much-needed shot in the arm for everyone involved, especially for her and Barbara. She took added satisfaction in how it would show their tormentors that they were not giving up or backing down, no matter what.

There couldn't have been a better day for the conference. The sun shone clear and bright, and although it was warm, the heat was not insufferable, as was often the case during Carolina summers. The press had turned out in force, taking seats along with church supporters facing the podium that Willie and Deacon Smith had set up. Members of the congregation and committee milled around while waiting to take their places behind the podium. Ammie was to read a statement for the media and then help lead a tour of the church and the grounds to exhibit what they were doing.

She chatted with various people, checking her watch with repeated nervousness. Catching the quizzical glances from several of the reporters, she knew she should have started the press conference fifteen minutes ago, but she stalled for time. She had been looking forward to the day for weeks, and now she had a sinking feeling in the pit of her stomach. As she was half listening to the person who spoke to her, a question kept resounding in her mind: Where was Barbara? Barbara was a stickler about punctuality. Ammie had never known her to be late to much of anything, least of all something as important as this press conference. If for some reason she was going to be late, Barbara would have gotten word to her. Ammie tried not to jump to the worst conclusions, but considering the attacks on both of them, it was hard not to do so.

She checked her watch again for the umpteenth time and

noticed some of the reporters looking at theirs, too. She had wanted to wait until Barbara got there, but she realized she had better get started, otherwise people would start to leave.

The thought struck her that John wasn't there, either, although he told her that he planned to attend. She quickly dismissed the thought. His jam-packed schedule at the academy had probably demanded his presence there.

She went over to the congregation and committee and signaled everyone to take their place. Before starting to speak into the TV microphones, she wondered again where on earth her friend was.

As Barbara had made her way to St. John down Old Wire Road, she took note of the time—perfect. She was right on schedule and would be able to help Ammie get things organized and hand out press releases and other material.

Trying to avoid the bone-jarring spots on the unforgiving dirt road that was in as bad a condition as Old State, she barely paid attention to the sound of an engine cranking to life from through the trees. As she continued down the road, movement that reflected in her rearview mirror caught her eye. Through the billowy cloud of dust her car created, she saw that a large truck had fallen in behind her. Although it was caked with mud, she could distinguish its tan paint.

Thoughts of the press conference absorbed her attention. With everything else going on in the news, it was important that people be reminded what was happening at the church and that even though they were making a lot of progress, they still needed help. Although her appearance at the conference was sure to generate more harassing phone calls, she wouldn't miss being there for anything. She hoped that—

The truck following her cut into her thoughts. It had sped up until it was dead on her bumper. With consternation, she pressed down slightly on the accelerator. There was no excuse for anyone to be driving like that. The way was clear for the driver to pass if he didn't think she was going fast enough. Whatever had become of patience or courtesy?

She glanced again into the rearview mirror. Two grungy, mean-looking white men rode in the truck. Her breath caught as she thought about how Ammie had described the driver of the burgundy sedan. Could the same man be at the wheel behind her?

A cold wave of panic broke over her when the men accelerated behind her. "Lord, have mercy," she whispered. Images of what had happened to Ammie only a week earlier flashed through her mind. Had it not been for Willie and Butch, all of them would probably be attending Ammie's funeral instead of a press conference.

When she slammed her foot to the floor, her car shot forward as if it had been fired from a sling. The truck raced behind her, closing in, as if prepared to strike. Only a few yards separated them. Through the haze of flying dust, she caught an unmistakable expression on the driver's face—pure hatred.

Despite her speed, the few yards of separation shrank to a few feet. The growl of the truck's large motor told her that it was far more powerful than hers. There was no way she could outrace it, to make it to the safety of St. John.

Through an almost mind-numbing panic, she caught sight of a huge cornfield to her right with laden stalks. Without any idea of what to do next, she jerked the steering wheel and plowed right into the field. Tall cornstalks crashed against the car as she careened into them. Her old car rocked and lurched wildly. She had propelled it into the field with such force that the wheels momentarily lost contact with the ground before colliding back down only to fly up again. Barely aware of her own consciousness, she pummeled a narrow swath through the field until her car slammed to a stop, as if she had hit some unseen wall.

The impact caused her forehead to crack down against the steering wheel, and searing pain shot through her head and reverberated down her neck and spine. Dazed, she lightly fingered her forehead and then her neck—she wondered if she had broken it, but realized she could still turn her head and felt no loss of sensation. She almost wished she couldn't feel anything—the pain was excruciating. She didn't know which hurt worse, her forehead or her neck.

An image of the truck blasted into her mind again. Fighting against the pain, she forced herself to twist around and look behind, but all she saw was the path of shredded and smashed stalks flanked by high, upright rows. She strained to hear the growl of the truck's motor, but could only hear the cawing of blackbirds and the hum of distant traffic from I-26. Wincing, she turned back around and turned the key in the ignition. The motor made a weak try before giving up. It had even less to offer when she turned the key again.

"Jesus, please," she murmured, "I need your help." She was several miles away from the church. It would take the better part of an hour to walk there, if not more considering how much pain she was in. The press conference would be history, but given the current situation, she would be satisfied if she could simply make it to safety.

The flurry of dust her car had churned up as it barreled into the corn had not totally dissipated when she climbed out of her old sedan. Some of it settled on her as she stood beside the car, trying to figure out what to do.

The rumble of an approaching motor made her blood run cold. Her hope that the vehicle would pass was shattered when, through the corn, she heard the motor slow to a consistent idle just beyond where she stood. The men in that truck—they had come back. Her frantic dash into the cornfield had bought her only a few moments, time they used to turn the truck around and agree on how to strike.

Standing beside her useless car, she picked up the sound of one of them yelling something.

"Oh, God," she prayed, and took off running farther into the field. The cornstalks seemed to have joined in on the assault, tearing at her clothes, hair, and skin. She sobbed as she tried to flee from the man who, judging from the sound of his footsteps, was closing in on her.

"Hey! Hey!" the man yelled.

Barbara ran harder, the thumping of her heart exploding against her ears.

"Barbara! What's the matter?"

In her terror, it took her a split second to realize what she heard.

"Barbara!" someone called louder.

She turned around to see John gaping at her.

"What the—?" he asked, utterly bewildered, and then started over. "What's the matter?"

Between gasps for breath, she told him what happened. After putting her in his car, he sped off, hoping to catch sight of the truck, but it was long gone. The mixture of her fear and the thick haze of dust had prevented her from getting a license plate number.

Limp from the whole ordeal, she let the tears flow as John fumed about what he would do with the two men in the truck if he got his hands on them. He called in a report while keeping an eye out on the chance that the men had stopped somewhere on the road.

They drove up to the church, and she saw Ammie speaking from the podium. Dozens of people were there, and she recognized a couple of TV reporters amidst the crowd. She spotted Sheriff Metts and several of his deputies.

"I'm going to tell Sheriff Metts what happened and have a wrecker sent for your car," John told her before getting out.

She debated whether to get out of the car, cringing at the thought of how she must look. That morning, she had put on one of her best outfits as well as taking special care with her hair. Now her hair was a mess, she had a huge goose egg on her forehead, her blouse was ripped, and she was covered head to toe in dust and corn silk.

But something told her to get out and take her place among

the other members of the congregation. After running her hands over her hair that poked out in assorted directions and beating away the dust and corn silk as best she could, she straightened her clothes and stepped forward to take her place behind Ammie along with everyone else in the congregation and on the committee.

"A lot has—" Ammie paused in her speech as she saw John and Barbara drive up. Relief at seeing them, Barbara particularly, replaced the dread that had weighed down on her. But she couldn't help wondering why they had come together. A closer look at Barbara as she climbed out of John's sedan made her do a double take. She looked as if she had just been thrown down a steep hill, and she had a horrible lump on her head. She must have been in a car accident.

"Um—" Ammie scanned down her notes until she found her place again. "A lot has happened since we called the plight of this historic church to media attention in February. At that time, virtually all the windows had been broken. Now there are new windows. The water pump was ruined. Now there's a new well and pump. Graves were desecrated. Now, we've repaired most of the damage in the cemetery and even located some old graves that were not marked."

She looked up from her statement and smiled, partially at Barbara as she slipped behind her.

"The bell had been stolen. Now there's a new bell and a new bell tower. Light fixtures had been smashed. Now there are new light fixtures. Graffiti had been painted on the doors and walls. Now there are new doors and the buildings have been freshly painted. A crucifix that hung on the pulpit was broken. It has been repaired. The church and Sunday school building have new roofs.

"The sanctuary has been remodeled. There's a new parking lot. Now let me tell you about how all of this has come about—it was a miracle."

"Amen," Deacon Wally Smith said.

"Volunteers have contributed more than one thousand work-days of labor and have donated truckloads of material. Counted together, it totals up to something in the neighborhood of twenty-five thousand. Cash contributions have reached six thousand three hundred, and most of it has been spent on material and skilled labor that we've gotten for bargain prices.

"There have been some fantastic volunteers down here, but before I close, I would like to recognize two in particular who have really shown the rest of us what selfless giving is all about—

"Lorenza Mathews of the State Criminal Justice Academy has worked countless hours here at the church. Matt is always the first one here—and usually the last to leave."

Hearty applause broke out as Matt grinned, though he seemed embarrassed by the spotlight.

"Butch Spires, a longtime member of the County Council, has won the contributions of things the rest of us never thought we could get. He's sent trucks and men out here from his company, Aggregate Trucking, and paid them out of his own pocket. Butch has dedicated the next several months of his Council pay to purchase carpeting for the sanctuary."

Butch gave a nearly imperceptible nod of his head as others clapped around him.

Ammie went on. "There are so many good people working on this project. These two guys, though, have really been the spark plugs.

"Compare what you see to what you saw back in February. Tell me it's not a miracle."

After the end of the conference, Ammie joined the group of people bunched around Barbara.

"Good God, are you all right?" she asked after she listened to Barbara recount the entire incident to Sheriff Metts and the deputies.

"I think I'll be okay, Miss Ammie. I've got to put some ice on this egg though." She gingerly felt the lump above her brow that was in fact about the size of a bluebird egg.

John signaled the reporters over. "Somebody just ran this lady off the road! You guys need to do a story on this. Take some pictures of her car and send a crew out to see if you can help us catch the guys who did this to her."

"They ran her off the road?" one of the reporters asked as if he hadn't heard what John said only a second ago.

"Yeah," John said. "If you really want a news story, you ought to do one about what happened to her. Her car is still stuck out in the middle of that cornfield right off that road."

"What road?" another young reporter asked.

"That road up there!" John pointed toward it. "Old Wire Road."

"Well." The young woman smoothed down her tailored silk skirt. "How are we going to know how to find her car, which one it is?"

It was becoming apparent to John and everyone else that some of the reporters were more into covering the news in safety and comfort than in putting themselves in potentially dangerous situations.

"Miss, it's red." His patience splintered more with each word. "And it's the only goddamned red car sitting in the middle of the damned cornfield!"

Barbara couldn't help but laugh along with Ammie, not knowing something worse was yet to come.

The lump on Barbara's forehead shrank over the next few days, and the soreness in her neck eased up a bit. She wished her memory of what had happened subsided as easily as her physical injuries. Closing her eyes, she could see that truck bearing down on her with those two men inside. And if she had a dollar for every time she had been called "nigger bitch" and other hate-filled slurs, she would be one of the richest women in America. She didn't know how much more of this she could take.

The strain was showing on Ammie also. Barbara wanted to stay strong for Ammie, and she knew that Ammie wanted to do the same for her. It was as if they had an unspoken pact between them that neither would be the first to break. They shared every detail of the harassment that they suffered, but they didn't speak of their fear. As if pretending it didn't exist could make it go away.

One hundred degrees. A heat index of 110. Barbara mopped her face as she slid inside her blazing hot car after finishing work one afternoon. The dog days of summer had set in, and the coolness of fall seemed a forever away. It was far worse inside a car that had sat in a heat-absorbing asphalt parking lot for most of the day. Weather like this made parking spots beneath shade trees valuable commodities, despite occasional smatterings of bird droppings and pine sap.

She was glad that the scorching heat wasn't deterring volunteers. If the numbers sagged one workday, they rebounded the next. Ammie was never without her notebook to jot down the names of each volunteer and donor. Amazingly, more than two thousand people had helped so far. Some, like Matt and Butch, had logged in hundreds of hours, while others had been able to mail in only a few dollars.

Many businesses had made significant donations, as well. Ammie passed their names on to Jerry so that he could mention them in his weekly update of their progress for the *Dispatch-News*.

Turning the air-conditioning to full blast didn't offer much relief as Barbara pulled out of the parking lot. Too drained by the heat to consider cooking that evening, she swung by a fast-food restaurant called the Golden Skillet and picked up dinner.

She was carrying the food to her car when someone called out, "Hey, you! Wait up a minute there, I want to tell you something."

Looking around, she saw a white man coming toward her from around the driver's side of a beat-up truck parked next to her car. Apparently, while she was inside, he had driven up in the old green truck loaded with bales of hay, farm tools, a bundle of crumpled drink cans, and a pair of old boots caked with dried mud. Stickers of the Confederate flag plastered the bumper. Another white man sat in the passenger seat. He scowled at her, but she couldn't focus on him because the other man closed in on her and snarled, "I saw your black face on the TV. You got this white woman helping you down at your church, that nigger church down there."

Stunned, Barbara tried to back away.

Wearing dirty jeans, a faded shirt, and cowboy boots, he had advanced on her until he stood only inches away, and his stench nearly made her vomit. The horrific odor was a nauseating combination of sweat and manure. As he spoke, dark tobacco juice bubbled at the corners of his mouth, staining his broken teeth and thin, wind-chafed lips.

"Now, nigger, I don't want to see your black face on the TV or talking on the news anymore, because we'll blow that motherfucking church off the map."

Out of the corner of her eye, Barbara saw his companion inside the truck twisting around, as if trying to grab hold of something. A gun? A knife? Were they going to force her into the truck and later leave what was left of her body on the road?

Almost frozen in place from terror, she backed into the door of her car, still clutching the box of food. "I've done nothing to you," she managed to say. "We're just trying to get help for the church. I didn't say anything about anybody."

"It's niggers like you that we like to grab and rape." He closed in on her again, taking a lecherous scan of her body.

It felt as if every drop of blood drained out of her.

"So I suggest you keep your mouth and your black face off of the TV. What y'all need is a good beating again. You understand what I'm saying, gal?"

Sneering, he shot a stream of tobacco juice onto her white shoes. It hit with a soft splat and sprayed onto her ankle. She felt its warm wetness seep into her skin.

Half turning to keep one eye on the man in front of her and the other on his partner in the truck, she opened her car door with shaking hands and slid in as fast as she could. The hateful sneers remained on both of their faces as she jetted out of the parking lot.

She made it as far as a convenience station a few blocks away where an acquaintance worked before her nerves gave out and she shook too much to drive any farther. Going inside, she related what happened to her friend. "I think you need to let the law know about this," the lady advised.

Taking her advice, Barbara made a report to the South Congaree police department, which had jurisdiction. She also talked to Stick Harris, who told her to report anything suspicious to him immediately. She had known Stick for years and continued to be impressed by his professionalism and dedication.

Before she went home, she stopped by her parents' and confided what had occurred.

Her mom sank into a chair in the kitchen. "Barbara, please, if you keep on with this, you're going to end up getting killed. You don't know what some of those white people will do to you. Look at what's happened already."

"I can't quit," she replied, and gave a resigned shrug of her shoulders. "If I've got to go, maybe this is my way to go out."

"Lord, they're going to kill our child." Her mother covered her face with her dark hands.

"How can I quit and leave Miss Ammie down there along with everybody else? It's because of me that she got involved in the first place."

"Mrs. Murray is a beautiful lady." Her mom wiped away tears. "And she's done some wonderful things to help the church, but now your life and her life are on the line."

"If you won't quit St. John, at least move up here where we are," her dad pleaded. "You and the kids. At least if you're here with us, we can protect you better. You see how Mrs. Murray moved out of the country up into Cayce. You need to move out of where you are, too. Them Klan people are all around over there. They could do anything. You've got to think about not only yourself, honey, but the kids, too."

Her parents' pleas resounded in her mind as she drove home. For his own peace of mind, her dad followed her to make sure she arrived okay.

She left the boxed meal on the stove for the kids. She had lost her appetite.

EIGHT

Do You Have a Death Wish?

August had barely begun before trouble visited St. John once again. During a patrol at three in the morning, a sheriff's deputy named Jim Williams noticed a blue truck parked near the front doors of the church, which were open. Ax marks cut across the wooden doors near their deadbolt locks.

Inside the building were six white teenagers. The oldest was a nineteen-year-old woman; the youngest, a fifteen-year-old boy. They had a soda can with gasoline in it, some hammers, screwdrivers, hatchets, and cutting tools. By the looks of it, they tried to set the place on fire but only succeeded in scorching the belfry roof and burning the bell rope by the time they were arrested. They had also punched a gaping hole in the belfry's ceiling.

Ammie, Barbara, and everyone else who had labored on the church were beyond disgust.

Assessing the damage with Ammie, Matt said, "It's a shame some people got nothing better to do with their time." He shook his head. Another setback. The last thing they needed.

"This is a church, for God's sake!" Ammie fumed. "If these people don't respect a church, what will they respect? They've got to be the dregs of society." Pointing to the scorch marks and the hole in the ceiling, she said, "They must have gotten aggravated when they couldn't get a fire started, so they knocked that hole up there."

All the people of St. John had ever wanted was to worship in peace, and all she wanted was to help them. And yet, the church continued to be under assault; her and Barbara's lives were in jeopardy; others, including Matt and Butch, were being threatened, too, and there was no end in sight.

They hadn't finished the sanctuary, had barely begun on the Sunday school building, and the church desperately needed some type of security system. But after they paid for the last round of supplies, only about three hundred dollars remained.

Ammie went outside and sat on the old stump, trying to fight back a growing wave of despair. She kept telling herself that she couldn't quit but didn't know how she could go on.

Closing her eyes against the harsh sunlight, she opened them again to look at Deacon Sulton's grave. She wished she had been able to meet him. In a way, she felt like she had. Barbara and Willie spoke of him often, as did others in the church. In her mind's eye, she imagined him coming there before each service, opening the building and preparing it for the arrival of others. She saw him shopping for a piano, taking special care to pick just the right one for his beloved St. John and using his life savings to buy it. Her heart ached for him as he paced amongst desecrated graves in the cemetery, wringing his hands as tears ran down his face. "Why, Lord? Why?" She could almost hear his cries as she gazed at his headstone.

During a recent visit to her daughter's home, Scott, her four-year-old grandson, apparently picked up some of the conversation about the church's hardships. "Why would anybody want to hurt God's house?" he asked with wide-eyed innocence.

She didn't know what to tell him, except to say that some people in the world were cruel. His small face screwed up in confusion. His confusion matched her own. Why? How could anyone do such a thing? If she lived a thousand years, she would never truly figure it out. Releasing a heavy sigh, she stood up. Walking to Deacon Sulton's granite headstone, she ran her hand over it.

"Whatever you do, keep the doors of the church open." That's what he had told Willie shortly before his death. Those words had been sustenance for Willie and Barbara, and Ammie drew strength from them as well. Deacon Sulton had given his all to St. John, as had many before him. To quit now would render their sacrifices in vain. It would strip hope away from future generations.

Her grandchildren would never have to leave their church at the end of services worrying if it would still be intact the following week because of vandalism. The children of St. John deserved the same. They deserved to have their ancestral house of worship rebuilt. They deserved to have it protected.

Folks occasionally sang "I Ain't Noways Tired" at the church. The words came back to her:

> I don't feel no ways tired.
> I've come too far from where I started from.
> Nobody told me that the road would be easy.
> I don't believe He's brought me this far to leave me.

They repeated the last line over and over—"I don't believe He's brought me this far to leave me."

Summer loosened its grip, and milder fall temperatures took hold. Ammie and Barbara met one late September morning at

St. John. They couldn't disguise their nervousness from each other or from the others joining them, including several reporters and photographers. Bill Moyers and a film crew from CBS were on the way to meet them.

Ammie inspected herself for the umpteenth time. She wore a light blue jacket with a matching skirt, a white blouse, and white pumps. It was nice enough for TV. She hoped.

As if they had coordinated their outfits, Barbara had on her best dress—a short-sleeved white knit that she accented with white pumps and light blue earrings shaped like hearts. Unlike Ammie, she didn't wear makeup. Her hair gleamed from the oil sheen she had sprayed in it. Because of local press coverage, Barbara had been on TV a number of times, but being interviewed by Bill Moyers was altogether different. After all, the man used to be an adviser to presidents, not to mention being a highly respected journalist.

Though the Sunday school remained in bad shape, the sanctuary was presentable enough. Despite being devoid of floor covering or wall paneling, the place was clean and solid. It was a lucky thing that the weather was still mild; they had no heat pump to warm it had an early cold spell set in.

Several vehicles pulled up, and Moyers emerged from one of them.

Someone behind Ammie and Barbara whispered, "Hey, he looks just like he does on TV!"

He greeted each of them with a warm handshake, and his unassuming personality quickly put them at ease. Within no time, they felt as comfortable with him as if they were chatting with a neighbor over a cup of coffee.

"I am more interested in the two thousand people who have volunteered to help the church than the dozen who have damaged it," he told them. "It's encouraging to me to come back to the South and see that there are good hearts here, that people are working together to defeat the demon, racism."

Wanting to learn the events that led to the rebuilding effort,

Bill asked Barbara what she had seen when she came to the church after New Year's.

"It was horrible," she told him. "It was like a massacre had been here. When I came up and got out of my car, the first thing I came to was 'KKK' scratched on the doors."

The two of them sat on the front pew. Barbara soon forgot about the presence of the cameramen as she relived for him what she found when she entered St. John that morning—the shot-up pews; the smashed chairs, woodstove, and water cooler; the hacked piano, the desecrated sacramental cloth, the crucifix with Christ's arms hanging by nails—everything. It all came back to her as if she saw it before her once more.

He looked at her with eyes that had witnessed more conflict across the world than most people would see in ten lifetimes.

"Were you surprised at how so many people responded to the needs of the church?" he asked, referring to Ammie and the multitude of others who had helped.

"I really was," Barbara responded in her soft voice. "I truly was. I was amazed and I was astonished. I was just overwhelmed by seeing all of this being said and done by these people."

"This was the first time in your recollection that the two races had worked together on something in this area to this extent?"

She nodded. "In this area, yes."

"Does this signify that things have changed for the better, or is it a special circumstance that's not likely to be repeated?"

Choosing her words carefully, she answered, "I would say that this was done, in my opinion, in an act of Christian love, but I can't say that it will continue."

A part of her wished she could be more hopeful, but given what had been going on, that was as optimistic as she could be.

They rejoined Ammie, who had been talking outside with Estelle Simmons, Barbara's mother-in-law. Ammie, Barbara, and Bill walked out to the cemetery with the camera crew and local media following as several church members looked on.

Barbara pointed Deacon Sulton's grave out. "This is the grave that was desecrated by the vandals, by the wheels of their vehicles dropping down and bruising the casket. We had to call the funeral home over to redo the grave."

Bill asked Ammie to recount her first images of the church and then what she found in the cemetery. Ammie spoke of what she found inside the sanctuary, her words similar to Barbara's. As they moved closer to Deacon Sulton's burial place, she said, "Well, I had just started back here and I had a feeling and I, well, I just broke down and cried."

They had walked until they stood right beside the old man's headstone.

"You just had to have seen it," Ammie continued. "The grave desecrated. A new grave, and the cross and flowers and everything—"

As with Barbara, the image of what she saw came back, hitting her hard. Forgetting the cameras and the fact that she was speaking to a world-renowned journalist, Ammie started crying. The emotion caused by what she had seen was always there, right below the surface. Most of the time, she was able to keep it in check, but sometimes it gushed out like water breaking through a dam.

Digging in her jacket pocket for a tissue, she found one and wiped away tears.

Gently, Bill asked her, "Did you say, 'We can do something about this'?"

Ammie took a moment to try to compose herself, but her voice still cracked when she answered. "I didn't say anything. I had a feeling that I had to do something, but I didn't know what."

They moved back inside the sanctuary and sat down as Ammie described how she pulled a committee together and how they set to work along with the people of St. John to rebuild. Bill sat in front of them as they sat on a pew behind.

"Have you experienced any harassment?" he asked.

"Oh, yes," Barbara answered quickly.

Though they didn't discuss every incident, neither of them sugarcoated the attacks that happened on Old State Road and

Old Wire Road. They had been hesitant to talk about them before. Bulldog and Stick warned them against discussing it with the press for fear of copycats.

"What about mail, phone calls? Have you had that sort of thing?"

"A lot of phone calls," Ammie said.

Barbara echoed her statement.

"What kinds of things do people say?" he asked, looking at Ammie.

"Do you really want me to say?"

"Yes."

She grinned, trying to figure out how to answer without her words getting bleeped out. "Nigger-lover," she replied, leaving out the *bitch* part and some of the nastier stuff.

When the conversation shifted to the outpouring of support, Ammie and Barbara were able to speak more freely.

What began as an act of friendship between them had enveloped an entire community. Continuing to speak about the diverse people who were helping, Ammie said, "It's shown what the people of Lexington County are really all about now. I've seen some people change so much in their attitude." She smiled. "Well, I would know that they were known as racists. You ought to see them now."

Bill interviewed Barbara's mother-in-law in front of the church. She recounted the dark days. "I felt that a lot of times, people would come in and throw something in the church and try to kill us or something like that, you know. There were people riding around on motorcycles, all around the church, and shooting different places. You can get afraid."

"Do you think some members just stopped coming out of fear?"

"That's right. That's right. They told us so."

As Ammie and Barbara had experienced, Bill's genuine concern over what they had gone through helped Mrs. Simmons to forget about the camera crew recording her every word and movement.

"Do you think the church is stronger today for having over-come these acts of vandalism?"

"I believe so, and I hope and trust the Lord that they won't bother us anymore."

"Do you think they might?"

"Well, a little bit." She sighed. "Kind of."

"But you're going to keep on coming."

"I'm going to keep on," she answered resolutely. "Yes, I will."

He told them that the show would air the next month. The segment would be put together using footage from that day as well as from when a camera crew filmed back during the spring. They took a short break before wrapping up. The morning had gone by so fast, Ammie could hardly believe it was drawing to an end already. Bill's return flight home was scheduled for early that afternoon.

She and Bill leaned against her car during the momentary break. He surprised her by asking, "Ammie, do you ever think that you've got a death wish?"

"No, not really. Why?"

"Well, you're a big Democrat in one of the most Republican counties in the United States, and you're a business manager in a state that hates labor unions, and you're helping a black church rebuild not two miles from where the KKK meets every month."

"Well, I really never thought about it like that," Ammie said, and then started to laugh. "But now that you mention it, maybe I do."

He joined in her laughter.

His visit reminded Ammie that they weren't alone. There were people out there, like Bill, who cared. Once the story aired, who knew how many others would be touched, too.

One of the reasons she had wanted to rebuild the church

was so it could serve as a beacon of inspiration for the young African-American children in the area. What hadn't occurred to her was that it could also offer hope to the entire country that the chasm between races might someday be bridged.

Along with a psychological boost, Bill's visit also resulted in tangible help. After local media coverage, three security companies—SC Alarm, Southeastern Security Systems, and Home Safety Equipment—donated and installed an extensive alarm system. Dick Park with SC Alarm Company pledged that in addition, his company would provide free monitoring.

Overjoyed, Ammie was sure this would go a long way toward stopping the ongoing attacks. At the next committee meetings, she told everyone, "If vandals ever come back, they'd better have their toothbrushes with them, because they're going straight to jail!"

All of them set to work on the sanctuary and Sunday school with renewed energy and focus. That completion was now within sight energized them all the more. Ammie announced to the media that they may possibly finish as early as Thanksgiving. It was almost enough to help Ammie and Barbara forget about the harassment they still received. Almost.

After she got run off Old Wire Road, Barbara noticed several suspicious-looking trucks slowly driving back and forth in front of her house. It wasn't anything that necessarily warranted police surveillance, but it gave her the creeps just the same. Not to mention the calls that continued streaming in, especially during the weekends.

Though she hadn't seen the burgundy sedan again or seen anything out of the ordinary since midsummer, the phone calls Ammie kept getting were enough to keep her guard up. She continued with the safety precautions Stick and Bulldog taught her. Betsy and Christy didn't need more than one to two fingers to count how many times they had seen the inside of her new home. Despite being near the police station, she remained reluctant for her daughters, or anyone else close to her, to visit her at home. She nearly always met them somewhere else and on the way there she made a series of sudden turns to see if another vehicle mirrored her movements.

It would be over soon, she told herself. They were nearly done. After that, things would return to normal, although she knew that in so many ways, she would never be the same. Barbara, either. Both of them had been forced to draw from strengths they never knew they possessed to battle pure evil.

Ammie wasn't in the habit of missing church, but the first Sunday in November was a special exception. She wouldn't have missed *CBS Sunday Morning* for all the oil in Texas. After checking the VCR again to make sure it was ready, she settled back down on the sofa.

"Dixiana, South Carolina." She heard Bill Moyers's voice as the segment opened with footage of Old State Road leading up to the church. "A long way from everything but trouble. A lot of history has happened on Old State Road. Once it connected Columbia to Charleston. Now it ends in the woods by a little Baptist church—"

Her breath caught as St. John appeared, and tears of joy stung her eyes. St. John on *CBS Sunday Morning*! The reality of it finally sank in as she continued to watch.

"Folks worshiped on this site back in the Revolutionary days, when slavery flourished."

As he spoke, images of the destruction filled the screen—the bullet-ridden pews, the chopped crucifix.

"Sunday after Sunday, the folks of St. John left their troubles at the door, or hoisted them with hymn and prayer to the mercies of heaven. But the singing and praying almost stopped last winter. Vandals came and did the work of the devil—"

After showing some of the destruction, there appeared snippets of the church service that took place when the film crew had come in early spring. They stayed for a Saturday workday and then for Sunday services. Their footage featured Barbara singing with others members, little Michael looking as cute as a button, and Reverend Shepherd starting to preach.

"Soon and very soon," they sang in a brief portion, "we are going to see the King! Hallelujah! Hallelujah! We are going to see the King!"

There was Barbara sitting there describing the New Year's desecration to Bill as they sat together on a pew. "It was horrible. It was like a massacre had been there—"

Ammie nearly squealed with delight. Barbara was on national TV, looking as if chatting with Bill Moyers was something she did on a daily basis.

Then Ammie saw Miss Estelle, Willie's mom, talking to Bill in front of the church. "Just like I said, I felt that a lot of times, people would come in and throw something in the church and try to kill us or something—"

"Oh, my goodness," Ammie said when she saw herself for the first time. While the segment showed her, Bill, and Barbara walking near Deacon Sulton's grave, Bill continued: "The vandals didn't stop at trying to destroy the church. That wouldn't have been hard to do, anyway. The congregation is poor, and the building had fallen into disrepair. But the vandals also invaded the cemetery behind it, raging against the dead. Tombstones were toppled and graves ripped open.

"Ammie Murray heard about the devastation the next morning when she came to work to the office where she and Barbara are both employed. They had been friends for several years—"

She saw herself starting to cry while describing how she found Deacon Sulton's desecrated grave.

"Ammie Murray is not one to weep for long about the sins of the world. She'd rather plow them under. She's a believer in miracles. The kind wrought by willing hands and hearts and the sweat of a good day's labor. A miracle, says her friend Barbara Simmons, is exactly what Ammie made happen here."

They showed footage of the spring workday. Nearly one hundred volunteers had showed up that Saturday. They swarmed all over the place, raking, clearing, hammering, sawing, painting, scrubbing.

"At Ammie's call, the volunteers turned out—as many as two thousand at one time or another—men, women, children, black and white, of different faiths, and from very different histories."

Tom appeared raking and planting a rose bush.

"Tom Turnipseed's grandfather belonged to the Ku Klux Klan, and Tom, an attorney now, was once a campaign director for the then unreconstructed George Wallace."

Tom, having once been a lay minister, had preached at the Sunday service following the workday. The film crew captured part of his sermon. In the African-American "call-and-response" tradition, members of the congregation punctuated the end of each of his sentences with "Amen!," "That's right!," "Yeah!," and other responses to show their agreement with his message:

"KKK—we all know what that means. That's intended to frighten God's people. But God's people—black and white— aren't going to be afraid anymore. Hate and fear are not going to come back in this country. We've had enough of it—"

"Say, so!" someone shouted louder than before.

"Amen!" others called out.

He had to pause before the shouts of support died down. "It's out there. We've got to always stand up and speak out and fight it wherever we see it. And I look at this diverse group of people brought together by good, God-fearing human beings, good Christian people—women like Ammie Murray and Barbara Simmons, all of the people who have worked so hard. We are not going to let it come back here in Dixiana, South Carolina! We're not going to let it come back here in Lexington County, South Carolina!"

As the segment came toward its end, Ammie saw herself talking about the healing gift of St. John—"I've seen people change so much. Well, I would know that they were known as racists— you ought to see them now."

Indeed. Miracles did happen, Ammie thought. She was seeing it with her own eyes.

NINE

Rebirth

The workday on the first Saturday of February was special. It was the last. St. John stood proudly in the quiet clearing beneath tall pines. Winter sunlight shone brightly as if to extend its blessing to the day.

From the new, earth-toned carpeting to the solidly rebuilt roof, the church had been reborn. Warmly hued wood paneling decorated the interior walls and complemented wooden pews that were painted a soft khaki tone. Donations that came in after the airing of *CBS Sunday Morning* purchased a heat pump that guarded the church against winter's chill. The windows gleamed with new panes of glass, and the exterior cinder-block walls sported a fresh coat of dazzling white paint.

While he was in Vietnam, Matt had found some pieces of

teakwood. He didn't know what he could do with it, but the wood was so pretty that he packed it in one of his duffel bags and brought it back home. For nearly two decades, he kept it stored, waiting to find just the right use for it. He knew he had found a home for it in St. John. For the crowning touch to its completion, he fashioned the teakwood into a cross and hung it behind the altar.

Ammie dabbed away tears of joy. For so long, she had wondered if this day would ever come—after everything they had been through—not only her and Barbara, but also the scores of others, including Matt and Butch, who had practically put their lives on hold to help. They didn't have to do what they did. None of them had had to. They could have just walked away. They could have quit. God knew that there were moments when thoughts of doing that crossed her mind. She was only human. But she hadn't. They hadn't. And because of that, St. John survived.

It was a simply constructed 660-square-foot building, but as far as she was concerned, Westminister Abbey couldn't have been more spectacular.

Before walking into it, Barbara paused to gaze at St. John. It was so beautiful that it nearly made her heart ache, especially when she thought of all the atrocities it had suffered. Bringing it back from destruction had almost ended her life and that of her friend. God had been with them, though, and their faith in Him and in each other had seen them through.

From the time she was a child, she had heard people quote the Biblical verse, "All things work together for those who love the Lord and are called according to his purpose." Tragedy had struck them—the people of St. John—but they had emerged stronger for it, and the building was in better shape than when she first saw it nearly fifteen years earlier. Their story had spread all across the United States and beyond. After the CBS segment, reporters from Japan and Germany had come, too.

A producer had even contacted them from Hollywood about doing a "movie-of-the-week" for one of the TV networks. The producer's company had made more than fifty TV movies, mini-series, and documentaries. She was attracted to the St. John story, not only because of the rebuilding effort, but also because of the friendship between Barbara and Ammie that spawned it.

The producer had written: "We believe that your special friendship and the events in your community that united you tells a story that deserves recognition. Racism should be exposed and denounced wherever and whenever it rears its ugly head. Your courage and persistence to right a wrong is a message well worth conveying."

When Ammie showed the letter to Barbara, neither of them could hardly believe it was real. The good fortune that arrived, especially in light of all that they had been through, boggled their minds. And it was because of St. John.

Ammie held a press conference on Tuesday, February 11, 1986, to announce the church's completion and that the Save St. John Baptist Church Committee was officially disbanding, exactly one year to the day after the first committee meeting had been held.

"Looking back over the past year," she told reporters and others gathered at the church, "at times I had become convinced that we had committed ourselves to a totally unrealistic project, but we kept on, and here we are."

Jerry and several other photographers snapped pictures as she read from her notes.

"Not one brick has been laid, not one wall painted, or one nail hammered by people who didn't love this church," she said. "People have contributed thousands of volunteer man-hours, more than fifty thousand dollars' worth of building materials, and we've raised more than eleven thousand in cash. There have been so many people who have helped, I can't name them all. Over two thousand have come at one time or another, but the real spark plugs have been Lorenza 'Matt' Mathews and Lowell

'Butch' Spires. There's no way we could have done this without them."

Applause broke out for the two men, who sat near each other.

"We have completed this mission with fourteen hundred dollars left, which we are donating to the church for them to use as they see fit. While it is time for the Save St. John Baptist Church Committee to step back, its goal accomplished, we'll always be here whenever the congregation needs us. Always."

The day was a triumph that each of them savored. Squeezing Barbara tight, Ammie said, "I never thought we'd see the day, but we did it, Barbara."

"We surely did, Miss Ammie," Barbara replied, hugging her back. "Thank the Lord, we sure did."

They gazed at the church in all its simple splendor. Both they and St. John had endured dark times, but brighter ones lay ahead. Or so they thought.

TEN

Halloween

Not even a full year passed before trouble returned. A few weeks before Christmas, a deputy checked on St. John at around four o'clock on a Sunday morning and discovered that the back door had been forced open and its lock broken. Nothing inside the church had been damaged. However, outside in the cemetery, several headstones were smashed and thrown about. The deputy found a parked Honda Accord nearby and traced it to a white seventeen-year-old boy. Questioning the boy and a buddy of his didn't reveal enough evidence to charge the two, so the police had to release them.

With her hands on her small hips, Ammie stared at the ruined graves in sickened frustration. Would St. John ever be left in peace? She hated to think what would have happened had the deputy not driven up. Apparently, those two boys stopped what they were doing when they heard the cruiser approach. The church had a sophisticated alarm system that had also given off a silent alarm, and Sheriff Metts's deputies had kept a careful watch on the property, and yet neither precaution had prevented this latest attack.

The graves bore ugly tire tracks, and the silk flowers that had rested on them were torn and scattered across the ground. "Here we go again," Ammie muttered to herself.

The recurrent vandalism pushed Barbara and Willie's charity toward the church's assailants past the breaking point, and the rest of the congregation shared their sentiments. Last year's break-in by the six teens who tried to set the church on fire had forced them to reconsider the wisdom of going easy on anyone caught harming the church, and the way Tony Allen acted after they had pleaded for leniency for him added to their change of heart.

As if to punish them for their leniency toward the three young men, the six teens got off with mere slaps to the wrists. The harshest sentence given was three years of probation and a hundred-dollar fine. Judge Owen T. Cobb Jr. gave that sentence to a seventeen-year-old boy who lived in the area. He had pleaded guilty to third-degree burglary. In sentencing him, Judge Cobb spoke of the boy's age, his lack of a criminal record, and regular school attendance. The teen's lawyer also said his client's parents had abandoned him when he was a young child.

The teenager claimed he went there only to help play a joke on one of the other teens in the group. "I had never been there before. I heard it was a place where they did Satan worship and all that good stuff. We wanted to scare this guy. The joke just got out of hand."

Ammie and Jerry attended the court proceeding with Barbara and Willie, who both sat in shocked disbelief at the light sentence. Ammie fumed to Jerry, who sat beside her, "I'm sick and tired of hearing people try to use the excuse that they think St. John is for devil worshipers. Anyone who looks at that beau-

tiful little church knows it's a house of Christian worship. It's
open to all on Sunday mornings. If they have any doubts, let
them come then."

Judge Cobb mentioned that he had a seventeen-year-old of
his own and could understand how young people got into trouble from time to time.

"He's almost congratulating the kid," Ammie seethed.

Whether he heard her or not, the judge said, "Some people
may have a problem with this sentence, but the fact that the
church has had vandalism problems in the past doesn't mean I
can take it out on this boy."

Willie shook his head with disgust after it was over. He told
Jerry and a reporter from *The State* newspaper, "I ask, is it right
that a person breaks into a house of God and goes free? We
can't keep sentencing these people to probation. It won't keep
others out. We have to have someone sent to jail for them to
stop messing with us."

"I guess they'll have to burn the church down before someone goes to jail," Barbara said, standing on the courthouse steps
with the others. "That's about the only thing they haven't done
yet."

The following week, Jerry used his weekly editorial to vent
his frustration and closed the column by writing:

> What happens the next time a group of high-spirited young peo-
> ple decide to break into the church? Must it be burned to the
> ground before somebody gets the message straight?
>
> Willie Simmons knows what the message should be. Judge
> Cobb hasn't learned it yet.
>
> Frank Rizzo's words came back to me from his days as mayor
> of Philadelphia. A liberal, Rizzo said, was a conservative who
> hasn't been mugged.

A week later, charges were dropped against the two young
women in the group of six. They were allowed to wipe their

records clean through entering the Pre-Trial Intervention program, paying a fine and doing some yard work at the church. Ammie told everyone, "It looks like we're not going to get a sentence that amounts to a hill of beans."

A vandalism attack in December closed out 1986 on a disappointing note—a year that had started with so much optimism. Ammie and Barbara's disappointment grew after a call from the Hollywood producer. She apologetically explained that she couldn't get enough funding to cover production costs, so there wouldn't be a TV movie after all.

Ammie and Barbara tried to be philosophical about the whole thing—apparently it hadn't been meant to be—but it was hard not to feel let down. It would have been better not to have been contacted in the first place than to have their hopes raised, only for them to be dashed. Not only their hopes, but others', too. Jerry did several stories about the proposed movie project in the *Dispatch-News,* as had reporters for *The State* and local news stations. Everybody had been so excited. It wasn't every day that people wanted to make a movie about anything happening in South Carolina, especially in Lexington County.

Fortunately, the ongoing vigilance needed for St. John focused attention away from the failed movie project. Despite the Save St. John Baptist Church Committee's having officially disbanded, Ammie and the other core members often gathered at the church to check on things and help out in any way needed. It was if they were homing pigeons programmed to return to St. John over and over again. Matt attended services regularly, often more than some members of the congregation.

Although the first half of 1987 passed uneventfully, they all worried that another attack was just around the corner. Stick and Bulldog were particularly concerned about what might happen on Halloween. The assaults on St. John always intensified around holidays—the most severe destruction having occurred during New Year's. Halloween potentially held more danger. The detectives worried about the kind of people who might be tempted to come to the church as a result of listening to the constant swirl of talk that the church was haunted and was a front for witchcraft and devil worship.

The area where the church was located—deserted and seemingly forgotten by time—heightened the rumors. The eerie quality of the surroundings and frightening rumors led to self-fulfilling prophecies luring thrill-seekers in search of a scary experience who, indeed, got scared and then spread more talk about how scary the place was. Aided by liquor and drugs, they embellished their daring exploits by coming up with all sorts of creepy, supernatural tales like the one about an old man getting murdered near the church and his spirit crossing Old State Road at midnight, moaning and screaming curses into the darkness.

The mutilated animals and satanic symbols periodically discovered over the past few years indicated that, at the very least, some people who had a fascination with the occult had been among those targeting the church for vandalism. At worst, they were serious satanic practitioners who weren't above committing the most lurid of crimes.

One day Barbara and her sister-in-law, Pat, were walking through the cemetery when they came upon a sheet of paper with some handwriting on it, blown against one of the headstones.

Barbara picked it up and studied it for a moment. "Oh, my God."

"What?" Pat asked.

"These look like instructions for some kind of satanic initiation thing." She started reading out loud. "Number one: Find a grave of a young child, slay a small animal on it, and sprinkle fresh blood in a complete circle around the tombstone. Number two: Remove the marker from the grave of a slave woman, kneel on it, and pray to the Dark One—"

Her skin crawling, Barbara balled the paper up and threw it into a large old oil drum that they used for burning trash. "Lord have mercy."

Was this somebody's twisted attempt at harassing the congregation, or were there people who actually believed in this kind of garbage? She thought back to the other things she had seen—the words *Kill* and *Death* written in blood on the walls, mutilated animals thrown in the baptismal pool, the six dead possums lined up in front of the front doors. It sickened her to think that satanic worshipers actually existed. That they trespassed on her church's property to carry out their ghoulish practices made it all the worse.

Someone vandalized the church two weeks before Halloween by pulling up a six-foot cross from the cemetery and smashing it against one of the sanctuary's windows. Luckily, the Plexiglas covering the window protected it from shattering.

Stick headed up an effort to get volunteers from the department for a stakeout. He figured the stakeout would have to extend through the entire holiday weekend; Halloween fell on a Saturday, and many would start partying—or troublemaking—on Friday night.

Bulldog was one of the first to volunteer. So many other officers wanted to be in on it that Stick had to turn some of them down with the promise that he would select them the next year. The tiny church held a special place in everyone's heart at the department, from Sheriff Metts on down. Many made checks on it even while off-duty and had helped with construction and cleaning during workdays in addition to donating money.

They notified the public through the media that they planned to stakeout the church the entire Halloween weekend—Friday night to Sunday morning. Their primary purpose wasn't to make arrests—they hoped that they wouldn't have to arrest anyone. The primary goal was to protect St. John. But they were determined that anyone they did catch would have the book thrown at them. To make sure that happened, they devised a strategy that would maximize the charges against them.

According to the plan, Stick would be outside with the majority of the officers while Bulldog would be inside the church standing near the door. If any of them saw anyone, they wouldn't arrest them on the spot, as the only thing they could probably get them for was trespassing—a misdemeanor. However, by staying hidden and allowing the vandals to act, they could nail them for more serious crimes, such as grave tampering, which carried a sentence of up to five years. Another serious charge would be breaking and entering. So if someone attempted to break into the church, Bulldog would be ready for them. With his .357 Magnum, he'd probably scare the living daylights out of them, too.

On Halloween night, Stick, Bulldog, and a small army of police officers gathered at the church. Bulldog gave Ammie a quick call before they took their positions.

"How's it going down there?" Ammie asked.

"So far, so good. How has it been for you? Okay?"

She caught a hint of concern in his voice and knew what he was really asking. His and Stick's lingering regard for her safety touched her. The horrible calls had eased off quite a bit since they finished the church a year and a half ago. She still occasionally got them, but that had been the extent of the harassment lately. They pretty much left Barbara alone, as well. Ammie wondered to whom they had turned their hateful attention. But at least it was drifting away from them.

"Oh, can't complain," she replied. "As long as we can keep the church safe, things will be great."

Peeking through the window, he saw a car drive up.

"Hey, I gotta go, somebody's just pulled up."

"Call me again when you can," Ammie said quickly. "I'll probably be up most of the night."

"Okay. Bye." He hung up the phone and took his place near the door.

Taking in slow and steady breaths, he listened to muffled laughter and talking from in front of the church. The voices became louder, and soon, Bulldog also heard footsteps on the porch. He lightly rested one hand on the locked doorknob and felt it start to twist as someone on the opposite side tried to force the door open. The voices were more distinct now. It sounded like at least four, maybe five people out there, some of them women.

With a sudden harsh clank of metal on metal as they broke the lock with a tool, the door gave way, and three young men and two women scampered inside, giggling and laughing.

"Police!" Bulldog bellowed at them, his Magnum drawn.

Several of them screamed in terror and nearly fell over one another as—almost at the same moment—several other cops jumped from out of nowhere, terrifying them even more.

"Oh, my God! Oh, my God!" one of the women screamed hysterically, unable to look away from the long barrel of Bulldog's .357.

The detectives and deputies had barely gotten that group arrested and headed for the jail before another group showed up. Cars streamed onto the property as if it were a drive-in theater on a Saturday night. Bulldog, Stick, and the other cops nabbed people right and left.

One teenager apologetically explained that he and his friends had come because the two charity-supporting haunted houses in the nearby towns of Cayce and Irmo had closed, so they figured they'd have some fun at St. John. Carloads of people came. Few groups seemed to know one another. Several of them had coolers of beer and blankets on backseats or in trunks.

All in all, police had arrested twenty-one people on charges ranging from trespassing to illegal possession of alcohol to grave tampering. The ages of those arrested ranged from fifteen to thirty-one. Thirty others who didn't actually make it onto the church's property were questioned and warned never to return. Before letting them go, the police recorded their names and addresses.

The number of arrests astonished everyone at the sheriff's department and St. John, too. News of the weekend stakeout had been published in the papers and broadcast on TV and radio. Stick and the other officers had done everything except use sky banners to let people know that they would be down there, and they still ended up arresting or detaining dozens.

Sheriff Metts held a news conference at St. John on Sunday after services.

"With a history of vandalism to this historic church, I was certain that it would be the target of partygoers and vandals," Sheriff Metts said to the gathering of reporters and church supporters inside the sanctuary. Ammie sat beside him to the left and Barbara to the right.

"Detective Sergeant James 'Stick' Harris was responsible for setting up all-night stakeouts from dusk until dawn throughout the Halloween weekend. He had officers inside the church, in the woods around the church, and patrolling in unmarked cars around Old Wire Road and Old State Road."

After listing the charges of those arrested, the sheriff said, "There's little doubt that this historic old church would have been destroyed this weekend if it hadn't been for Sergeant Harris and his detectives."

He passed out a listing of the people arrested. "If others come here to destroy, I'll do the same again until the message is clear that this community will not tolerate vandalism."

ELEVEN

Stick and Bulldog

Over the next few years, Halloween continued to be the most dangerous night on the calendar for St. John. Despite publicizing their presence at the church each year, Stick, Bulldog, and others in the sheriff's department kept racking up more arrests.

One year, all the officers were still in hiding when they saw two men drive onto the property, get out of their car, and start digging into a grave. A few of the police were about to close in, but Bulldog motioned them away. He sneaked up behind the two guys as they worked up a sweat in the cool October night, shoveling into the sandy ground.

Pulling out his trusty .357, Bulldog cocked it behind the men's heads. In the eerie dark silence, the click of the gun resounded almost as if the Magnum had been fired.

The young men froze with shovels in midair.

"Police!" Bulldog hollered. "Don't move!"

The very sight of the vandals repulsed him. Assaulting the burial place of the dead—how much lower could somebody go?

"On second thought," the detective added, "Keep digging. I don't think that grave is deep enough for the both of you."

One of the men's scrawny body shook as he began sobbing. "Please, man, don't shoot us! Please, for God's sake!"

"We're begging you, man," pleaded the other. "We'll give you whatever you want. Just don't kill us!"

"You're under arrest," Bulldog said, managing to suppress his laughter at being taken so seriously.

Later, during the men's court hearing, Bulldog found out they were both transients from Texas.

After Bulldog summarized his case against the men in court, one of the men told the judge, "Your Honor, you don't have to ask me one question because everything Detective Yarborough said is true, and then some. I'm a drug addict, Your Honor. I'm not saying that as an excuse, but just to say that we were going to steal gold and stuff from out of them graves to buy drugs.

"You give me whatever time you see fit, and I'll go up and do my time. I want to do my time as soon as I can, because once I get out, my ass will be Texas-bound. I'm not ever coming back to South Carolina again, not even to pass through on the highway."

"Not even to pass through?" the judge asked, peering down at the greasy-haired man who stood beside his accomplice.

"No, sir."

"Why is that?"

Motioning toward Bulldog, the man replied, "Because he took ten years off my life when he came up on me with his gun. He said he was a cop, but I didn't believe him. I thought for sure he'd cap me and my buddy in the back of the head. I ain't never gonna get over that, Your Honor. Never, ever. Once I do my time, South Carolina's seen the last of my ass."

No one ever saw him near St. John again.

On another Halloween, the thirty-five-year-old manager of a

local store brought about a half-dozen of his employees with him to the church. Bulldog took position inside the church, and Stick stood nearby. From through the doors, they could hear the manager telling the women, "Aw, what are y'all so scared about? Nothing's going to hurt you."

The moment they jimmied the door and came into the church, Stick flipped the lights on, and Bulldog leveled the .357 on the manager. "Police! Trick or treat, you son of a bitch!"

Above the screams of terror that broke out, Bulldog said, "Come right on in, everyone, have a seat on the front pew, and let's have a word of prayer."

Near hysterics, the manager fell flat on his face, spilling beer all over the floor. One of the employees was beyond hysterics. Shrieking and crying uncontrollably, she yelled at her boss, "Why did we ever let you talk us into coming here?"

"Oh, God!" screamed another. "We're dead!"

Bulldog, Stick, and others with the sheriff's department made arrest after arrest for everything from simple trespassing to burglary. Though they never had to arrest the same person twice, more kept coming. It was as if some bottomless pit existed somewhere that vandals kept crawling up from. Officers arrested nearly as many women as men, and though most of those captured were teenagers, many, like the restaurant manager, were much older. While the vast majority were white, a few were black.

A black teen told Stick before being taken to jail, "I heard about this place and wanted to check it out for myself."

"Why didn't you come for services on Sunday, then?" Stick asked, but got no reply.

Despite their best efforts, even those off the clock, the sheriff's department couldn't put an end to the assaults. Crime occurring in other parts of the large, primarily rural county added to the impossibility of the limited department keeping St. John under continuous surveillance. Often, by the time the nearest deputy raced to the church in response to a signal from the burglar alarm, the vandals were long gone.

Sometimes months went by between attacks, sometimes only weeks. Sometimes the damage was only superficial, other times, life-threatening.

Willie, who had inherited the duty of opening the church from Deacon Sulton, arrived at St. John early one November morning to get the place warmed up before he and Barbara took off to start picking up elderly members.

He was about to light the pilot light of the heat pump's fuel tank when he realized someone had tampered with it. Had he lit it, both he and the church would have been blown to bits.

After they started rebuilding, Ammie offered to take on the responsibility for being St. John's contact person with the police and county prosecutors. If there was any retaliation from those arrested, she would rather it be directed toward her than at members of the congregation. They had suffered enough already. It was an offer that church members gratefully accepted.

One of St. John's apprehended assailants was a teenager whose father called Ammie about his son's arrest. At first he was fairly pleasant. "My boy's really sorry about what all happened. We've raised him better than that, but you know how kids can act when they get with the wrong crowd."

"I sure do," Ammie replied.

"He won't think of setting foot in Dixiana again," the man went on, "much less St. John. We cracked down on him really hard, and he's learned his lesson. What do you say we just make him pay a fine and drop the charges."

Ammie's grip on the phone tightened. So that was what the call was about.

"I'm sorry," she said. "That's not possible."

"Why not?"

"Your son, sir, committed a crime. He tried to burglarize a church, a church that has not done anything to him. He's got to face up to it like the others who were caught with him. The charges will not be dropped."

"I see," the man said icily, and then hung up.

A few days later, she came home to discover that a louvered glass door that served as a second front entrance to her house was shattered. Fragments of glass lay scattered over the carpet of the room she used as a home office.

She quickly looked around, the house was empty, and nothing appeared to be stolen. Still, maybe it had been an attempted burglary. She called the police.

Within minutes, a patrolman came over and searched the house but, like her, couldn't find anything amiss other than the shattered door.

"What in the world could have caused it to break like that?" Ammie searched for a rock or anything that could have been thrown through the door to cause the damage.

"I don't know, ma'am," the officer said before leaving. "But if anything else happens, give us another call."

Once he drove off, Ammie got a wastebasket, squatted down, and started to throw shards of glass into it. She stopped when something small and metallic caught her eye.

"Good Lord." She stood up and called the police again.

The same officer returned.

She pointed out the small object nestled in the carpet. "I was trying to clean up the glass when I saw it. Isn't that a bullet?"

Squatting down, the officer used his pen to position the spent shell so that he could see it better. "Yes, ma'am. It looks like it was fired by a .357." He looked up at her. "Somebody out there doesn't like you."

"You can say that again." Ammie crossed her arms resolutely.

After he left, she attempted to pull away a chunk of glass dangling from the door when it fell loose, slashing into her right hand, between the thumb and forefinger. Blood gushed from the deep cut, and she grabbed a towel to stanch the flow. As she wrapped it tightly around her hand, it didn't dawn on her to call for help. Instead, she drove herself to a hospital across town. It took twenty-six stitches to close the wound.

Because of the repeated hits to St. John, Ammie arranged occasional workdays to repair damages. The faithful diehards showed up—Matt, Butch, John, Tom, and Judy, along with a handful of others and, of course, Barbara, Willie, Deacon Wally Smith, and the other few church members able-bodied enough to help. Their camaraderie tempered some of the discouragement they felt about the reasons for their frequent reunions.

Ammie maintained a fund-raising drive, too. Nearly every dollar she raised went toward replacing or repairing something torn up by vandals—the air conditioner, fuel tank valves, Plexiglas window coverings, doors, locks, and dead bolts. Lots and lots of locks and dead bolts. One after another was smashed or jimmied apart.

What time she didn't spend either at work or helping the church went toward caring for her mom, Jean Evins, whose health had been fading during the past few years. Ammie drove to see her so often at Providence Hospital, a medical facility in downtown Columbia, that it seemed her car could maneuver its way there on its own. She imagined that was the reason she went to Providence when she injured her hand instead of going to Lexington Medical Center, which was closer to her house.

She discovered that the accumulation of struggle and stress over the past several years finally caught up with her when she became horribly ill. Figuring it was just a bad bout with the flu, she kept dragging herself back and forth to work and around town for nearly a week while trying an array of over-the-counter remedies. She didn't want to go to the emergency room, fearful that they would admit her. Her meager salary barely afforded her enough money for visits to the doctor. She sure didn't have enough for a hospital bill, as her insurance would only pay a portion of it.

Growing steadily worse as the week approached its end, she collapsed in bed one night, burning with fever. When she woke up, she was in the hospital. Betsy sat beside her hospital bed.

"What?" Ammie looked around in confusion.

"You're in the hospital, Mom," Betsy said soothingly, covering Ammie's small hands with hers. "You've got pneumonia."

"Lord have mercy." Ammie tried to sit up. "How did I get here?"

"I called the ambulance after I spoke to you on the phone. You weren't making any sense when I called you, so I knew something was awfully wrong."

Ammie felt as if she had cotton stuffed inside her head. She couldn't remember any of what Betsy was telling her, yet she knew it was true.

"The paramedics had to break down your door to get to you." Betsy went on. "They told me they had to practically fight you to strap you down in the stretcher. You were raging, yelling, and screaming about how everybody ought to stand up against managed health care."

Picturing herself strapped down and carrying on wildly, Ammie laughed. "Well, what they're doing with managed health care is bad. Maybe I wasn't as delirious as they thought."

She stayed in the hospital for six weeks. When she came out, the pneumonia was gone. But in exchange, she had a huge hospital bill that would take an eternity to pay.

Ammie's recovery was a huge relief to Barbara. She had long been concerned about how her friend kept pushing herself. Too hard, in Barbara's opinion. She felt much of that was a result of what they had been going through at the church.

As if Barbara didn't have enough to trouble her mind, in July of 1989, an intruder broke into her mother-in-law's home and, though there was nothing much of value to be stolen, Mrs. Simmons was beaten so badly that she ended up in the hospital for a month. No signs connected the attack to the church. Apparently, it was a random act of violence—just another sign of a society going mad.

Barbara had also been worrying lately about her son, Jonathan. Of her three oldest children, who were all in their twenties, Jonathan had had the roughest journey into adulthood. For him, life seemed to be a confusing maze in which it was too easy to lose his way. From the time he was a young boy, people had been slapping labels on him: "developmentally delayed," "emotionally handicapped," "exhibits oppositional-defiant personality disorder."

Now the system had an additional label for him: criminal. On December 14, 1989, he was convicted of attempted rape. The police said that he had grabbed a woman coming out of a Cayce restaurant and tried to rape her before she fought him off and got away. Jonathan told his mother he didn't do it. She believed him.

She wished that the police, along with all his teachers and school psychologists, who saw him only as an assortment of problems and mental disorders, could see him the way she did. He was a sweet boy, so desperate for love and approval, wanting to fit in—somewhere, anywhere. His need for acceptance concerned her. That kind of need could lead to people getting in with the wrong crowd.

But she had brought him and the other kids up in the church, and that would be a solid foundation for him. He loved to sing in the choir, and he was certainly a hard worker. He worked like a dog at the church, he and his older brother, Willie Lee. Even the police keeping watch over St. John spoke well of him for that; so did Ammie, Matt, and others on the committee. He was respectful to her and Willie and he doted on little Michael, who, at age six, was fourteen years younger than he.

The attempted rape conviction would make life even harder on him than it already was. It branded him as none of the other labels had done before. How was he supposed to get a decent job with a record? How could he support himself, much less any future family?

She would pray. Her prayers would see him through this.

TWELVE

Lost Soul

But Barbara's prayers couldn't save him from the vortex of destruction that was sucking him in. On July 18, 1990, he was charged with the murder of a seventy-nine-year-old white woman, Josie Lamb, who was found beaten to death in her home. For Barbara, the only thing more shocking than the gruesome, vicious murder was that the police thought Jonathan committed it.

Dazed from shock, she and Willie tried to absorb the case against their twenty-one-year-old son as detectives with the Richland County Sheriff's Department laid out their evidence.

According to police, one week before the murder, Jonathan had gone to Josie Lamb's house and knocked on her door. When she opened it, he tried to force his way in, but he ran off after she started screaming.

Despite the incident, she told a close friend who lived nearby that she wasn't fearful, reasoning that their neighborhood remained safe. They lived in Olympia, a small hardscrabble mill village bordering the town of Cayce. Everyone knew practically everyone because they had all, at one time or another, worked at Olympia Mill, an aging textile plant in the middle of the village that had been the main employer for generations.

Mrs. Lamb had retired there after working as a cloth inspector. Following her divorce, she lived alone, enjoying her garden and visiting with family and neighbors. Not only had she worked alongside most of her neighbors, but she had grown up with them, too. So little crime occurred in Olympia that many didn't bother to lock their windows and doors at night. Even after the attack, Josie Lamb didn't secure hers, either, hoping to get relief from the July heat with cooler nighttime temperatures.

But from what investigators pieced together, sometime between the afternoon of Monday, July 16, and the small hours of the next day, Jonathan returned through an unlocked door. He found Josie Lamb sitting on her toilet, half-naked. Earlier that month, she had broken her leg. The injury made it impossible for her to get away. Jonathan lifted the lid covering her toilet tank and brought it down on her skull, again and again until it shattered like fine porcelain, splattering blood and bits of brain tissue against the wall and onto the tiled floor.

Once he killed her, the detectives said he rifled through her house and stole about two hundred dollars' worth of jewelry.

Josie's cousin found her the next morning.

Eyewitnesses reported seeing a young African-American man recently near Lamb's home who fit Jonathan's description. Indeed, Jonathan had been walking around the neighborhood that week. He told police that an acquaintance who lived in Olympia owed him some money.

Crime scene investigators lifted prints from Lamb's blood-stained bathroom walls. They matched Jonathan's.

That news was only the beginning of an unbelievable nightmare for Barbara and the rest of her family. No sooner had she found out about Jonathan's arrest than she discovered that he failed a lie-detector test and then signed a confession.

The next few days passed by in a surreal haze that Barbara desperately wished she could dispel. She and Willie saw Jonathan in jail. At least the man they saw behind plate glass had her son's body, but Jonathan was gone somewhere else, and she didn't know how to reach him.

"Jonathan," Barbara called, but her voice came out in a choked whisper. Tears burned her eyes as if someone had tossed acid against her face.

"We've got a lawyer for you, son," Willie said, struggling to keep his composure.

Jonathan only looked at his parents with the eyes of a dead man.

The nightmare got worse. Sheriff Metts announced to reporters that in addition to the murder of Josie Lamb, he suspected Jonathan in the rapes and beatings of three elderly women in Lexington County. One of the victims was Estelle Simmons, Willie's mother. It had not been some unknown intruder who had beaten her so unmercifully that she was hospitalized for a month, but her own grandson—and he had done far worse.

"He raped me," Mrs. Simmons finally told investigators. "Jonathan raped me."

Jonathan tried to hang himself later that week. Fashioning a noose out of his jail jumpsuit, he was putting it around his neck when a guard discovered him. After being taken to a psychiatric center, he was returned to the jail and put on suicide watch.

Along with her son, another of the casualties the tragedy claimed was Barbara's marriage. "Hard times," old folks said, "either pull you together or drive you apart." These hard times had driven her and Willie apart. They split wide open the small hairline cracks that had developed over decades of marriage—unresolved hurts, unsettled disagreements—and turned them into things that wounded more than ever. What her mother-in-law said Jonathan had done to her had been one of the most destructive blows. She and Willie couldn't have a discussion about Jonathan without arguing about who was to blame for what had happened. They couldn't talk about much of anything anymore.

The crowning blow to their relationship had been the decision Barbara felt she had no choice but to make. She did it to save Jonathan's life.

She realized that, considering the evidence, the only possible way of saving her son from receiving a death warrant was to show extenuating circumstances for his behavior. So she said that Willie had been an abusive father. As weeks passed, her desperation mounted, and her charges became more explosive—not only had Willie been abusive, but his family had been, too, especially his mother. Reprimands and spankings Jonathan received as a child evolved into psychological torture and violently brutal whippings and beatings.

Barbara didn't know what else to do. What did other people do when their whole world had gone insane?

The breakup of her marriage had led to another painful loss—St. John. She had put her life in jeopardy, sacrificing endless days and nights for the church, but that didn't change what it was: a small church mainly made up of Willie's relatives and longtime friends of his family. Perhaps it was because her emotions were already scraped raw from everything that had happened recently, but it seemed that each of the few dozen members, from Reverend Shepherd on down, was taking Willie's side instead of sympathizing with her. It wasn't so much anything that anyone said or did, but more of what they didn't say or do.

She didn't feel like she could go there anymore. At a time

when she most needed her church's support, she mourned its absence.

Any one of these tragedies—Jonathan's troubles, her crumbled marriage, her estrangement from St. John—would have been hard enough to deal with, but one happened on the heels of the other. She couldn't get her bearings from the first stunning blow before being hit with another and another. Within a short space of time, her entire world had been torn from its foundation and ripped to pieces.

Ammie could scarcely believe what was happening, either. She had known Jonathan since he was a child. She couldn't count the number of times he had been over to her house to do yard work and other chores to earn spending money. He had been nothing except well mannered and determined to do a good job. Sometimes she had to make him stop working because he was so conscientious.

And she didn't know what they would have done at St. John without him. He and his brother Willie Lee had worked like seasoned construction workers, though they were just teenagers.

It devastated Ammie to see what Jonathan's problems were doing to Barbara—and Willie, too. If only there were something she could do to make it better. During her life, she had been able to accomplish so much through sheer willpower and resolve, and yet when the world of one of her closest friends was shattering, she felt completely helpless.

She did what she could—listening to Barbara when she wanted to talk, holding her when she needed to cry, and praying for her—but she desperately wished there were more she could do. Jonathan's situation appeared hopeless; the cases against him, airtight.

He could face the death penalty. If his life hung in the balance, the only thing working in his favor was that the murder occurred in Richland County instead of Lexington. Under the fiery persuasion of prosecutor Donnie "Death Penalty" Myers,

arch-conservative Lexington juries handed out more death penalties than did any other county in the state. In contrast, only
two people had been sentenced to death in Richland County
since the U.S. Supreme Court had made capital punishment
legal again in 1976.

Though Richland County was less conservative, Ammie still
worried that its prosecutor, Dick Harpootlian, would seek capital
punishment. The combination of his aggressiveness and political
ambitions coupled with the sensationally heinous nature of the
murder raised the stakes that, if convicted, Jonathan would pay
with his life. It didn't help matters that he was African American
and Josie Lamb an elderly white woman—a fact sure to inflame
a jury, especially one with a white majority.

Ammie held out hope that at least Barbara and Willie could
put their relationship back together. She loved both of them.
Willie was a good man, no matter what Barbara felt forced to
say about him. Ammie had grown close to him through working
with him at St. John, and his love for Barbara and their children
was as clear as day. Ammie knew that although he might not
show it as much as Barbara did, what was going on with Jonathan
crushed him, too.

Like Barbara, he was a parent losing a child, but in many
ways, he was a child losing a parent. What Jonathan had done
to Willie's mother had nearly destroyed her, not only physically,
but also emotionally. To Ammie, Miss Estelle now seemed a faint
remnant of herself. With her shoulders hunched and her gaze
often downcast, she looked as if she was trying to escape within
herself to another world.

Ammie worried that Barbara was shutting down into denial.
Despite all the evidence against him, including his own confession, Barbara insisted on his innocence. Ammie reasoned she
would probably do the same if the tables were turned. It wasn't
easy to be logical when your child's life was at stake. As a mother,
she knew how strong the instinct was to back one's child, no
matter what.

She wished Barbara could receive solace from her church. She needed St. John as much as it needed her. She and Willie constituted most of the driving force that kept the church going. Although St. John was enjoying a rare stretch of calm—nothing much had happened over the past seven or eight months— there was still the day-to-day business of running it, much of which Barbara did, including serving as treasurer, organizing Sunday school, and arranging various programs. If she pulled out for good, Ammie didn't know how St. John could survive.

But Barbara couldn't bring herself to return, no matter how much she wanted to. She didn't know when she would return, if ever. Her anguish deepened over the next several months as she and Willie filed for divorce and she was forced to use energy she didn't have to adjust to single parenthood. What weighed on her more than anything else was Jonathan. What were they going to do with her boy?

It broke her heart to visit him in the detention center, but she did it anyway, trying to hide her pain from him. What he had to do was to focus on saving himself, not worry about her. He had a team of court-appointed lawyers, psychologists, and social workers, and she took heart that he was starting to open up to them, to help them help him. They had to know every detail of his life—including things he was ashamed to talk about—but he was opening up. His defense team had to understand him even more than she did. They had to gather enough information so that even if the jury did not believe in his innocence, they would at least believe how unstable he was and realize he needed to be in a hospital, not in a prison.

In late January 1991, Dick Harpootlian announced he would seek the death penalty. The trial would start that June.

His announcement stunned Barbara, but Willie tossed it

aside. "The law can say all it wants," he told Ammie shortly afterward, "but Jonathan ain't going to go to any electric chair. He didn't kill that woman."

She was amazed at his words, especially given what Jonathan had done to his mother.

"I'm not saying that he wasn't involved," Willie went on to say. "He was there, but so were others, and they were the ones who actually killed her. I just know it. There are some other fingerprints there. I don't know who all they belong to or why Jonathan's covering up for them, but it was some others with Jonathan who did it. I keep telling Jonathan, 'Boy, don't take the rap. This is a murder charge.' But he won't say anything."

Ammie groped for something to say in response. The only set of prints found at the murder scene other than Lamb's were Jonathan's. And the reason Jonathan didn't speak of accomplices was because there weren't any.

Despite their divorce, Barbara and Willie shared a faith in their son's innocence that defied logic. Ammie hoped that faith would sustain them in the days ahead.

One week before his murder trial, Jonathan pleaded guilty to raping his grandmother and the second elderly woman in addition to one count of first-degree burglary. Judge Julius Baggett sentenced him to life plus sixty years. Because he had committed more than one violent crime, he would never be eligible for parole.

Even that sentence wasn't enough to quell the heartache of the son of his second victim. The man spoke during the sentencing. "From what we've gone through the last twelve months, 'Hell' is not the word for it. I've lost everything I could possibly give to make sure my mother's okay. For this man to walk around and breathe is not right."

Jonathan had little to say other than to enter his guilty plea. He seemed cocooned in his own pleasant, daydreamy world, occasionally smiling at the Lexington County deputies who waited to take him away.

His murder trial lasted only a few days, but it was more than enough time for Harpootlian to prove his guilt beyond a shadow of a doubt. "It was a foul murder," he told the jury, who sat transfixed by his words. "He crushed Josie Lamb's skull like an eggshell. He picks on old ladies. This is a man whose sexual release is assaulting elderly women."

In acknowledgment of the overwhelming evidence of Jonathan's guilt to the murder, Jonathan's lawyers conceded that he had killed Lamb, but tried to prove he hadn't robbed her of the two hundred dollars' worth of jewelry. Because of South Carolina law, gaining an acquittal on the robbery charge meant the difference between life and death. The death penalty could be applied only to someone who committed a murder in combination with an "aggravating circumstance," meaning another crime such as robbery, assault, kidnapping, or rape.

As in his rape trial, Jonathan did not take the witness stand. He looked on as if he were an uninvolved observer.

The trial ended Thursday afternoon, June 27, and the jury filed out of the courtroom to begin deliberations.

Within twenty-five minutes they returned.

"We find the defendant guilty," the foreman said as the judge read out each of the charges.

"Oh, my God," Barbara moaned, and covered her face with her hands. Jonathan seemed not to hear the verdict, or if he did, didn't seem to understand that it applied to him. He just stared straight ahead.

The hearing to determine whether he would get a life sentence or death in the electric chair would start Saturday.

"I feel so awful for both of y'all," Ammie said, giving both Barbara and Willie compassionate embraces. She wished she could utter words that could convince them that everything would be okay, but she knew none existed. She could only hold them and show how much she cared for them.

They had been to court together so often over the last few years to get justice for St. John; now they prayed for mercy.

That Saturday, Jonathan's legal team hoped to persuade the jury to spare his life through testimony from Barbara, other family members, and mental health professionals. All of them tried to point out reasons why he had little control over what he had done, but Harpootlian showed the horrific photos of Lamb's body and demanded death. "Simmons is a mean, sick psycho, and the community is sick and tired of violent crime. We have a person here who preys on people who can't fight back or resist. He looks for the old and infirm, like a jackal circling a herd."

The jury reached a decision the next day: death by electrocution.

As the guards ushered Jonathan to death row, Barbara collapsed sobbing into the arms of her oldest son, Willie Joe.

"I think justice was done," one of Mrs. Lamb's relatives told a reporter standing nearby. "It's been a long year, but with God's faith, we've made it."

After Jonathan appealed the sentence, attorney David Bruck took over the case, and his involvement offered hope to Barbara and Willie that Jonathan's life could be saved. Bruck, based in Columbia, was a nationally recognized expert in handling death penalty cases. His most well-known client was Susan Smith, the young mother who eventually confessed to drowning her two sons in a Union County lake.

The next three years were a mind-numbing series of hearings and court procedures as the case made its way toward the U.S. Supreme Court. Barbara and Willie followed each legal move. They understood that Bruck was basing Jonathan's appeal on the fact that the jury was not informed that Jonathan was ineligible for parole because of his convictions on the earlier rape charges. During deliberations, jurors had asked Judge Ralph King Anderson if Jonathan could be paroled. Following an earlier South Carolina Supreme Court ruling, Anderson wouldn't say one way or the other. Instead, he told them to consider the words *life* and *death* "in their plain and ordinary meaning." In light of this, Bruck said the jury had no alternative except to assume that Jonathan could possibly be freed one day unless he was executed.

Bruck was not trying to have the conviction for the murder overturned, but rather the punishment. He was struggling desperately for his client to be able to live out the rest of his life behind bars. He had a fight on his hands. Recent appellate and Supreme Court decisions were making it harder to overturn death sentences, and few people had much sympathy for death row inmates. As far as most people were concerned, executed criminals were getting just what they deserved.

No matter what she was busy doing, her son's situation was never far from Barbara's thoughts, and she tried not to think of what would happen if Bruck was not successful. She could only imagine how it weighed on Jonathan's broken mind. She could only imagine because he wouldn't let her come to visit him on death row anymore. "I want you to forget about me," he told her. "Forget you ever knowed me."

He cut off contact with pretty much everyone except for Bruck and other members of his legal team. Not being able to visit made Barbara's mind race. She had seen movies and TV shows about how awful prisons were. Was he all right? Was he being abused? Was he taking care of himself?

His order was nearly more painful than the news of his arrest back in 1990. She knew that, in his own way, he wanted to save her from more heartbreak, but not being able to see him made her pain worse. Forget about her own son? It would be easier to stop breathing.

Willie doggedly held on to his belief that his son would never face the electric chair, and his work at the steel plant and St. John helped make the days, weeks, and months pass. With Barbara gone, more of what had to be done at the church fell to him. After twelve or thirteen hours at the plant, he fought against exhaustion to keep the church maintained, buy supplies, ferry elderly members back and forth, set up for services, and help Reverend Shepherd in leading the congregation.

He was thankful that, for the most part, St. John had been left alone over the last few years. There was still sporadic vandalism—a damaged dead bolt here, a defaced headstone there— but no serious structural damage since back in 1991 when the air conditioner got stolen. The tight surveillance by the sheriff's department appeared to be effective, though not completely impenetrable. The stakeouts continued each Halloween, and Stick, Bulldog, and the rest of the guys always netted some arrests, though the numbers had dropped since that first Halloween. Word had gotten out not to mess with St. John, exactly what Willie had hoped for.

It was also reassuring to him to see how Ammie was sticking with St. John, even though Barbara wasn't involved anymore. Since it was Barbara who had gotten her involved in the first place, it would have been natural for Ammie to lose interest, but she hadn't. She was as devoted as ever, and she kept organizing workdays periodically to do some of the heavier maintenance and cleaning.

Willie hated to think of what would have become of St. John if it hadn't been for her.

With things relatively quiet at St. John and her long career with the union winding down toward retirement, Ammie was able to spend more time with her family, which had grown with the births of Christy's two children: Nicholas and Lindsay. Although Ammie couldn't shake the caution ingrained in her by Stick and Bulldog, she enjoyed visits with her family, knowing that the danger had passed.

Looking back, she was still stunned by everything she had gone through—what they had all gone through. Tom Turnip-seed theorized that the destruction of St. John had been one of the things that had warped Jonathan so. The brutality of it had probably been too much for his developing mind to handle. Ammie didn't know. The only thing she was sure of where Jonathan was concerned was that he was severely disturbed, and his crimes had ripped apart his family and driven Barbara from St. John. Not only had they fueled the destruction of Barbara and Willie's marriage, but they had also pitted other family members against one another, even within Barbara's own family.

Ammie wondered how it would all turn out. Jonathan's execution would only foment more bitterness and divisiveness than his conviction had already created. For Barbara and Willie's sake, she hoped David Bruck would win a reversal. In the meantime, the only thing she could do was to be supportive as possible to both of the Simmonses.

Out of the thousands of cases submitted to the U.S. Supreme Court, only a small fraction is selected to be heard. Jonathan's case was among those. As David Bruck and Dick Harpootlian went to Washington in January 1994 to argue their cases in front of the nine justices, the waiting was hardest on Barbara and Willie. Seven men and two women hundreds of miles away had the final say in whether their son would live or die. Neither Barbara nor Willie had any way of talking to those people, of begging for mercy. They couldn't do anything but put their trust in God and David Bruck. Even after oral arguments, they would have to wait until the summer for the decision to be announced.

Waiting—Barbara thought—was sometimes the hardest thing to do in the whole world.

On Friday, June 17, 1994, the Supreme Court issued its ruling. In a seven-to-two decision, with Justice Harry Blackmun writing the majority opinion, Jonathan's death sentence was overturned. Antonin Scalia and Clarence Thomas dissented.

The court ruled that Judge Anderson should have instructed the jury that Jonathan was ineligible for parole. Blackmun wrote:

> The jury may reasonably have believed that [Simmons] could be released on parole if he were not executed. To the extent this misunderstanding pervaded the jury's deliberations, it had the effect of creating a false choice between sentencing [Simmons] to death and sentencing to a limited period of incarceration.

For Barbara and Willie, the announcement brought relief, but no joy. Too many lives were destroyed for any celebration, not only in their family, but others—especially Josie Lamb's.

A reporter from *The State* interviewed one of Lamb's cousins about the reversal of Jonathan's sentence. The cousin said bitterly, "He gets to live and watch TV and eat three squares a day while she's dead. Her death took a lot out of all of us. You just don't get over losing someone like that."

Barbara and Willie's relief was very short lived. The day after the announcement of the reversal, Harpootlian said he would seek a second death penalty.

"What!" Barbara cried when she heard the news. "But he can't do that! The Supreme Court said they can't give him the death penalty."

Jonathan's legal team explained that the Supreme Court's decision did not shield her son from receiving another death sentence during a resentencing trial. Their ruling meant only that his 1991 sentence was unconstitutional. A second jury could be convened, and if they voted for death—as long as they were aware of Jonathan's ineligibility for parole and no other unrelated legal errors were made—Jonathan could constitutionally be put to death.

The lawyers' explanations sounded like legal gibberish to Barbara. From what she saw, the bottom line was that the state was set on killing her boy, and there was nothing she or anyone else could do to stop it.

Two months later, in early August, Jonathan sent a letter to Brenda Shealy, the deputy clerk for the state Supreme Court. In writing on about the level of a third-grader, he told her to tell the state justices that he wanted to die.

> You see I need you to tell them that I need to get Excicuted. simply because theres no life or future in prison. yes its true you can't blame nobody for where you are today but yourself. . . . I don't need anybody's sympathy. I don't want it. remember Eye-4-Eye and Tooth-4-Tooth—Im not even going to put up a fight to live.
>
> . . . I told my Mother to forget she ever knowed me or had me for that matter b-sides She wont miss nothing simply b-case She has two other Sons . . . it would be different if I was the only child.

The last part of the letter was particularly crushing to Barbara. Jonathan's mind must be more broken than before. He had lost his will to live. He had tried to commit suicide before. Maybe this was his way of doing it again.

However, by the next month, he changed his mind, indicating to a judge that he wanted his lawyers to argue for a life sentence.

Ammie hated the emotional roller coaster that Barbara and Willie and their families were on, and there was no end in sight. It might take months before another jury was selected to decide whether to put Jonathan to death. If they voted for death, there was probably less chance of the sentence being reversed on appeal because now Harpootlian knew to tell jurors of Jonathan's ineligibility for parole.

They were back to waiting again. And praying.

It was all getting too much for Barbara. One day as she and Ammie were eating lunch, Barbara looked out the window wistfully at the passing traffic.

"Sometimes I think about taking Michael and just packing up and leaving," she said after taking a bite of her sandwich.

"Where would you go?"

"I don't know, don't care really. I just want to get away where I can make a fresh start, somewhere where I don't know anybody and nobody knows me. Have you ever felt like that, like you wanted to run off and start over?"

"This is your home, though. Most of your family is around here. What about your mom and dad? The rest of your family?"

"I think about that, too." Barbara picked at her food. "But I don't know how much more I can take. I trust in God, but I'm only human."

"I sure would miss you if you were to go."

A sad smile creased Barbara's face. "We're sisters, Miss Ammie, remember? Even when we're not together, we're with one another. Can't nothing change that. But anywhere I go, I'll come back and see you. You can't do without me, and I can't without you. It's like I always say, we season each other, just like salt and pepper."

"That's right." Ammie laughed. "Just like salt and pepper."

Within a few weeks, Barbara made up her mind to strike out for Charlotte, North Carolina. Charlotte was as good as anywhere else to make a fresh start and yet close enough that she could get back within a couple of hours to visit. She just couldn't take life in Lexington County anymore. The bad times outweighed the good. She didn't know how long she would live up there, how long it would take to cleanse her soul of the piercing agony she was going through. It could be only months—it could take years.

When she went to Ammie's to say good-bye, Ammie hugged her tight. For some reason, Ammie had an undeniable feeling that Barbara wouldn't be gone long, and she took comfort in that.

"Take care of yourself, Barb. Now you promise to keep in touch, right?" Ammie held Barbara's shoulders firmly.

"I sure will, and I'll call as soon as I get settled in," Barbara promised. "And I'll be down here visiting before you know it. I won't be a stranger. You've got my word on that. I just need to get away. I need time to get my head together."

"I know. I know." Ammie pulled her into her arms again.

Fall turned to winter, then winter to spring and spring to the summer of 1995, and still they waited to learn of Jonathan's fate. According to his attorneys, it probably wouldn't be decided until later in the fall.

On Wednesday, August 16, 1995, Ammie had other things on her mind. She had spent the entire morning at an early meeting of the Lexington District Two school board. She was elected to the board five years earlier, the first female ever to serve on it, and in January 1995, her fellow members selected her to be the chairwoman.

The volunteer job was turning out to be a lot of work. As chairwoman, one of her major goals was to push through a $19 million bond referendum, and the going was tough. Griping about higher taxes, many people without children in schools didn't understand why the district needed more money.

On her drive home from the meeting, Ammie made a mental checklist of what needed to be done before they met again. She was still thinking it over when she walked into her home. Noticing that the message light on her answering machine was blinking, she hit the PLAY button. There was a message from her mother. From the way her mom first called her name, Ammie instantly knew something terrible had happened. "Ammie Jean! Ammie Jean! I just heard that St. John is on fire!"

THIRTEEN

Smoke and Ashes

Grabbing her purse, Ammie raced out the door to her car and sped off. This couldn't be happening, she told herself. St. John had already been through so much. A fire. "Lord, please let it not be true," she prayed.

Smoke reached her before she was within a half-mile of the church. It wafted through the air in a thick haze, stinging her eyes and filling her car with acridity. "Oh, God, no," she moaned.

Barreling down the dirt road, she turned into the church-yard. It was filled with fire trucks, police cruisers, pickups, and cars. Her breath caught as she stared straight ahead. St. John had burned to the ground. The only thing left was the cinder-block skeleton of the vestibule and the bell, but even the bell had been grotesquely warped by the heat. Ashes hung in the air and smoke floated up from blackened debris.

As she got out of her car, her legs shook so much she had to lean against the car to keep from collapsing. Everything they had put their lives on the line for, had sacrificed for, now lay in a smoldering heap.

Ash settled on her face and mixed with her tears. Through the despair that threatened to overwhelm her, she noticed Paul Willie Davis. He was one of the police officers who had made countless checks on the church, often while off the clock. An African American, he was a huge monolith of a man, but as he climbed out of his cruiser, Ammie saw that he was crying, too.

Unable to speak, Ammie pushed away from her sedan and used the momentum to stumble toward him, her arms outstretched. He made his way to her. As they grabbed hold of each other, their pain overflowed into aching sobs. She clung to him, grateful for his strength that kept her from sinking down onto the ground. Despair—an utter lack of hope—seared through her heart, leaving it as burned and charred as the remains of St. John.

She had thought they had been through the worst ten years ago. But what had happened then couldn't begin to compare with this. She pressed her face into Paul Willie's chest, shaking with sobs. This was unbearable. Everything they had done had been in vain. This truth was too bitterly cruel. What had been the point? What was the point of anything anymore?

Paul Willie gripped her shoulders while she forced herself to look once more at what remained of the church. Smoke drifted around the few dozen others milling around or standing in small groups. Ammie recognized some arson investigators from SLED—the State Law Enforcement Division—as well as sheriff's deputies, detectives, and firemen. She saw Willie Simmons huddled with his sister Pat, Miss Rosa Bell, Miss Magnolia, and a few other women from the congregation. They bore expressions of stunned grief. All of them were crying.

Patting Paul Willie on his arm, Ammie eased out of his em-

brace and walked over to Willie and the women. As she walked
toward them, her eyes stinging from the smoke and tears, she
heard Katherine Brown singing. Her voice stopped Ammie in
her tracks. She was hearing things. Katherine had died several
years ago. But she heard her beautiful, pure voice as surely as if
she were standing beside her—

Amazing Grace, how sweet the sound
that saved a wretch like me.
I once was lost,
but now am found,
was blind, but now I see.

Ammie only heard the singing for a moment, but it was
enough to soften some of her pain.

Wiping away tears, Willie put an arm around her. "The Lord
will make a way, somehow," he told her and the women.

"Something good can come out of this," Ammie said, leaning
against Willie and trying to believe her own words. "At times,
when the worst happens, later, we can see that it was for the
best, that good results from it."

"Lord, have mercy on us." Miss Rosa Bell blew into her handkerchief. Gray ash powdered her black, curled hair that had
been glossy from hair pomade.

"I can't believe any of this is happening," Pat said. "When I
got the call that it was on fire, I thought somebody was playing
some kind of sick joke. This is worse than somebody in the family dying. What in the world are we going to do now?"

No answer came to any of them. They were in too much
shock to think clearly. A thought filtered in and out of Ammie's
mind—insurance. Was there enough to rebuild? Would the congregation even want to rebuild there, given what they had gone
through? If they were to rebuild, what was to stop someone from
torching the place again?

The one thing she was sure of was that the cause of the fire was arson. She didn't need to wait for some SLED report. Someone—or some people—had slipped through the sheriff's department's net of protection and set the place on fire. They weren't satisfied anymore to just smash windows, break doors, steal equipment, and desecrate the sacred. They wanted to destroy St. John completely. And they had.

Later that afternoon, Ammie was rocked by more bad news. St. John had no insurance. Because of the problems over the years, the monthly insurance premiums had been high, and the tiny, struggling congregation hadn't been able to keep up. Coverage had lapsed more than two years earlier.

Arson investigators had encircled the ruins with bright yellow tape marked with the words CRIME SCENE—DO NOT CROSS. The tape fluttered in the breeze as Ammie slumped down on the old stump that had been far enough from the fire to survive it. Still numb from shock, she watched investigators and deputies pick through the rubble. Willie had left to take some of the women back home. Others who lived in that section of the county stopped by after learning of the fire to take a look at the destruction.

Ammie covered her face with her hands. Rebuilding St. John before had nearly cost her life. "Hell" didn't come close to describing it. She didn't think she could go through it again. It had been hard enough with Barbara, but her friend was gone now, and even the fire wouldn't be enough to bring her back. Barbara's pain was too deep, her divorce from Willie too bitter.

And Matt. He had been their Rock of Gibraltar, but now his health was so poor that he wasn't able to do much except to go back and forth to the hospital and his doctor's office.

Deacon Wally Smith was already dead; so was Gus Simmons, Willie's brother. They had been among the few men in the congregation physically able to do much work.

Ammie gazed at the charred ruins. The church had persevered for over two hundred years, but what fire failed to do in 1781 had been accomplished today—it had brought St. John to its end.

Barbara got word of the fire. The news only confirmed that she had done the right thing in deciding to move. Heartache came on top of heartache in Lexington County.

She had been able to move and start over, but she knew that few people in St. John's congregation could. St. John was the only church most of them knew, and Lexington County the only place they had ever lived. Most were old, and change was too hard.

At this point in their lives, their main hope was that after being buried in the church's cemetery, they would be allowed to rest in peace without someone desecrating their burial sites. She wondered what the congregation would do. It didn't sound like Ammie was able to lead another campaign to build it again. No one could understand Ammie's decision more than she could. She had reached the same one herself, though for different reasons.

Perhaps the congregation would join nearby churches. St. Paul AME wasn't too far away from St. John, and many in the two congregations were friends with one another. In fact, members of St. Paul had pitched in to help rebuild St. John. And, of course, there had been Katherine Brown. When she was alive, she used to attend St. John so often that many people thought she was a member. Barbara would never forget how that woman could sing. She could sing in a way that made time stop, that brought heaven to earth. It was best when she sang without any music. That way nothing else competed with the sound of her mesmerizing voice.

Though several years had passed, Barbara still mourned her friend's death. So many losses, one behind the other. The destruction of St. John was among the most painful. With everything they had done, it hadn't been enough. It had pulled every fiber of strength out of them and left nothing else to start over again.

During a visit back home, Ammie had told her that she believed that, somehow, something good could come out of this. Barbara prayed she was right.

A few days after the fire, Ammie received a note through the mail. There was no return address or any signature. She read it—

> I have reason to believe that the fire may have been caused by some young men who were at the church learning how to make firebombs and while making up a bomb, they accidentally set St. John on fire. I can't call the police about this because my call could be traced and I would be putting my home and safety in harm's way. . . .

She turned the note over to SLED. Because SLED investigators had confirmed the fire had been arson, they had taken over the case from Sheriff Metts's office. Sifting through charred debris, police had found remnants of bottle rocket firecrackers, a twelve-pack Bud Light container, an empty Zima bottle, some Marlboro cigarette butts, and a plastic bag from a Winn-Dixie grocery store. Lab technicians weren't able to lift fingerprints off any of the objects. There wasn't much else to go on. If any evidence had existed that identified the assailants, it had gone up in flames with the rest of the church. Probably the only way the case would be solved would be if investigators received an anonymous tip.

If there were some reward money, it might loosen someone's tongue, but Ammie didn't see any way to get donations for that. She forced herself to consider the possibility that the police would never find who torched the church.

That thought tore her up nearly as much as thinking about how devastated the congregation already was. They were divided about what to do. Some wanted to try to rebuild where they were while others wanted to find other property that was less isolated. With no insurance money, Ammie worried how they could do either.

Though they hadn't asked for any assistance, Ammie felt she had to warn them that she didn't know if she could muster the stamina to marshal another rebuilding effort. She told Jerry Bel-lune the same when he asked her if she was going to reconvene the Save St. John Baptist Church Committee. But she couldn't get the church off her mind. Images of it and its people even invaded her dreams.

Through deaths and desertion, the congregation had dwin-dled back down to about two dozen members after reaching a high of between fifty and sixty shortly after the church was re-built in 1986. The burden of rebuilding would fall to Willie, but without help, it would be impossible. More than two thousand volunteers had helped before, and still it had taken more than a year to finish. Even if St. John were reconstructed, what was there to stop someone from destroying it again? Nothing.

County officials dealt the congregation another blow. They de-termined that the church was in a floodplain, so they wouldn't be able to rebuild it at its current site even if they wanted to. The news was devastating to those who clung to the hope of remaining where they were.

After attending Sunday services at her church, Ammie went over to Willie's, where what was left of St. John's congregation gathered for makeshift services. He had removed a wall in his single-wide trailer to enlarge the den enough for everyone to sit together.

It broke Ammie's heart to see them. All they ever wanted was what others took for granted—a church to worship in without fear—but they had been denied that over and over again. A flash of anger raced through her with such intensity that it nearly took her breath away, but the more she thought about it, the angrier she got. How dare anybody destroy St. John. They had to do something. She had to do something.

"Have y'all decided what to do?" she asked, once the closing prayer was said.

"Well, we've got to move, there's no question about that," Willie said. "I hate to do it, but the county hasn't given us much of a choice. Maybe we can find a few acres of land on Old Charleston Highway or Old Wire Road."

"Or maybe down around Silver Lake," Reverend Shepherd said.

Willie scratched his head. "Wherever we go, it's going to cost us, and getting land is just the beginning."

"Y'all have been the only thing I've thought about lately," Ammie told them. "I don't know how much good I can do, but if it's all right, I'd like to help out as much as I can."

"If it's all right?" Willie repeated. It was the first time Ammie had seen him smile since before the fire. "Are you kidding? Of course it's all right, Sister Murray. You didn't even need to ask that after all these years."

"I know, but I wanted to, anyway."

In all the time she had been involved with St. John, none of them had ever asked for help. Though buffeted by injustice, they had maintained their dignity and pride, and Ammie wanted to do everything in her power to honor that.

They sat in Willie's den for more than another hour tossing around ideas and deciding which steps to take next. One of the first things that had to be done was to clear away the burned ruins. Ammie said she would get in touch with a local company called C. R. Jackson, Inc., to see if it would lend some volunteer labor and machinery to do it.

The only thing left to do with the land was to use it as a cemetery. If they could raise the money, they wanted to put up some type of memorial marker at the entrance to the grounds and maybe put a nice wrought-iron fence around the property, as well.

After returning home, Ammie took out her address book and started calling. It was time to reconvene the Save St. John Baptist Church Committee.

On Monday, September 25, Ammie arranged a press conference on the steps of the Lexington County Courthouse to announce the re-forming of the committee and that St. John Baptist Church would be rebuilt.

With Willie and others from St. John standing beside her, Ammie said to the cluster of reporters and onlookers:

> Ten years ago, St. John was destroyed by vandals. The Save St. John Baptist Church Committee rebuilt it. Five weeks ago, on August 16, 1995, arsonists destroyed the church, but I'm here to tell you that we will rebuild it again.
>
> We could dwell on all of the negatives that have happened, but we prefer to think about the positives and move forward. We will have our first workday this Saturday. Anyone who wants to come out and help us is more than welcome. C. R. Jackson Company has already agreed to donate a crew and equipment to clear away some of the debris.
>
> The real story of St. John is not the attacks that have been made against it. The real story is the coming together of many, many people from all walks of life, different religions, different races, different politics. They put aside their differences and worked together for the greater good.
>
> They came together to help the people of St. John to have a place to worship. The only wish of the church members is to be able to worship near the graves of their ancestors who had suffered in slavery.
>
> But the vandalism has not stopped. In the past ten years, the sheriff's department has made more than two hundred arrests.

It would probably be hopeless to rebuild in the same isolated place where these sick individuals would probably continue the vandalism.

Besides, we couldn't rebuild there even if we wanted to because the church is located in a floodplain. What we are looking for now are a few acres of land perhaps along Old Wire Road, the Old Charleston Highway, or in the Silver Lake area. These sites would be close to the cemetery but in public view to help keep vandals away.

We want to build a chapel about twelve hundred square feet in size. We estimate the cost will be seventy-five thousand dollars, but that doesn't include any furniture. Everything St. John had was destroyed—its piano, pews, altar—everything. Many have agreed to serve on the committee again and several churches, including Congaree Presbyterian, Cayce First Baptist, and Brookland Baptist, are onboard, too. I pray many more churches will become partners to help us raise the funds and materials necessary to rebuild.

That Saturday, two dozen people came out to the workday. It thrilled Ammie to see Matt climbing out of his truck. He had always been rail thin, but he looked even thinner now.

"Golly, gee, Matt." She threw her arms around him. "How are you?"

"I'm ready to work."

But Ammie could tell that just the trip to the churchyard had taxed him. She worried that he would push himself too much.

Butch came. So did Jerry. As usual, Jerry made sure to snap everyone's picture to accompany the story he planned for the next edition of his paper. He had tried to retire, but his retirement had been cut short because of county residents pleading with him to renew his newspaper career again. After coming out of retirement, he started running the *Lexington County Chronicle*, another weekly.

In many ways, it was just like old times for Ammie. Some of the best days of her life had been spent at St. John on Saturdays working and enjoying the company of other volunteers but Barbara not being there left an empty place in her heart.

Workmen from the C. R. Jackson Company rumbled onto the grounds in dump trucks and a huge backhoe. Within no time, they had cleared away the debris. The cinder-block outline of the vestibule topped by the warped bell stood as a desolate reminder of what used to be.

Ammie raked hard at the ground to clear away small chunks of cinder block, charred wood, and glass that the heavy equipment couldn't pick up. They had a long road ahead of them. Poring her way through her address book to make phone calls, she had raised a little over two thousand dollars so far. Seventy-three thousand more to go. It may as well have been a million.

In late October, a local Seventh Day Adventist church heard about the fire and offered to let St. John use their property to hold services until the church could finish rebuilding. Willie and others in the congregation gratefully accepted the offer, though the Seventh Day church was about fifteen miles away, and the drive to ferry members back and forth threatened to wear Willie's car out. Still, it seemed better than being jammed together in his den.

Another church, St. Stephen's Lutheran, donated solid oak pews and chairs. Ammie had Jerry include an appeal for storage space in one of his articles, since they didn't have anywhere to put the furniture yet.

In the hopes of raising money, Ammie arranged interviews with anyone in the media who stood still long enough for her to talk to. Donations were trickling in, most only for five to ten dollars at a time. But the notes that many enclosed with their contributions gave her spirits a much-needed boost. One fellow, who described himself as an eighty-three-year-old white man, wrote: "I want to have a small part in the rebuilding of your church. You are in my thoughts and in my prayers. I asked God to forgive those that did such a terrible thing and for Christ to enter their hearts."

She deposited his money and that from a few others in the account the committee had set up at a local bank. Every little bit helped. She tried to remember that.

By late November, they had another thousand. So far, they were averaging about a thousand dollars a month. Ammie quickly crunched the numbers. At the rate they were going, it would take another six years to raise enough money for a modest building, and that didn't include any furnishings.

She jabbed the OFF button of the calculator so hard that the small device clattered on her desk. The hopelessness of it all spiked a throbbing headache. Her mother's deteriorating health added to Ammie's stress. Lung disease was ravaging her eighty-five-year-old body, although she maintained the same tenacious spirit that helped her make a way for herself, Ammie, and Emmala after she became a young widow.

One of the things Jean Evins hated about being so ill was that it prevented her from helping out at St. John. She had spent many a Saturday working there in 1986, and she shared her daughter's anger that it had been destroyed again.

Ammie checked in on her every day. Her mom was in pretty bad shape, but she had managed to bounce back before, and Ammie hoped she could do it again.

Jonathan's situation weighed on her, too. His mind was more twisted than before. Lately, he had been trying to take on the identity of a death-row inmate named Michael Torrence who had been convicted of killing three people, including a prostitute whose body he dumped alongside a freeway. Why Jonathan wanted to mirror Torrence was beyond anything Ammie could comprehend. Torrence was an avowed racist who freely offered his white supremacist views to anyone who cared to listen. But to show his identification with him, Jonathan had carved "KKK" on his chest, and when Torrence fought to have his appeals dropped so he could be executed, Jonathan mimicked his actions.

Before a second jury was seated to hear arguments about whether or not to impose another death sentence, Jonathan told Circuit Judge Costa Pleicones that he wanted a bench decision. That meant he wanted Pleicones to decide his fate instead of a jury, even though the likelihood of receiving capital punishment was greater through bench decisions than with juries. The judge agreed to his request. As if to further seal his fate, Jonathan told Pleicones that if he were ever freed, he would rape and kill again.

Ammie didn't go to court to see what was going on, but she did follow the case in the paper. She could only sadly shake her head when reading of how, later that week, Jonathan stood before the circuit judge and announced, "If you do sentence me to life in prison, I will viciously attack, rape, and kill innocent people. As God is my witness, a death sentence is the best thing for me. I have no remorse. I'm ready to go on and face up to my responsibilities."

Ammie closed the newspaper, not able to imagine how it must be searing Barbara and Willie with pain all over again. Although she had turned the situation over and over in her mind, she couldn't figure out how things had gone so wrong for that young man. From one month to the next, he was determined to live, then be executed, then live again. It was crazy, and it spoke to how disturbed he was.

The next week, Judge Pleicones thwarted Jonathan's wish to be executed. "Your worst fear is remaining alive," he told Jonathan before addressing Jonathan's lawyers. "On death row, this defendant enjoys a perverted celebrity status."

Execution offered an easy way out, too easy as far as Pleicones

was concerned, and one that attracted the attention that Jonathan appeared to crave. As he sentenced him to life imprisonment without the possibility of parole, the judge spoke of
removing the young inmate from death row, "You will give up
those comfortable surroundings. You'll lose your celebrity status.
You'll grow old. You'll grow feeble."

Jonathan stared back at him, his jaw tightened.

"You, the predator, will become the prey."

With a rap of the gavel, guards closed in on Jonathan to take
him away to the prison to live out the rest of his life.

Ammie was glad that the ruling sealed the last chapter in Jonathan's case. Now, maybe people could start getting on with
their lives. Not only Willie, Barbara, and their families, but the
families of Jonathan's victims, too. A spokesperson for Josie
Lamb's family said the ruling offered closure, and they were
satisfied in knowing that Jonathan would never walk the earth
again as a free man.

With Christmas nearing, Ammie struggled to get into the holiday spirit. It was bad enough that the committee was tens of
thousands of dollars short of what was needed to rebuild St.
John, but her mother was sicker than ever and was in the hospital again.

Ammie visited her every day, and December 11, 1995, was no
exception. She found her mom propped up in her hospital bed
watching TV. Afraid of wearing her out, Ammie didn't want to
stay long. After they had chatted about general things going on
in the family, Ammie stood up to go.

"Well, I'm heading for Toys 'R' Us to pick up that present
that I had told you about that I ordered for one of the kids."
She fished out her car keys from her purse. "A lady at the store
called me and said it was in."

"All right. I'll see you tomorrow."

But when Ammie opened the door to leave, her mom called her back.

"Aren't you forgetting something?"

"I don't think so." Ammie scrunched her brows together, trying to figure out what she was referring to.

"You're forgetting to give me a kiss good-bye!"

Laughing, Ammie went over and kissed her. "That just goes to show you how scatterbrained I've been lately. I sure do love you."

"I love you, too, Ammie Jean." Jean Evins smiled at her daughter warmly.

After saying good-bye again, Ammie left, not realizing that would be her last time seeing her mom alive.

Her mother's death devastated Ammie. Although her mom had been in poor health for years, Ammie had not been ready for her to go. She sought solace in knowing that Jean Evins had been released from her suffering and was in the arms of God.

Still, her passing made that Christmas a bittersweet one and reminded Ammie and the rest of her family of past Christmases when she was with them. Ammie welcomed the end of the holiday season. Maybe the next year's would be easier. She had heard the saying, "Time heals all wounds." It would take lots of it to heal hers.

Another thousand dollars came in before the end of the year, bringing the total to about four thousand, and someone donated a piano and an organ. The going was slow, but Ammie was buoyed by her contact with Tim McConnell, president of Victory Savings Bank, the state's only black-owned bank. It had been cofounded by one of Ammie's heroes—Mary Modjeska Monteith Simkins. For decades, Victory had supported social causes affecting African-American communities, and it had served as a financial lifeline during the Civil

Rights era to people who were fired from their jobs or had loans prematurely called in when it was discovered that they were participating in the movement. Many were threatened with the loss of their livelihoods and homes if discovered to be NAACP members, regardless of whether they participated in protest activities.

Tim proposed staging a one-day fund-raising drive in the offices of the bank in downtown Columbia the second Monday of January. He planned to invite all the city's corporate heavy-hitters to come and make pledges of financial support. Each of the three local news stations agreed to provide coverage, as well as radio and print media.

Neither Ammie nor anyone else at the church or on the committee could get over the generosity of his proposal. The very idea of a bank wanting to help them that much was encouraging. With so many influential people showing up, who knew how much money could be raised?

That Monday, January 9, 1996, Ammie spent the day in a conference room at Victory Savings. She was so excited, the day went by in a blur. The room was jammed with executives and reporters, and she couldn't turn around without someone holding a microphone in front of her, asking for a comment.

By the end of the day, Tim announced they had raised $37,750 in pledges and that he would do everything possible to secure the rest of the money needed to rebuild St. John.

Ammie wanted to take the middle-aged African-American executive by the hands and whirl him around the room. Almost thirty-eight thousand, and that didn't include pledges still coming in! Combined with what they already had, the day had brought St. John more than half the money they needed.

She wrapped her arms around Tim and fought back tears. "I don't know how I can ever thank you enough. This is just incredible! I still can't believe it."

"This is one of the most worthy community projects this bank has ever been involved in," he answered. "I'm just glad we can be of assistance."

Tom Turnipseed was on the board of directors for a civil rights organization based in Atlanta called the Center for Democratic Renewal (CDR). Founded in 1979, its original name was the National Anti-Klan Network. Rev. C. T. Vivian, a former aide to Dr. Martin Luther King Jr., helped start the group in response to a sharp increase in Klan membership and activity. Although the number of Klan members had fallen to a mere few thousand by the end of the 1960s—in part due to the national backlash against the horrifying crimes they committed during the bloodiest days of the Civil Rights movement—membership had risen to an estimated 12,000 by 1979. In Decatur, Alabama, on May 26, 1979, Klansmen shot into a crowd of civil rights marchers who had gathered to protest the continued detention of Tommy Lee Hines, a retarded black man who had been arrested a year earlier on charges that he raped a white woman. He was later convicted of the rape charges by an all-white jury. Two black marchers during the Decatur protest were wounded and another arrested when he fired back in self-defense. Seven months later, on November 3, 1979, a group of Klansmen, American Nazis, and other white supremacists shot and killed five anti-Klan protesters in Greensboro, North Carolina. Despite footage from local news stations, which filmed the shootings, each of the defendants was acquitted of murder charges.

Alarmed at both the Klan's resurgence and the inadequate local legal response to it, the National Anti-Klan Network fought to make perpetrators of racially motivated violence face legal consequences for their crimes. One of NAKN's actions toward this goal included a 1983 lawsuit against the Justice Department for its failure to aggressively prosecute violent white supremacists. NAKN members also organized conferences, rallies, protests, and workshops to keep the problem of hate groups and related crimes in the public forefront. And in addition to using informants and covert surveillance to monitor the Klan and other like-minded organizations, it documented the rate of occurrence and general trends relating to hate crimes.

It was a small organization with a full-time staff of only about a dozen, and had very limited funds, mainly from grants and donations, but what it lacked in resources, the group made up for in tenacity. It had also established links with larger organizations with deeper pockets like the NAACP, the Southern Christian Leadership Conference, and the National Council of Churches (NCC), the country's largest ecumenical organization.

Tom explained to Ammie that the CDR had discovered a disturbing recent rash of arsons destroying black churches across the country, but particularly in the South. South Carolina was among the states hardest hit. Already, they had uncovered at least seven arsons, including two churches within ten miles of each other—Mt. Zion African Methodist Episcopal in Williamsburg County, destroyed on June 20, 1995, and Macedonia Baptist Church in neighboring Clarendon County, burned June 21, 1995. Police had two young white men in custody. Both of them admitted to being Klansmen.

The problem was growing to epidemic proportions in other states, as well—four were destroyed in Louisiana on one day, February 1, 1996. Even a church co-pastored by NFL great Reggie White was not safe—Inner City Church in Knoxville, Tennessee, was reduced to ashes January 8, 1996. A team of CDR field investigators and attorneys was working to determine exactly how many other churches had been harmed. After traveling and talking with pastors and members of congregations, it realized local law enforcement personnel and arson investigators had ruled many fires to be accidental in the face of clear evidence that pointed to arson. For example, one church was told that a faulty refrigerator sparked a fire, even though church members adamantly repeated that the gas line—which powered the appliance—was shut off at the close of each church service to save money. More important, the area surrounding the refrigerator was not nearly so damaged as other sections of the building.

What the team had found so far led the CDR to believe there was a nationwide conspiracy under way to annihilate the African-American community's bedrock of strength—its churches. The CDR pointed to the arrests of the two Klansmen in the Clarendon and Williamsburg fires as proof that the fires were not isolated incidents but part of an organized campaign of terror. Other examples of this conspiracy were the convictions of three white teens in Pike County, Mississippi, who—after igniting a fire that consumed Rocky Point Missionary Baptist on April 5, 1993—rode away screaming, "Burn, nigger, burn," and "That will teach you niggers!" In addition, three white men in Maury County, Tennessee, pleaded guilty to burning crosses and then setting fire to two black churches.

Another factor that lent itself to a conspiracy theory was the timing of the arsons, such as the four Louisiana churches burned on February 1—the first day of Black History Month. Rocky Point Missionary was torched close to the anniversary of Martin Luther King's assassination. In addition, the fires often occurred either in clusters, like the Louisiana fires, or in pairs, like at Little Mt. Zion Baptist and Mt. Zoar Baptist in Greene County, Alabama; and Springhill Freewill Baptist and Rocky Point Missionary Baptist in McComb, Mississippi.

In light of the growing national crisis, the CDR found the response of law enforcement officials and judges on the local, state, and federal levels to be woefully inadequate. To bring assailants to justice was an uphill fight beginning with basic investigation, which was often not adequately done and resulted in many arsons being mistakenly ruled as accidents. More pitfalls lay in the prosecuting of the small percentage of assailants who were apprehended. Because of the ineffectiveness of state laws and the barriers to having cases transferred to federal court, few defendants faced serious prison time. A large number of them were allowed to plea bargain their cases down to lesser charges, often resulting in only probation. In conjunction with documenting the severity of the crisis, the CDR was gathering information to elicit greater involvement by the federal government so investigations could be more thorough, prosecution more aggressive, and punishments more harsh—to prevent future arsons. It also had joined with other organizations to raise money to help burned churches start to rebuild. Tom asked Ammie for permission for the fact-finding delegation to visit St. John.

"Yeah, tell them to come on," she replied. "We'd love to talk to them." She was astounded that so many black churches shared St. John's plight. Maybe with everyone working together, they could do something.

The delegation came the next month and spoke of the worsening crisis. Even by the extremely conservative statistics from state law enforcement agencies, more than forty African-American churches in the South had been burned in just the last fourteen months. Most of them were like St. John—located in rural, isolated areas. And as St. John had experienced, the anguish of church members was immeasurable. The elderly pastor of one church became so distraught that he had to be hospitalized. The churches were more than simply buildings where people worshiped. They were centers of small communities, where people gathered for everything from family reunions and picnics to political rallies and vote casting. And in addition to carrying personally sacred memories of christenings, weddings, and funerals, the structures frequently held historical significance. Elam Baptist in Gray, Georgia, was built in 1808. Gen. William T. Sherman and his troops made the church an exception to their scorched earth policy when they stopped there to rest in the midst of marching across Georgia toward South Carolina. They used Elam's pews as feeding troughs for their horses. Elam withstood a civil war from a previous century only to fall victim to an arsonist's torch on July 21, 1994.

The CDR, in collaboration with other civil rights groups and religious organizations, was determined to put a stop to the destruction. It was going to have a conference in Atlanta in April about the heightening emergency. Over lunch in Tom's downtown office, one of the CDR attorneys turned to Ammie, who was sitting beside Willie's sister, Pat Lowman. "Leaders from all of the major civil rights and religious organizations will be there, but we'd also like to have representatives from churches that have been burned to give their input. It would be great if one or two of y'all from St. John could come."

Willie and everyone with the church opted for Ammie and Pat to represent St. John. The two women traveled to Atlanta and stayed at a motel near Ebenezer Baptist, where Dr. Martin Luther King had served as pastor. Touring the historic church, Ammie could almost feel the presence of the great civil rights leader, and it gave her chills. In the course of attending one meeting after another, she unexpectedly met King's widow, who came by the conference to show her support.

Coretta Scott King shook Ammie's hand warmly and spoke with her briefly. Ammie was so excited, she couldn't remember much of what the woman had said, but she did remember the compassionate kindness that radiated from her, as well as her beauty. Despite the advancing years, Mrs. King was as lovely as she had been in the sixties, and to Ammie, she epitomized how a queen should look.

Seeing her was the highlight of the productive trip that resulted in the development of plans for meetings in Washington, D.C., with House and Senate leaders, as well as with officials from the Justice Department, the FBI, the Treasury Department, and other government agencies. The Treasury Department played a major role in church burnings because it oversaw the Bureau of Alcohol, Tobacco and Firearms, a lead agency in investigating arsons. The NCC, led by Rev. Dr. Joan Brown Campbell, headed up arranging the meetings in Washington. The meetings could possibly include President Clinton. In addition to raising awareness, the coalition wanted to raise money to fund rebuilding efforts. Most of the affected churches either didn't have enough insurance coverage or had no insurance at all. To make matters worse, some insurance companies were canceling the policies of churches deemed to be in high-risk locations.

As with the meeting in Atlanta, the NCC wanted representatives from burned churches to participate in the Washington meetings, and Tom relayed word to Ammie and Pat to plan on traveling to the capital. NCC would cover their travel and lodging expenses. Ammie was thrilled by the invitation, but she was also glad that she could go home for a while.

Although the conference had been exciting, it saddened her that there was a need for it in the first place. She'd seen so many pastors and members of other burned churches there. It struck her how, almost to the person, people described how the destruction had felt like the death of a close family member. The places of worship had been so much more than bricks and mortar. They were the central force of the communities—what people's lives revolved around—and yet within a flash, they had been reduced to ashes.

FOURTEEN

Different Colors, Same Message

As Ammie suspected, it took an anonymous tip to breathe life back into the investigation of St. John's case. Toward the end of April, a young woman called the arson hot line and reported that a white seventeen-year-old named James Brenner bragged to her that he and four other teenage boys set fire to the church. Brenner, who went by the nickname of "Smokey," also boasted of being a Klansman. Once, he passed a Klan application form to the informant and tried to convince her to join the Klan, too. Though still a minor, he had already had several brushes with the law, including arrests on forgery, breaking and entering, and runaway charges. He had been a disciplinary problem in high school, as well. He was expelled three times from ninth grade three years in a row before being permanently expelled.

The first week of May, Lt. Terry Alexander with SLED and Detective Bill Allen with the Lexington County Sheriff's Department took statements from each of the five young men who had, at one point, attended high school together. Three of them—Brenner and two brothers named Robert "Bobby" and Roger Emerson—gave statements that implicated themselves and one another. Like Brenner, both of the Emersons, respectively aged seventeen and nineteen, had had run-ins with the police on charges ranging from shoplifting to assault.

Initially, Brenner claimed that he used drugs and stayed drunk so much that he couldn't remember whether or not he had been at the church at the time of the fire. He added that he also had brain damage because his father used to slam his head against the walls of their trailer. But as he spoke, he told investigators that if he had burned the church, he was sure he would have remembered it even through his drugged and alcoholic haze, and he didn't remember burning anything of the sort.

In spite of claiming a poor memory, he attempted to cast blame on his brother, William, who he said broke into the church during the night of the fire. According to James, William was a "pyro" who had also vandalized one of the church's graves in addition to breaking into the building.

But when James Brenner failed a lie-detector test on May 9, a day after giving his statement, his story shifted. He said after picking up Bobby and Roger Emerson in his parent's brown Toyota van, they stopped at a Winn-Dixie for beer and then went to St. John. The drive to the church was a familiar one for Brenner. He admitted having gone there about twenty-eight times to practice satanic rituals. He said that he watched the Emersons shoot fireworks and drink beer, but that he didn't do either.

However, he was smoking, as were both his friends, and in his signed statement, he said that while "taking a leak" behind the church, "I may have dropped a cigarette in some pine straw and caused a fire." He denied seeing anything start to burn though and tried to steer the blame for the arson over to the

Emerson brothers—"I think Bobby or Roger set that fire on purpose. They would have done it just to see if they could get away with it."

He asserted that after he came back from urinating behind the church, he saw the brothers standing next to a side door that was half hanging from its hinges. As soon as they saw him return, Brenner said they appeared in a hurry to go back home. All three piled back into the van, and they sped off with only the parking lights on.

In his statement, he admitted to telling friends that he had burned St. John but said he did that only to show off and "act big." He also denied being a member of the Klan despite admitting he had frequently bragged that he was in the organization.

Roger Emerson's account of what happened that night proved to be almost as changeable as Brenner's. Though he altered his version of events, each version implicated James Brenner as the arsonist. In his first recounting, he said that he, his brother, and Brenner had gone down to the church and were shooting fireworks when Brenner went around to the back of the church. Roger estimated Brenner was gone for about fifteen to twenty minutes and upon returning ran to the van and called out, "Let's get out of here." When the Emersons asked him what he had been doing behind the building, he told them to never mind.

In his statement, Roger said, "I thought he [Brenner] was up to no good. Maybe he was trying to break in or something." Roger said he saw no evidence of a fire and didn't have any idea that one had occurred until his mother told him the following day.

But the same day Roger gave Alexander and Allen that account, he changed it and said he actually saw Brenner light the fire. In his second version, he said that after shooting fireworks for a while, Brenner tried to break into the front windows and a door that he had partially knocked from its hinges. When he couldn't force his way in, he went around back, after which Roger said he heard glass breaking. Again, he estimated that Brenner was gone about fifteen to twenty minutes, but when he returned, Roger saw him light a piece of cloth and set it on top of some pine straw and leaves near the church. After sparking the fire, he yelled, "Let's get out of here!"

When Roger asked him why he set the fire, he replied, "Don't worry about it. I did it for a good reason."

Bobby Emerson gave an account that contradicted those of both the other young men. He agreed that the three of them had gone down to St. John the night of the fire, but said six other people went with them, too. He said Brenner first drove by the church, then turned around and parked in the yard. Everyone except Brenner and an unnamed friend stayed in the van and shot fireworks from the windows.

Bobby said Brenner stood in the churchyard shooting fireworks and then kicked at the church's sign, trying to knock it down. Leaving the sign, he walked around the church alone before he and his friend got back in the van. Brenner was gone "no more than a minute," and after getting back in the van, he sped off down the road without turning on his headlights, saying he wanted to avoid the family living next to the church being able to get his license plate number.

Though his statement wasn't as forceful as his brother's in pinning the blame onto Brenner, Bobby did say that Brenner despised black people and whenever he caught Bobby socializing with blacks, he gave him a hard time about it.

On May 10, investigators arrested Brenner and the Emerson brothers. They were each charged with arson and burglary. The brothers indicated they would be willing to testify against Brenner if their charges were downgraded.

News of the arrests was a major relief to Ammie and everyone else involved with the church. They hoped that the piecing together of the case by SLED and the sheriff's department would make any future arsonist think twice before torching the church again.

Shortly after the teens' arrests, Ammie received a surprising phone call. At first she thought it was someone's idea of a practical joke, but as the caller spoke, she realized he was who he said he was. Bob Herbert, the acclaimed op-ed columnist with the *New York Times*, explained that he was doing a column about church fires and thought St. John made a compelling example of the escalating crisis.

His relaxed tone of voice quickly put her at ease. She spoke from her heart about how she had gotten involved with St. John; what she had seen on her first visit; and the threats that she, Barbara, and other committee members had received from people who hated what they were doing. "These no-good ding-blasted slime balls," she said. "Excuse my language, but that's what they are—they couldn't stand to see black people and white people working together on anything, not even to rebuild a church. The television would show blacks and whites down there working side by side, and that would make them crazy and they would feel they had to break up that black-white thing."

She could easily talk about St. John for hours and hoped that she wasn't going on too much, but he assured her that everything that she had said was useful.

The State newspaper carried Herbert's syndicated column on May 24. He had used many of her quotes. Ammie had to smile as she read it. Along with the publicity it gave St. John and the church-burning epidemic, it would probably be the first and last time she ever saw the words "no-good ding-blasted slime balls" in newsprint.

A couple of weeks after the column ran, Ammie found a large box that had been delivered to her door. Opening it, she found dozens of Bibles and a letter written in neat block print lying on top of them. She opened the envelope and read the note inside.

June 11, 1996

Dear Mrs. Murray,

My name is Pete Critsimilios and I am a fireman in New York City. A week or so ago in the N.Y. Times newspaper, I read about the St. John Baptist Church in Dixiana, South Carolina.

As I read what was done to this little country church, I felt very bad. Sometimes, feeling bad is not enough. Sometimes, you have to stand up and be counted.

Ms. Murray, you are a true American hero, and I stand with you. And I know that many other Americans stand with you too. I am not a religious person, Mrs. Murray. I am a Greek Orthodox Christian married to a Roman Catholic woman. My wife and I try to walk the straight and narrow and we teach our girls to do the same. My wife showed me the story and simply said, "There's a brave woman down south who needs our help." Now what do you ladies want to go and do—change the world? You mind if I tag along for the ride?

Enclosed, please find 100 Bibles. Those poor people might not have a church, but at least they will have the word.

Take heart, Mrs. Murray. We stand with you. May God continue to give you the courage to fight the good fight. Take heart!! Be strong, be careful and keep the faith. I remain your fellow American, and your friend—

> With Devotion to God, Duty and Country,
> Pete "The Greek" Critsimilios
> Engine 37, Ladder 40
> F.D.N.Y.

She laid the letter on her kitchen table and looked at the Bibles. They were of different colors, but all bore gold-embossed lettering in the bottom right-hand corner: ST. JOHN BAPTIST CHURCH, DIXIANA, SC. It struck Ammie that they symbolized all the people who had rebuilt the church in 1986 and who had come together once more to build it again—they were of different colors, but St. John Baptist Church had imprinted itself on each of their lives forever.

The date of the Washington trip drew nearer, and Ammie and Pat grew more excited as they prepared to leave, even more so after NCC officials said they wanted to include the two women in a video the NCC was making about the convergence of leaders and church representatives in the capital. Because St. John's story was so compelling, the NCC wanted its film crew to follow Ammie and Pat as they went to some of the scheduled meetings, press conferences, and church services.

Over the course of the three days they would spend in the nation's capital, the NCC had arranged for them to meet individually with South Carolina lawmakers Sen. Fritz Hollings and Rep. Floyd Spence. They were also to attend meetings and press conferences with Attorney General Janet Reno, Treasury Secretary Robert Rubin, and other government leaders, as well as NCC president Rev. Dr. Joan Brown Campbell, Rev. Dr. Mac Charles Jones, more NCC staff, and representatives from dozens of organizations and churches.

Rev. Terrance Mackey, pastor of the church burned in Williamsburg County, had already testified before the House Judiciary Committee, along with several other ministers.

Judging from the itinerary, the three days would be jam-packed from dawn to dusk. Ammie was cautiously optimistic that she could keep up with a pace that threatened to be grueling.

The NCC had given them plane tickets, but Ammie and Pat ended up driving through the night to Washington because Pat didn't want to fly. They arrived at the first light of Friday morning, June 8. Dragging her suitcase into her hotel room, Ammie collapsed onto the bed. She was bone-tired and regretted not taking advantage of the plane tickets. Pat was in a room downstairs. Her body throbbing from fatigue, Ammie dug out the itinerary and glanced at it. She shot up like a rocket, grabbed the phone, and punched in Pat's phone number

"Pat, we've got to go!" she shrieked. "We're supposed to be

over at the Capitol to attend that meeting with Janet Reno! Meet me downstairs as soon as you can!"

"Oh, my Lord," Pat exclaimed. "I'm on my way."

Bolting out onto the sidewalk from the lobby, they frantically flagged down a cab that took them to the Capitol. By the time they ran up the steps, sweat poured down their faces and they panted for breath. Running into the ornate structure, they stopped a building employee and received a series of Byzantine directions that got them lost. A guard noticed them pulling on locked doors and sent them to the right room.

An NCC official stopped in midsentence as they opened the door. The paneled conference room was packed with people. There were so many there that there weren't any empty chairs, and some people stood against walls. Seated at the top of a long, polished mahogany table was Janet Reno. She looked up at Ammie and Pat as they squeezed their way into the room. Ammie felt her face grow warm from embarrassment from their late arrival.

A tall man leaned over and whispered into Ammie's ear, "We've all introduced ourselves. Announce what your name is and which church you're representing."

Praying that she looked more confident than she felt, Ammie firmly said, "I'm Ammie Murray with St. John Baptist Church, Dixiana, South Carolina."

Pat introduced herself, too. "And I'm Reverend Patricia Lowman, associate pastor of St. John Baptist."

Ammie wondered if she could find out what they missed. The attorney general discussed at length the federal government's keen awareness of the church burnings and its commitment to bringing the guilty to justice. Nearly 250 federal agents had been assigned to investigate the crimes—the largest federal arson investigation in the history of America. Staff with the Justice Department, FBI, and ATF (Treasury Department) were working together with unprecedented closeness to halt the crisis. For the first time, the FBI and ATF combined their computer files to search for patterns and potential clues. If a conspiracy existed to burn black churches—as many civil rights leaders asserted— investigators would uncover it. Anyone—whether as a lone individual or member of a group—who torched churches would face the full retaliation of the United States government.

After giving her remarks, Janet Reno met with each person in the room, shaking their hands and briefly chatting with them. No sooner had Ammie and Pat exchanged pleasantries with her than they had to dash off to meetings with Rep. Floyd Spence and Sen. Ernest Hollings with the NCC film crew in tow. The congressmen cordially welcomed them, and while Ammie figured their staffs had probably briefed them about the rising epidemic, she gave them copies of newspaper clippings, photos, and fact sheets all the same.

As it turned out, she discovered both lawmakers were already involved in developing a congressional response. Representative Spence vowed support for HR 3525, a House bill that made it easier for federal agents to investigate arsons. If passed, the bill would eliminate the ten-thousand-dollar minimum that current law required damages to religious property to exceed before triggering federal involvement. The bill further expanded federal powers to investigate such crimes.

Senator Hollings indicated there was strong support for the House bill, and indeed, the Senate planned to amend it to further expand federal powers in relation to stopping and preventing church fires. The senate bill, S1890, penned by the unlikely duo of arch-conservative Sen. Lauch Faircloth, R-NC, and liberal stalwart Edward Kennedy, D-MA, would extend the federal statute of limitations from five years to seven, increase maximum sentences from ten years to twenty, and allocate funding to help affected churches rebuild.

The last piece of information was especially good news to Ammie. After a Columbia architectural firm—GMK Associates— donated plans for a new building, the committee realized it had underestimated how much money was needed to rebuild St. John. Instead of $75,000, they needed at least $110,000. The ability of Tim McConnell and Victory Savings to help was diminished by the bank's own financial woes after a string of creditors defaulted on loans.

Following meetings with their elected representative, Ammie and Pat went to one of the press conferences held later in the day. Almost at each press conference, the controversy played out as to whether or not there was a national conspiracy behind the fires. The CDR, NAACP, and other civil rights organizations continued to assert one existed. Among other things, they pointed to the fact that 56 percent of the churches burned within the last eighteen months had been black, despite that the number of white churches in America far exceeded black ones.

Others, including officials with the Justice Department, said they had not discovered any evidence of a conspiracy and that if anything, results from current investigations disproved the theory. For starters, approximately one-third of those charged with burning black churches were black themselves. This included one nineteen-year-old in Clinton, Mississippi, who—in what may have been a play for attention—went next door and set fire to Lynch Chapel United Methodist, then returned home and called the fire department to report the blaze. Eventually, he pleaded guilty to the arson and received a three-year sentence.

Another issue that undermined the conspiracy theory for many people was related to psychiatric disorders amongst some white assailants. At least three black church fires were solved when volunteer firefighters admitted both to the crimes and to the fact that they were pyromaniacs. In their cases, it appeared to police that they were driven more by mental instability than racism. Apart from the three firefighters, two other whites who pleaded guilty were so unstable, they had to be committed.

State and federal agents also discovered that sometimes the torching of black churches was done to cover up other crimes like burglary. Nonetheless, officials acknowledged that racism was the primary factor in the overall epidemic. Assistant Attorney General Deval L. Patrick, who headed the Department of Justice's civil rights division, said, "It's plain that racial hostility is behind many of the fires." In addition to directing DOJ's civil rights division, President Clinton had appointed him to lead a new task force to address the issue of church fires. Information from investigations under way led Patrick to a conclusion far more frightening than a conspiracy—that what existed was "an epidemic of individual terrorists." As opposed to foot soldiers in some centrally organized group, these were individuals who carried out their crimes in secrecy, proving much harder for police to track and apprehend. Patrick told reporters, "The prospect of a conspiracy is a chilling thing. But the prospect that these are separate acts of racism is even worse."

In concurrence, Noah Chandler with the CDR said, "The conspiracy is racism itself."

Although his schedule had not permitted him to attend the meetings, President Clinton used his weekly radio address on Saturday, June 8, to discuss the crisis. Normally, the weekly addresses were merely taped, but this time, news programs televised him reading it.

After a long, tiring day, Ammie returned to her hotel room and saw the event on TV. She was pleasantly surprised to see one of the pastors at the meetings, Rev. Terrance Mackey, pastor of Mt. Zion AME in Williamsburg County, standing beside the president as he read the address:

> Good morning. This morning I want to talk with you about a recent and disturbing rash of crimes that hearkens back to a dark era in our nation's history. Just two days ago, when the Matthews-Murkland Presbyterian Church in Charlotte, North Carolina, was burned to the ground, it became at least the thirtieth African-American church destroyed or damaged by suspicious fire in the South in the past eighteen months. And over the past few months, Vice President Gore has talked with me about the pain and anguish these fires in his home state of Tennessee have caused. Tennessee, sadly, has experienced more of them than any state in the country.
>
> We do not have evidence of a national conspiracy, but it is

clear that racial hostility is the driving force behind a number of these incidents. This must stop.

It's hard to think of a more depraved act of violence than the destruction of a place of worship. In our country, during the fifties and sixties, black churches were burned to intimidate civil rights workers. I have vivid and painful memories of black churches being burned in my own state when I was a child. In 1963, all Americans were outraged by the bombing of the Sixteenth Street Baptist Church in Birmingham that took the lives of four precious young children. We must never allow that to happen again.

Every family has a right to expect that when they walk into a church or synagogue or mosque each week they will find a house of worship, not the charred remnants of a hateful act done by cowards in the night. We must rise up as a national community to safeguard the right of every citizen to worship in safety. That is what America stands for.

As President, I am determined to do everything in my power to get to the bottom of these church burnings as quickly as possible. And no matter what it takes, no matter where the leads take us, we will devote whatever resources are necessary to solve these crimes. Today, more than two hundred federal agents from the Bureau of Alcohol, Tobacco and Firearms and the FBI are working with state and local authorities to solve these cases. Fire investigators, national response teams, polygraph examiners, and forensic chemists are combing through fire sites, interviewing witnesses, and following leads. A task force chaired by our Assistant Attorney General for Civil Rights, Deval Patrick, and our Assistant Secretary of the Treasury for Enforcement, James Johnson, is coordinating these efforts. FBI Director Louis Freeh and ATF Director John Magaw are also serving on the task force. To date there have been a number of arrests. Two of those in custody are known members of the Ku Klux Klan. So we are making progress, but we must do more.

That is why today I am announcing four steps we are taking to fight back. First, I have asked the task force to report back on their progress and to let me know if there are other actions the federal government can take beyond those under way to stop these crimes.

Second, I have instructed the ATF to inform churches of any steps they can take to protect themselves from arsonists. Churches throughout the South will be visited by ATF special agents to answer any questions church leaders and parishioners may have. We are also making this information available to national church organizations for distribution to their members.

Third, I am announcing my support for the bipartisan legislation introduced by Congressmen John Conyers and Henry Hyde to make it easier to bring federal prosecutions against those who attack houses of worship. I look forward to working with Congress to make it even stronger.

And finally, I'm announcing that we are establishing a new toll-free number that is now available twenty-four hours a day, seven days a week. If you have information about who is responsible for these church fires, please call it. It's 1-888-ATF-FIRE. That's 1-888-ATF-FIRE.

In the end, we must all face up to the responsibility to end this violence. We must say to those who would feed their neighbors what Martin Luther King called, "the stale bread of hatred and spoiled meat of racism"—that is not America. That is not our way. We must come together, black and white alike, to smother the fires of hatred that fuel this violence.

Amen, Ammie thought. Amen.

Once all the meetings wrapped up on Sunday, June 10, Ammie and Pat left Washington. As they had been on the go nearly nonstop from Friday morning to Sunday afternoon, the nine-hour drive back home was more exhausting than the one up. In two days, President Clinton would be in Williamsburg County, South Carolina, to celebrate the rebuilding of Mt. Zion AME.

Pat was planning to go, but Ammie was simply too worn out to consider it. But she wouldn't have missed the trip to Washington for anything. The series of meetings and press conferences, which had been extensively covered by the national media, had made the entire country sit up and take notice of what was happening. Indeed, because of coverage by foreign journalists, now the whole world knew.

The next month, another writer with the *New York Times* contacted her. This time it was national correspondent Fox Butterfield. He and *Times* photographer Wade Spees came down for interviews and photos of the church ruins. She took them to meet members of the committee, and Willie couldn't get over having a *New York Times* reporter in his trailer.

In addition to interviewing Ammie, Willie, Jerry, Tom, Sheriff Metts, and Pat, Butterfield also got in touch with Mary Emerson, mother of Roger and Bobby Emerson. She told him one of the worst things about the whole ordeal was that it was causing her sons to be labeled as racists when they weren't.

"Most of our neighbors are black," she said, "and most of the boys' friends are, too. They've spent the night at each other's homes plenty of times. In our family, skin color doesn't make no difference."

Her sons were out on bail, but James Brenner had been unable to post his twenty-thousand-dollar bond. Apparently figuring out that he was being fingered to take the brunt of the guilt, Brenner had tried to retract the statement he had given detectives. He claimed that he had been forced to give the incriminating statement through police brutality. When detectives told him to contact his attorney regarding his allegations of abuse, he replied that he fired his lawyer because the lawyer had advised him to plead guilty.

Butterfield's article ran July 21 in a Sunday edition of the paper. Ammie read it and looked over the photo of her and

Patricia standing amidst the ruins. The *Times* had done pieces about St. John two months in a row. Not bad, she thought, not bad at all.

St. John was continuing to hold services at the Seventh Day Adventist church, and Willie confided to Ammie that the trip out there was taking its toll on everybody. By the time he made his rounds to pick up elderly members and took them to the Adventist church, many of them were worn out. His car was taking a beating from the long trip, too.

Ammie hated the thought of them having to crowd into his den again, so she made a series of phone calls to create another option for them. In August, she called several people and organizations, and her calls yielded the donation of a large tentlike fabrication from Sprung Instant Structures Company and the nonprofit AmeriCares organization. The structure had sturdy aluminum framing and was covered by weather-resistant material. One hundred people could fit in easily, giving the twenty or so who normally came for services more than enough room. Members from a labor union in Augusta, Georgia, and employees from a local crane company were among those who helped put it up.

Ammie hoped they wouldn't have to use the temporary building for long. The recent news coverage had generated close to twenty thousand dollars in contributions. They still weren't where they needed to be, but they were on their way there. With luck, they would be able to break ground for the new building in early spring.

A Roman Catholic church in Winfield, Illinois, contacted her about making a donation. Its priest, Father Guy Vaccaro, had read about St. John in the *New York Times* and was struck not only by what had happened to it, but by its name. His church was called St. John the Baptist.

By chance, Ammie was going to be in Illinois in late August to attend the Democratic national convention. She had been selected by the state party to be a delegate for President Clinton. She told Father Vaccaro this, and he invited her to speak before several Masses after the convention ended.

She stood before the parishioners and told St. John's story and how she had gotten involved and what she and others had been through to help the church. Although she had lost count of the number of times she had told the story, the raw emotion from it came back to her as if it had all happened yesterday.

A special collection was taken up at each of the Masses. By the end of the weekend, the Catholic church raised ten thousand dollars. Ammie was astounded by the outpouring of support, and the love she felt from them was almost palpable. She could barely hold back tears when Father Vaccaro said, "Our churches are tied together by a profound faith. We believe that wherever there is a dying, there will also be a rising."

St. John received an early Christmas present from the NCC. Seven major foundations, including Annenberg, Rockefeller, Kellogg, and Ford, had donated monies to the NCC's burned-churches rebuilding fund. The NCC was channeling the funds to affected churches, and they sent a check to St. John for thirty thousand dollars. Ammie, Willie, and everyone with the committee and congregation celebrated. They had no doubt that before the end of 1997, St. John would stand once again.

FIFTEEN

A Stranger from Texas

But that was not to be. Part of it was because county officials revised the flood maps, determining that St. John was not in a floodplain after all, meaning the church could rebuild where it was if it wanted to. The redrawing of the maps divided the congregation about what was best to do. Some wanted to rebuild where they were while others wanted to maintain the grounds as a memorial and cemetery, but make a fresh start somewhere else that offered more visibility and protection.

They went back and forth about it. Ammie didn't feel it was her place to try to influence the decision one way or the other. Though she would risk everything for the church, she constantly reminded herself that she was not a member and had no right to participate in internal decision making.

Meanwhile, the search to find the right contractor proved more challenging than they had ever imagined. They were stymied at every turn in getting one who was both available to get started and willing to do the necessary work within the budget.

As the spring months of 1997 melted into summer, Ammie grew more frustrated. It was as if they were running in place. The congregation had reached a consensus to rebuild where they were, but their decision was met with disappointment from several of the core committee members.

Butch couldn't shake the feeling that the congregation was making a serious mistake. After working through his contacts, he had managed to get someone to donate to the church a half-acre of land close into town. While he had a deep appreciation for why they decided to remain where they were, he worried that they were only setting themselves up for more heartache. The repeated vandalism that culminated in the fiery destruction two years ago proved the police were limited in what they could do to safeguard it.

The insurance premiums were bound to be up in the stratosphere, too. The architectural plans called for the structure to be rebuilt with fireproof material, but each of the contractors the committee met with said that using such material would add tens of thousands to the total cost. The next best thing was to have a brick exterior, but even that wasn't cheap.

The same concerns dogged Ammie. What would happen if the tiny congregation fell behind on the insurance premiums again and someone torched it? How many times would the public respond to her calls of help to rebuild it? Besides that, she was sixty-four, and although she had been enjoying fairly good health lately, she wouldn't live forever. She wanted to think that someone else would step forward to lead another rebuilding effort, but she couldn't count on that.

At least she was grateful that, because of the efforts from the NCC, CDR, NAACP, and other organizations, the issue of church arsons continued to stay in front of the American public. Later that summer, a PBS television producer called her. PBS was making a documentary about hate crime called *Not in Our Town* and wanted to include a segment on St. John and other burned churches.

A producer and film crew came down and spent a day doing interviews and shooting footage. They shot clips of her, Matt, and Sheriff Metts. She looked forward to seeing the program that was supposed to air the following February. Anything that kept the issue in the spotlight was helpful.

The year 1997 ended on a dispirited note. The singed cinderblock frame of the vestibule stood forlornly amidst the weeds and underbrush that stubbornly defied Willie's efforts to keep them shorn to the ground.

For Ammie, the entire year had been a series of steps forward, and then back. They didn't have much to show for all the work they had done, and she could only hope that 1998 would turn out better.

In mid-February, one of the women in the congregation found a contractor willing to take on the job for what their budget allowed. Members of the church and the committee gathered with local media in the churchyard to watch construction workers break ground.

Ammie couldn't contain her joy. Her heart leapt at the sight of bulldozers and heavy trucks rumbling into the churchyard. "I'm so happy, that I'm numb," she said to Doug Pardue, a reporter for *The State*. "The good Lord has been working overtime."

The contractor anticipated being finished within three months.

"Praise the Lord," Willie said, raising his hands toward the heavens.

Ammie said, "This is beyond wonderful."

The completion would make for the sweetest spring she had ever experienced.

Everyone chatted excitedly while watching the workers. Ammie had turned away briefly to wave to a committee member pulling up into the drive, but a thundering crash made her whip back around. Someone on the construction crew had charged his bulldozer directly into the remains of the vestibule. Chunks of cinder block tumbled to the ground.

"Oh, no," she said, her hand flying to her mouth.

Pushing up the bill of his baseball cap, the contractor looked at Ammie quizzically. "What's the matter? That was just an old outhouse."

"No, it wasn't," she told him. "It was the vestibule. We wanted to save it to be part of the new building."

"Sorry." He shrugged. "Our mistake."

"Well, what's done is done," she said with a short sigh. "Maybe we couldn't have saved it, anyway."

The PBS documentary *Not in Our Town* aired shortly afterward. In the segment about church burnings, each of the places of worship featured was shown rebuilt at the end of the program; every one of them, that is, except for St. John. But that would be remedied soon, Ammie thought.

In a small southeastern Texan town called Sinton, Al and Linda Hoelscher watched the same program. Al owned a small roofing company, and Linda, his wife, did the bookkeeping. They were channel surfing when they came across the documentary, and it immediately grabbed them. The sad sight of St. John lying in ruins while the rest of the churches had been rebuilt jabbed at their hearts and the anguish etched on Matt's face as he looked at the ruins haunted them. By the time they finished watching it, tears streamed down Linda's face, and Al felt like shedding some, too.

Wiping her cheeks, Linda turned to him and saw that he shared her feelings. It didn't surprise her. She knew his heart was as big as the state they lived in. "You're gonna help build that church, aren't you?"

"I sure am thinking about it."

"No, you're not thinking about it. You've made up your mind to do it. When do you want me to start making phone calls?"

"I want you on the phone tomorrow."

Grabbing a pencil and notepad, Linda struggled to remember the name of the woman in the documentary trying to get the church rebuilt; then it came to her because her first name was so unusual—"Ammie Murray." Also jotting down, "Lexington County, SC," she figured her best bet to find out how to get in touch with Ammie would be through that county's sheriff department.

The next morning, Linda dialed information and got the number for the department. She dialed it and after she explained why she was calling, a deputy gave her Ammie's phone number, and Linda gave it to her husband.

Ammie was walking out the door when the phone rang.

"Mrs. Murray," Al said, in his Texan twang, "my name is Al Hoelscher, and I'm calling from Sinton, Texas."

They spoke for hours. Al explained that he and Linda wanted to help any way possible and that he had spent decades in construction and owned a business in the trade. In addition to volunteering with various charities, he and Linda were active with Habitat for Humanity and had recently helped construct three houses in nearby Corpus Christi and four homes in San Antonio, 135 miles to the northeast.

"We've just signed with a contractor here in the state," Ammie told him. "He's already started, and says he'll be finished in late April. He and his guys will be working on the foundation within the next week or so."

"That's great. We just wanted to make sure that y'all had somebody to get the job done. It tore us up to see that church was nothing but ashes."

Thinking about how the construction company had knocked down the vestibule, Ammie added, "Well, we may still wind up needing some extra help after all, though. Would it be okay for me to keep in touch?"

"Absolutely." Al gave her his number.

She thanked him and said, "I'll keep you up to date with how things are going."

Soon afterward, she stopped by the construction site to see how work was progressing. The contractor and his small crew were driving away in an old truck as she headed into the churchyard. Slowing her car, she rolled her window down to speak to them, but the contractor drove past, merely waving. She returned his wave and turned onto the site.

Getting out of her car, she walked around the site. What she saw concerned her. Short stumps of cinder block dotted the sandy ground. Apparently, the contractor planned to use them as the footings of the foundation. Cinder-block foundations were frequently used for small to medium houses, but she wondered if one was strong enough for a large building. She had expected the contractor to pour concrete into steel rods to form solid, fortified pilings that penetrated into the ground.

Making a mental note to talk with him about it, she drove away and shifted her focus to her daughter Betsy who was having major surgery the following Monday, March 9.

Betsy's jaw had been broken as a child. The surgery she had to repair it left her jaw misaligned and caused her chronic pain. Further procedures, including braces, still hadn't resolved it. Finally, she found an excellent orthodontic surgeon who had corrected many similar cases. The surgery meant rebreaking the jaw and wiring it shut for six weeks to allow it to re-form properly.

While she hated the idea of not being able to eat solid foods for six weeks, Betsy looked forward to the procedure that would relieve the pain that had burdened her most of her life. For at least the first few weeks or so after she had the surgery, Ammie felt she needed to be with her, especially during the daytime when her son-in-law Steve worked and the grandkids—Scott and Shannon—attended school.

Betsy called her on the Friday before the operation. She excitedly reported that she had hired someone to help out at her audiological practice while she was home recuperating from the surgery.

"That's great," Ammie told her. "I know how worried you were about finding somebody."

"Yeah, Mom, I really think she's going to be great. She's got fantastic credentials, lots of experience, and she seems like a really nice person. It gives me peace of mind knowing that I've got her onboard. You know how particular I am when it comes to my patients."

"I sure do."

Betsy's practice specialized in pediatric cases, and many of those cases were referred by social service agencies that provided care to children with special needs.

"So what are your plans for this weekend?" Betsy asked her.

Looking around, Ammie replied, "Ah, I guess I need to see what I can do with this house. It's a mess. I've still haven't sorted through all of the stuff I got out of Mom's house after she died. How about you?"

"I'm taking Shannon to that cheerleading camp up past Newberry."

"Okay, call me when you get back."

"All right."

But later on that rainy Saturday afternoon, Betsy didn't call. Her husband did. His voice was strained tight. "There's been a wreck—"

Bits and pieces of the rest of his words wedged their way through into Ammie's numbed mind—"roads were slick," "hydroplaned," "eighteen-wheeler," "they've been air-vacked to Richland Memorial."

Dulled from shock, Ammie robotically drove to the hospital, where she met her family who had gathered there along with a growing mass of Betsy's friends and neighbors. The trucker with whom Betsy had collided followed the medical helicopter to the hospital and told Ammie what had happened.

"I was heading down the eastbound lane, and she was over in the westbound. It was raining something awful. There was a lot of it standing on the road, and when she hit a slick, she lost control of her car. I saw her crossing over the grass median into my lane and heading straight toward me. I tried—" He voice broke.

Covering his face with his hands, he began sobbing.

Embracing him, Ammie said, "I know. I know."

Betsy and her teenage daughter stayed in surgery for hours. One of Shannon's lungs was punctured and, among other bones, her clavicle and jaw were broken. In an ironic twist of fate, the same orthodontic surgeon who was going to operate on Betsy two days later ended up operating on Shannon. But though her injuries were extensive, they weren't life-threatening.

Her mother's were. The wreck had crumpled Betsy's slender body like that of a small porcelain doll hurled against a stone wall. If she survived the surgery, which was doubtful, her doctors warned of massive brain damage and permanent paralysis.

As the numbness that enshrouded her began to wear off, Ammie's anguish became unbearable. If she could only change places with her child, she would do it a thousand times over.

She was sixty-five and had lived nearly a full life while Betsy's was just blossoming. It wasn't fair. It didn't make sense.

She prayed. She wept. She paced. She tried to sit still. One moment she wanted to strike at something; the next she felt weak as a rag doll. Family and friends made efforts to comfort her, but the only thing she wanted was to see her daughter and granddaughter.

Betsy hung on through the surgery and was transferred to ICU. They moved Shannon to a hospital room. Her surgery had gone well, but she still hadn't regained consciousness.

As desperate as she had been to see both of them, it devastated Ammie to see their broken bodies. Shannon's would heal, but the doctors continued to speak in somber tones about Betsy. Tubing and wires hung from her, and they connected to machines that beeped and hissed menacingly. Ammie searched the faces of all the medical staff that constantly streamed in and out of her ICU room for signs of hope, but found little.

She did draw comfort, however, from all the people who poured in as word spread of the accident. The hospital staff said they had never seen such a massive turnout of well-wishers. So many folks came bearing flowers and gifts for Betsy and Shannon and prepared meals for their family that a large table had to be set up in the waiting room. Willie and Matt were among the people from St. John who visited often.

Over the next couple of weeks, their visits and the phone calls Ammie received from Al and Linda were about the only things that made her think about the church. She told Al and Linda that she figured she would be able to concentrate on St. John once Betsy and Shannon were more stable. Expressing heartfelt concern, the Hoelschers said they would keep her daughter and granddaughter in their prayers.

During a sporadic visit to her home to shower and see to her new dog, Ammie decided to swing by the church on her way back to the hospital. With all the recent tragedy, she hadn't been able to see it since the cinder-block footings were installed.

The construction workers were nowhere in sight. In fact, not a bit of work had been done since her last visit. The cinder-block footings stood like small, petrified tree trunks.

"What the hell?" she muttered, and then backed up and turned around.

As soon as she got to a phone, she dialed the contractor's number. "We're sorry," she heard a computer-generated voice say, "but the number you have reached is no longer in service."

She tried the number again but got the same message. Feeling suddenly nauseated, she called others on the committee. "Have y'all seen any of the construction workers down at the church lately?"

None of them had.

They never saw the contractor or any of his workers again. Nor did they ever see the $27,000 that they had given him as a down payment.

Ammie buried her face in her hands. What kind of rotten low-lifes would scam a church, especially one that had already endured so much tribulation? There had to be a special place in hell for people like that. That fact that the contractors and his men were African Americans made it all the worse. They knew what St. John had been through and how ecstatic its congregation was when construction—or the so-called construction—started. That man and his workers were nearly as bad as the three teens who burned St. John in the first place. If she ever got hold of them, she'd tear them limb from limb.

The money was the worst part of it: $27,000. Every time she thought about it, she wanted to throw up.

She thanked the Lord that Al and his wife were still interested in helping. Calling him, she filled him in on what had happened.

"Good God Almighty, you've got to be kidding!" Al exclaimed.

"I wish I were. I'm just sick about it. We all are. You wouldn't believe how hard it was to raise that money and now it's long gone. That no-good, thieving, lying skunk of a contractor and his crew could be anywhere by now."

"You're right about that."

There wasn't much else to do but go forward. Al wanted to come out and look over the site and the blueprints and told her he would get out there as soon as he could.

Her conversation with Al eased Ammie's anxiety. He told her that after he visited, he would return to Texas, get some volunteers together, come back with them, and start building. They would work for absolutely nothing and complete as much as possible within the two weeks that he traditionally shut down the company for summer break.

Talk about a ram in the bush, Ammie thought. She felt as if he had lifted a heavy stone from off her. She had more than enough to worry about as it was, with Betsy and Shannon.

If she wasn't at Betsy's side, Ammie was at Shannon's. Once Shannon recovered enough to go home, Ammie stayed with Betsy practically around the clock. She had plenty of company. Steve and the kids were constants as were Christy, Emmala, Betsy's best friend, Betsy Dyches, and other close friends and family members. They nagged Ammie to get more rest and take care of herself, but she couldn't bear to be away from her daughter for any significant length of time. Betsy needed her. And although she still wasn't able to speak, she had regained the ability to open her eyes, and they lit up whenever Ammie talked or sang to her, read to her, held her hand, kissed her cheek, or stroked her face. She could rest later. Betsy needed her now.

Little by little, Betsy's condition improved. Her vital signs grew stable and, though unable to talk, she appeared more alert. What meant so much to Ammie was that her child was able to smile, a somewhat weak one, but a smile nonetheless. It was as clear a sign as the rainbow after the flood that she would recover.

Physical therapists began a passive regimen of exercises to help her regain use of muscles atrophied from weeks of lying in the hospital bed. When her doctors spoke of plans to transfer her to a physical rehabilitation center, Ammie felt like skipping up and down the sterile hallways.

Leaning over Betsy, she kissed her softly. "Do you hear that, honey? You're getting better! You're going to a place where they will teach you how to do some of the things you used to do."

Betsy smiled up at her. Ammie ached to hear the sound of her voice, but she contented herself for the time being with her ability to read her daughter's expressions. The neurologist persisted in speaking to them of brain damage and said that Betsy would probably need total care the rest of her life. Ammie brushed Betsy's sun-streaked blond bangs from her eyes. Doctors didn't know everything. They weren't God.

Betsy's two-week stay at the rehabilitation hospital proved to be a painful disappointment. Therapists there determined she had no potential for rehabilitation. Her injuries were simply too severe. The staff was compassionate but firm in their belief that Betsy would live the rest of her life in little better than a vegetative state. They transferred her to a nursing home.

Ammie tried to take the news in stride. Betsy would continue to receive therapy at the nursing home, though not so aggressively as at the rehab center. She would get better. Ammie didn't care what others said. And once she improved, those people at that center would see her again. Ammie would make certain of it.

During one of her visits home, she received another call from Al.

"I think I can make it out there around the twenty-eighth to look things over."

"The twenty-eighth?"

"Yeah, of this month. That will be on a Thursday, the last Thursday of this month."

Her brain blunted from the fatigue and monotony of indistinguishable days at Betsy's side, Ammie tried to recall which month they were in—May. It was May already.

"That sounds fine, Al."

"Are you okay?"

"Oh, yeah. I'm kind of dragging today, but I'm a tough old bird. We've got Betsy settled in the nursing home, but we're hoping we can eventually get her back to the rehab hospital."

"You know we'll keep praying for her and the rest of y'all, too."

"I appreciate it more than I can ever tell you, Al."

As promised, Al arrived on May 28. At a lanky six feet four inches and wearing a ten-gallon hat, cowboy boots, a checkered shirt with a pack of cigarettes tucked in the breast pocket, and faded jeans, he fit Ammie's image of a Texan. He caught her up in a big bear hug, and she hugged him back. They had spoken on the phone so much, it was as if they had know each other for years.

"Man, am I ever glad to see you," Ammie told him. "After everything that we've been through, we're finally going to get this thing off the ground."

His arrival renewed her determination. St. John was going to be rebuilt. If it were the last thing she ever did, she would make sure that happened.

Al realized that Ammie was going to get the church built whether he helped or not—and he wanted to put his shoulder against the wheel with her.

"I'm itching to see it," he said. "It's all I've been thinking about. How far is it from here?"

"I can get you there in about fifteen minutes. Willie and Matt are going to meet us. I let both of them know that you made it into town."

As with Ammie, Al felt as if he already knew Matt and Willie before he met them. He and Linda had spoken to them numerous times on the phone in preparation for his visit.

The men greeted him with hearty handshakes and pats on the back, and all four of them walked over the site that, except for the destruction of the remains of the vestibule and the cinder-block pilings, looked exactly the same as it had on *Not in Our Town*.

Inspecting the pilings, Al flicked ashes from his cigarette and muttered, "This has got to be about the sorriest junk I've ever seen in all my life."

"They're pieces of shit is what they are," Ammie agreed bluntly.

Placing his hands on top of them and examining them from one side to the other, Matt said, "You know, these things aren't even straight. See how crooked they come up? A blind man could have set this stuff up straighter than this guy did."

Al shook his head. "This is a mess. This is terrible. Before I come back, I'm going to need y'all to clear away this crap. Sand needs to be brought in, too, to fill in all these places where the ground has sunk in."

"Don't worry about that," Willie said. "I know a guy with a tractor who can haul this stuff off. I can get a few truckloads of sand in, too. But first I got to ask you how much are you going to charge us? We're on a tight budget."

"Nothing," Al answered. "Like I said before on the phone, me and my people are coming for free."

"For free?" Matt said.

"Yes." He understood their skepticism. Had he changed places with them, he would be far more skeptical. The people of St. John had paid a high price for trusting people before, especially those who had shown up from out of nowhere.

Still sensing some leeriness, he went on, "Look, I don't care about any money. I don't even want to know how much y'all have got. That ain't my objective. As long as when I need the materials, you can get them out here, we're gonna build this church."

They showed Al the blueprints, and he was astounded at the size of the planned structure. The design included seven bathrooms. The tiny congregation didn't need that many. Once he got back home, he thought he could rework the plans to cut down on the overall costs.

With the blueprints spread out on a table, they looked over them and discussed which suppliers might offer either donations of materials or at least significant discounts. If they kept building costs at around fifty thousand dollars, that would still leave St. John with reserves for insurance premiums and other necessities.

Over the three days he was there, Al shared most of his meals with Ammie, who filled him in on the church's extensive history. So much of what she told him had not been included in the documentary because of time limitations. Its history made St. John more special to him than it had been before.

Toward the end of his visit, Willie took Al to his trailer, where several elderly ladies of the congregation had gathered. Willie introduced him to each of them.

With tears in her eyes, one of the ladies clasped Al's hand. "Are you going to build my church?"

Looking down at her, Al felt like grabbing a hammer, running out the door to the church, and starting right then and there. "Ma'am—" his voice strained with compassion. "—I'm gonna do the best I can."

"We thank you." She squeezed his hand before letting go.

The only thing that made leaving St. John bearable was knowing he would return soon. July 10 marked the date he would come back with Linda and as many others as he could convince to join them. Since he was closing his business for two weeks, he hoped that some of his crew could come.

Before he returned to Texas, he predicted that they could get most, if not all, of the church structure up within two weeks. Of course, that depended on how many volunteers he could bring and how many Ammie, Matt, and Willie recruited.

"Two weeks?" Ammie asked.

"Yep, two weeks. I hope y'all will be able to have your first service here within a week of our arrival."

She blinked hard. Here was an angel standing right in front of her. And he chain-smoked and wore cowboy boots.

As soon as Al returned home, before he could say the first word to her, Linda knew St. John had completely won him over.

He unnecessarily reaffirmed that after releasing her from his embrace. "There's no way I'm not going to build that church. We're going out there to build it, and that's the bottom line."

"Just say when, and I'm ready to go."

Reworking the blueprints, he cut out four of the bathrooms. Remaining in the revised building plan was a large sanctuary with a hidden baptismal pool, two Sunday school classrooms, a kitchen with an airy dining area that could be sectioned off to create additional Sunday school classrooms, a pastor's study with an adjoining bathroom, two other bathrooms, two storage areas toward the front of the building that could double as small offices, and a vestibule. The building would have a brick exterior and central heat and air. In total, the square footage would be 4,250—six and a half times the original 660 square feet.

He lit up another cigarette. Lumber, especially what was needed to make trusses for the roof, stood a good chance of being the most expensive item. He didn't know how many trusses they needed or the specs for them. A company that specialized in producing them would have to have their engineers come up with that information.

Picking up the phone, he dialed the number for a truss manufacturer that he often worked with located in San Antonio.

"We could make 'em for you, but it would cost like hell to truck 'em all the way there," one of the employees said. "What I'd do if I were you is to get in touch with somebody in South Carolina."

"I don't know anybody out there who makes them."

"Me, either, but I'll tell you what I'll do—I'll surf the Web and see what I can find out and call you back."

"All right, I appreciate it."

Al told Linda about it.

"We'll probably never hear back from him again," she said as she prepared lunch for them.

But the guy called back a few days later.

"I found this company called Hipp Truss out of Simpsonville, South Carolina. How far that is from Dixiana, I couldn't tell you. I've never heard of either one of these places before talkin' to you."

"That's all right," Al said as he copied down Hipp Truss's phone number. "I'll take it from here. Thanks."

Al dialed the number and asked to speak to either the manager or owner. He was connected to the owner, Russ Hippensteel, who asked him to fax a copy of the building plan to him.

Once he did, they spoke on the phone again.

"They're going to come out to about fifteen thousand dollars," Mr. Hippensteel said.

Al whistled. "That's steep. Sir, this is for a church that got burned down a few years ago that we're trying to rebuild. If there's any way you can help us out, we sure would be mighty appreciative."

"Tell me about this church."

Al told him everything and about how he and others from Texas were going to spend two weeks reconstructing it.

"You're going to come all the way from Texas to build it?"

"Well, sir, I'm gonna do my best."

"Let me see what I can do. I'll call you back in a couple of days." Before getting off the phone, he mentioned that he had recently returned from Africa, where he had helped build houses through a Christian charity.

Two days later, he called Al. "I'm cutting that bill in half."

"Oh, my Lord!" The man was giving St. John more than seven thousand dollars. "Thank you so much! Thank you!"

"It's my pleasure."

Al immediately called Ammie with the news. It added to more good news she had recently received after so many dark months. Betsy was continuing to improve, and Richard Meyer, a national correspondent with the *Los Angeles Times*, had called to let her know that his piece on St. John was going to run in the July 11 edition of the paper.

He had spent several days in Dixiana the previous summer, and while telling him the story, she was impressed by his attention to minute details. He even went to the point of having her identify the names of plants and trees growing around the church. He combed through a stack of documentation compiled by Clayton Kleckey, who had headed up the church's history subcommittee twelve years earlier; read reams of old newspaper clippings; and spent hours interviewing everyone from her, Matt, and Willie to Stick, Bulldog, and Jerry Bellune.

In the course of working on the story, he and Ammie developed a friendship that only strengthened after he returned to Los Angeles. They frequently spoke on the phone, and although the subject of St. John almost always came up, they also chatted about general goings-on in their lives and those of close family members. On two occasions, he surprised her by having a gallon of her favorite ice cream, black walnut, delivered to her.

His piece in the *Times* would be 8,052 words, the longest article to ever appear in the paper.

By early July, Matt had grown more and more concerned. Al, Linda, and others from Texas would be arriving within a few days, and St. John still didn't have a building permit. Because of the size of the church once it was completed, they had to have a commercial building permit as opposed to a residential one.

Matt racked his brain trying to figure out which licensed contractor they might go through to get a permit, realizing that anyone willing to help them would be taking on enormous financial and legal risks in exchange for nothing except St. John's gratitude. Letting the church use his or her license exposed a contractor to tremendous liability if a catastrophe occurred during construction.

Matt didn't know any contractors well enough to approach and ask them to trust him with what amounted to their livelihoods and futures. But one day, he was driving through Lexington and caught sight of some men building a bank. He slowed his truck. If those guys were building a bank, someone with their company had to have a commercial building permit.

Figuring he had nothing to lose, he turned his truck into the construction site that had a large sign in front of it spelling out TYLER CONSTRUCTION.

"Hey, fellas," he called out.

The men turned around and looked at him with mild curiosity.

"Listen, I'm with St. John Baptist, that church down in Dixiana that got burned down a couple of summers ago. There's a bunch of us that's gotten together to rebuild it, but we need to get a commercial building permit some kind of way. Do you think your boss could help us out?"

"He might," said one of the men as he mopped his forehead with a handkerchief. "Mr. Tyler's a real religious man."

"Yeah," said another. "Go on over and talk to him. He'll do anything to help a church."

"Where is he?"

The men gave him the address and directions on how to get there.

Entering the company's office, Matt removed his cap.

"Excuse me, ma'am," he said to a secretary, who was typing.

She turned around. "May I help you?"

"I don't have an appointment, but I was wondering if I might speak to Mr. Tyler. My name is Lorenza Mathews, and I'm with a group that is trying to help rebuild St. John Baptist. That's the church down in Dixiana that was burned in 1995. We're in need of a commercial building permit, and I was talking to some of your employees who are building that bank over in Lexington, and they said Mr. Tyler might be able to help us."

"If you can have a seat, I'll let Mr. Tyler know that you're out here."

Matt had no sooner sat down than Walter Tyler came out to meet him.

Shaking the hand Mr. Tyler extended, Matt repeated the reason why he had come. "I know it's asking a lot, but we'd really appreciate if you could help us."

"I'll be happy to on one condition—that you follow building codes."

"We most certainly will."

Within moments, Mr. Tyler had his secretary type up and give to Matt the appropriate paperwork for the church to get not only a building permit, but also a zoning and grading permit under Tyler Construction's name.

He shook Matt's hand again and wished him good luck.

Matt stepped back out in the bright sunshine holding the precious papers. If that wasn't a miracle, he didn't know what was.

SIXTEEN

The Lord Is Standing By

After driving through the night, Al, Linda, their two children, and four of Al's crewmen rejoiced as they entered Lexington County. Their 1,031-mile trip from Texas had been a long, hot, miserable one. The two old vehicles they drove, a truck and a travel trailer, had broken down five times since they had left Sinton. They felt like they had spent most of the three-day journey stalled on the side of the road under the scorching sun.

Their racial diversity had also earned them more than a few openly hostile stares along the way. The eight of them were a microcosm of Texas—Al, Linda, their twenty-one-year-old son, John Ray, ten-year-old daughter, Mandy, and Al's foreman, Don Max-

well, were white. Roland Vega and his cousin Mike Garcia were
Hispanic, and Phillip "Casper" Hall was an African American.

Once they were within ten miles of Dixiana, Al called Ammie.

"Thank God," she said after he told her they were nearing
the church. "I was afraid that after all the problems y'all had on
the road, y'all would give up and go back."

"No way," Al replied.

"I'll meet you there. I'm going to call everybody and let them
know you're here."

With his body aching from fatigue and damp from sweat, Al
steered into the churchyard. Willie had been able to get someone to clear away the concrete footings that were now piled up
on the edge of the property. In their place was a layer of sand
leveling out the ground.

Linda looked across the land, as well. In her mind's eye, she
could see a new St. John filled with young parents dressed in
their Sunday best holding small children on their laps. She
heard a pastor preaching the word of God and saw older members fanning themselves to the rhythm of his sermon. And she
heard the music—the beautiful gospel music. It filled the
church and floated out beyond. God willing, she would help
make that dream a reality.

Ammie arrived within minutes, and she was quickly followed by
Willie, Matt, Emmala, Jerry, and dozens of people who streamed
in to welcome them. Besides Jerry, other reporters soon showed
up for interviews and photos.

The warm welcome made the Texans feel as if they were coming home. Finally, as the summer sun dipped down beyond the
trees, the crowd began to thin out. Laughter and chatter mixed
with cicada serenades that grew louder before quieting, then
rising again. By Monday, the cicadas and nearly everything else
would be drowned out by a different music—the hammering of
nails, the whir of saws, the rumbling of heavy machinery—the
rebuilding of St. John.

The Monday morning sun had barely risen before the crew began using post diggers to make holes for the pilings. Willie gave them a hand. He had taken a rare one-week vacation to help get the frame up. While the men did their work, Linda and Mandy focused on the graveyard that had become overgrown again. The high grasses on the periphery of the property almost completely hid both of them, especially since at four feet ten inches, Linda wasn't much taller than Mandy.

They didn't work long before Emmala arrived and staked out a portion of the graveyard to clear away. She chopped and whacked down underbrush until about eleven, when she stopped to get lunch together for all the volunteers. Twelve years ago, Barbara organized the meals, but she was gone, so Ammie asked Emmala to do it. She contacted a local restaurant that agreed to donate meals to feed each of the crew members and then some.

Emmala was glad to pitch in, and she had recruited some members from her church, St. David's Episcopal, to come later that afternoon. She also had contacted Warren Smith, a former high school classmate, and he agreed to help out, as well.

Ammie took a break from Betsy's bedside to come by. Not only did she want to visit with everyone, but she also came to pick up Al. They had been invited for an on-air interview at a local gospel station.

On their way out, they shouted greetings to Matt as he pulled up into the churchyard. They rode over to the station, WTGH, "The Gospel Highway," which was across the street from Brookland Cayce, Ammie's high school alma mater. She and WTGH's owner, Rev. Isaac Heyward, had been friends for years, and he used every opportunity to help out St. John. Back in 1986, he organized a gospel concert to raise funds for it, and since then, he frequently delivered guest sermons there. His short stature belied his powerful, roof-raising preaching.

Ammie threw her arms around the diminutive African-American man and introduced him to Al, who towered above them.

"God bless you, Brother Al." Reverend Heyward vigorously shook Al's hand. "You've come a mighty long way to do this, and I heard y'all had all sorts of trouble coming out here."

The memory of the trip nearly made Al wince. "Whew, it was tough, all right. Broke down five times, but we made it. We stayed strong. It's like I told Ammie, there was no way we were going to turn around. We came out here to build a church, and that's what we're going to do."

Reverend Heyward ushered them into the studio, and on-air, Ammie gave a brief summary of all that had happened to St. John, how she got involved with it thirteen years earlier, and the latest developments in the rebuilding campaign.

After the reverend introduced him to listeners, Al spoke of how watching *Not in Our Town* prompted his involvement and how he and the seven other Texans were spending their two-week vacation at St. John to aid in building it. Then he made a pronouncement, "We aim to have the frame up before the end of this week, and Sunday, we're gonna have church."

Reverend Heyward laughed at first, but then he realized Al wasn't joking. "You mean this Sunday?"

"Yessir, this very Sunday."

His confidence was infectious. After they were off the air, Ammie said to Reverend Heyward, "It would be wonderful if you can come and preach for us."

"I'll be there."

By the time she and Al made it back to the site, more volunteers had shown up. It thrilled Ammie to see Warren Smith again. They greeted each other warmly.

"Emmala called me the other night to see if I could help, but

I was planning to come down here, anyway," he explained. "I read in the paper about how the fellow who's helping y'all came all the way from Texas, so I said to myself, 'If him and his people can come all the way out here, then I can come down and see what I can do to help.' Where is he, anyway?"

Ammie pointed in Al's direction. "Right over there with his wife, Linda, and their daughter, Mandy. C'mon, I'll take you over to meet him."

She introduced him. He told Al, "I don't know what I can do, but I've come down to do what I can. I've done some construction before, including helping my brother build his house, but it's been quite a while ago."

"We're glad to have you," Al said, shaking his hand.

Ammie reveled in the sight of the construction under way. It had been so long in coming—almost three years. Sometimes she had feared it would never happen. She wished her mother were here to see it, and Barbara, too. Since moving to North Carolina, Barbara had moved again, and Ammie lost track of her. She hadn't heard from her in months and no one she knew, including Willie, seemed to have any information about her whereabouts, either. But this area was home for Barbara, and that assured Ammie her friend would turn up sooner or later.

Heavy trucks loaded with building supplies thundered onto the site, and driving one of them was Russ Hippensteel, owner of Hipp Truss. He personally drove the trusses from Simpsonville, one hundred miles to the northwest, despite that he looked to be in his seventies. Ammie, Al, and Linda embraced him and thanked him repeatedly for his generosity.

Jim Spearman and Jay Wedeking from St. David's Episcopal came to help with the pilings and prep work for the flooring Al wanted to start on the next day. Jay matched Al in height and surpassed him in solid bulk. He had experience in everything from carpentry to electrical work and was self-employed in general home repair and improvements.

One of the newer members of St. John, Tommy Lee Guess, arrived, as well, and he immediately dived into work. He had done some construction in the past also and looked massive enough to lift the front end of a pickup off the ground.

The mid-July heat made the work hot and grueling, but by the end of the day, all the pilings were poured and would be hardened by the next morning and ready for subflooring. Nearby, sheets of plywood, stacks of trusses, and planks of freshly milled lumber formed a small mountain.

Ammie, Linda, and other women helped Emmala set out dinner. They had made makeshift tables from a few sheets of plywood set on top of cinder blocks. Everyone heaped their plates with grilled hamburgers, hot dogs, pork and beans, coleslaw, potato salad, and various chips and cookies and took seats on the metal folding chairs that formed a misshapen semicircle under a big oak tree.

This was becoming Ammie's favorite part of the day. The time spent relaxing underneath the tree with old friends and new ones helped her to forget, if only for a couple of hours, the dark times she had been through.

Thankfully, she hadn't received a threatening phone call in ages, but she sporadically received disturbing letters. One of the more recent ones was a bizarre, convoluted one with each of its four pages on legal-size paper, crammed with either single-spaced typed print or cut-and-pasted pictures that venomously attacked Jews and African Americans. Whoever sent it to her referred to African Americans as *niggars* (sic):

> . . . The picture on the left depicts a dirty Niggar who had a "harem" of many white women. These white women and all of the Whites in the Jewnited [sic] snakes victims of Nazi-Red, Jew-Niggar propaganda and lies of the Jew Press, RadioTV, Movies. White political rat stooges and church "clergy" and deceived whites in press and courts are betraying Jesus. Graphic picture

of female Supreme Court "Jewstice" [sic]. These cowardly white "government" officials have sold out to the devil and will burn in hell. Iniquity abounds. Judgment is nigh . . .

Bulldog and Stick checked in on her frequently, as did some of the other deputies, and she continued to practice the safety precautions the two detectives had taught her. Perhaps the day would come that she could stop being so careful, but it hadn't arrived yet.

The guys worked on the floor all day Tuesday and once they finished, they jumped on top while someone snapped a picture of them. For Mandy, helping with the church was as much fun as it was hard work. The adults doted on her, and during the evening, she enjoyed exploring the woods with her older brother. Working alongside Emmala drew the two of them close, and before anyone knew it, Emmala became "Aunt Em."

Late that evening, the Texans sat out on the folding chairs underneath the big oak tree long after the stars peeked through the night sky, and Ammie, Matt, Willie, Emmala, and others had called it a night and left. The Texans didn't feel like turning in just yet, though they had been up since before sunrise.

They loved Al's jokes, and he had them all laughing, but as a car turned into the churchyard and neared them, their laugh ter died away. Immediately reminded of the danger they could be in, Al peered through the darkness. With relief, he recognized the vehicle was a Lexington Sheriff's Department squad car. A uniformed deputy emerged from it.

"Hey, how are y'all doing this evening?" he asked, walking over to them.

"We're doing great," Al said, and the others greeted him, as well. Sheriff Metts had told them that he would have deputies checking on them throughout their stay.

Offering him a seat, Al, Linda, and the crew pointed out the work completed so far.

Nodding approvingly, he turned back to them. "Well, I'm gonna tell you boys something. With these people messing around here up to no good, I know y'all didn't come all the way from Texas without bringing a little firepower with you."

Al shook his head. In the next moment the deputy was going to make them turn their weapons over to him—he just knew it. They had brought a small arsenal with which to protect themselves.

"Here's the deal, gentlemen," the officer went on. "Y'all shoot as many of 'em as you can out here, and I'll get the rest out on the highway!"

The Texans roared back, laughing.

"That sounds good to me," Al replied, slapping his thigh.

More volunteers streamed in. Many admitted to Al that he had shamed them into coming. "If you can come all the way from Texas, then by golly, I can get off my duff and come here when this church is only a few miles from where I live," one of them told him.

One fellow came despite harboring a bit of anxiety about the close proximity to potential danger. "What will you do if the Klan comes marching down that road?" he asked Al, pointing to the dusty road.

Al pushed back the bill of his cap. "When they get to the front gate, I'm gonna tell them to jerk them sheets off and grab a hammer 'cause we fixin' to build a church!"

The lighthearted response disguised the fact that a carload of guys had sped by late one night shouting, "Nigger-lover!" at the Texans while they sat around in front of the camper and tent. And Al and the crew were sitting around on another night when someone drove up and then suddenly backed up and sped off. After calling in to the sheriff's department, Al and the guys jumped in the truck and took off after the car. They didn't catch it, but the deputies did. Inside the car, they found a young man and woman.

The young man told the deputies he had driven to St. John to have sex with the woman, who was someone else's wife. When he saw Al and the others under the tree, he panicked and sped off, worried that someone had made out their identities.

The deputies let him off with a warning not to ever get within miles of the church.

"If I were y'all," Al told the deputies when they returned, "I would have hunted down that woman's husband and let him know what was going on."

Ammie's anticipation skyrocketed at the sight of the framed building. It was one thing to see a building sketched out in blueprints, it was another to see it standing tall under a bright July sun.

She told Betsy of the wonderful things taking place there. As her daughter smiled at her, Ammie knew she understood. She lived for the day that Betsy would walk into St. John with her. Giving Betsy a gentle kiss, Ammie said, "It won't be much longer now, darling. Everything will be all right soon. You'll see."

The crew worked like machines and continued hammering and sawing even into the night. Everyone was determined to have enough done to be able to hold services inside the framed struc ture on Sunday—the first time the people of St. John would worship at their ancestral site in almost three years.

Their hard work paid off.

Dozens of people came that sabbath day, completely amazed to see how much had been accomplished in such a short time. TV news crews buzzed around, filming and interviewing people and taking photographs as the crowd filed in and took seats on pews constructed from planks of pine laid over cinder blocks. The swelling crowd reflected the diverse army of volunteers who had came to St. John's aid over the past fifteen years—white, black, young and old, rich and poor, and everything in between. Some came in suits and dresses while others wore jeans, T-shirts, and work boots.

St. Paul AME sent its choir, and once Willie had led everyone through an opening devotional, the choir rocked the gathering with "I'm Glad to Be in the Service One More Time." Caught up in the exhilarating joy of the morning, Ammie tried to accompany them on the portable electric piano she brought from home, but all the classical training she received diminished her ability to keep up with their fast-paced, soulful tempo. She plinked at the keys until St. Paul's pianist mercifully took over.

Freed from the instrument, Ammie took a seat in the front row and rocked along with everyone else, singing and clapping. Being there nourished her soul and filled her with confident anticipation of the completed building to come. But for today, the frame was more than sufficient. It sheltered them from the hot sunlight, yet the view of the churchyard was blocked only by vertically spaced two-by-fours.

Although some of the volunteers had set up a microphone in front of the wooden podium, Reverend Heyward's voice resonated with such power that he didn't need it.

"I'm glad to be among people who have a determination not to let the devil get the upper hand. I'm happy to be among people who don't want to throw in the towel."

He punctuated his sermon about the need to persevere and depend on God with energetic movements. Grabbing the microphone from its stand and moving from one spot to the next, he said, "If the Lord doesn't come, He'll send somebody. He sent Sister Ammie Murray to head up the Save St. John Baptist Church Committee. He sent Brother and Sister Albert and Linda Hoelscher with those workers to come and rebuild this church. I said if He doesn't come, He'll send somebody. Have I got a witness?"

"Yeah!" the congregation shouted back in unison.

"He sent many others from the Christian faith and people who just love to do what's right. I tell you—the Lord is standing by! Hold on!"

At the close of services, Linda walked toward the big oak tree where a huge meal had been laid out to feed everyone. She met one of St. John's elderly members, who sat on the steps connected to a portable oxygen tank. The lady's name was Bessie Jackson.

"You know," she told Linda, "I told my daughter I wasn't going to die until I can die in my church."

The simplicity of her desire struck Linda, and she wondered if the church would be completed in time. With everything in her, Linda prayed it would be.

Only one week remained before Linda, Al, and the other Texans had to go home. They set to work with renewed energy on Monday.

As the week dwindled down, Al, Linda, and those with them attempted to find solace in knowing they were leaving St. John with the most difficult work completed and assurance by the committee that continuing community support could finish the rest. Still, they would miss seeing people they had grown so close to—not only Ammie, Emmala, Matt, and Willie, but also others who came every day, despite their own busy work and family schedules—folks like Tommy Lee, Jay, Warren, Jim, and an ironworker named Tony Aaron and his wife, Cricket.

The day they dreaded finally came Sunday, July 26. They walked into the framed shell for a simple church service, wondering when they would see it again. Most of the congregation was elderly, and many, like Bessie Jackson, were in poor health. Would they still be alive when Al and Linda made it back?

They had an answer to only one question: "If somebody burns this place down, we'll come back and build it again," Al told everyone. "And if they burn it down again, we'll be back again and again and again."

With tears sliding down her tanned cheeks, Linda said, "We're leaving, but a part of us will be here forever, a big part."

To say what words couldn't, Willie and the congregation gave each of the Texans one of the Bibles sent by Pete "The Greek."

Rough, callused hands caressed the Bibles as if they were sheathed in pure gold.

Enough tears flowed to start a river as the eight Texans said good-bye to everyone. They didn't want to leave, but they had no choice. Their lives and families were in Texas, as painful as that reality was to accept.

Hugging them all tight, Ammie told Linda, "Call as soon as you get home to let us know you got in okay."

"We will." Despite her best efforts, Linda's face had become blotchy from crying. "And keep us up to date on how things are going."

"Oh, you know we're going to do that, and we'll send pictures, too," Ammie assured her.

Climbing into the truck with Al and Mandy, Linda looked back at St. John one last time. What would become of it? Would it be safe? She knew she would worry about it until earth covered her coffin.

Two squad cars escorted them northward to the Columbia city limits. Before getting on Interstate 20, which would take them out of South Carolina, Al and Linda looked up at a highway overpass. It was lined with people waving farewell.

The tears of sadness Ammie shed while watching her friends leave mixed with tears of joy over how much they had accomplished. They had done much more than erecting the foundation and frame for the church. They had dealt a resounding blow to all the James Brenners and Roger and Robert Emersons of the world by showing them that attacks against black churches would not go unchallenged by whites and blacks, and that hate crimes would be countered with outpourings of fearless love.

The Christian Knights of the Ku Klux Klan were learning that same lesson in nearby Clarendon County. They had sown the seeds of their own disintegration and discovered that the harvesting of them was more bitter than they had ever imagined.

Ammie took pride in knowing that one of the people instrumental in bringing about that harvest was Tom Turnipseed. One of his cousins was the acclaimed civil rights attorney, Morris Dees, who had cofounded the Southern Poverty Law Center and made headlines by winning multimillion-dollar judgments against hate groups. When Clarendon Klansmen were convicted of torching Mt. Zion AME and Macedonia Baptist, he and Tom approached both churches about suing the Klan. Mt. Zion was forced to back out after elderly members reported receiving threats, but Macedonia plunged ahead. Dees led the church's legal team that included Tom, State Sen. John Land and his daughter—Ricci Land Welch—and Richard Cohen, an attorney with the SPLC.

In addition to suing the Klansmen already serving extensive prison sentences for the arson, Macedonia sued their Grand Dragon—Horace King. He was one of the first people put on the stand. As Ammie sat down to watch the trial on Court TV, he began his testimony. Ammie froze. His voice. After all these years, now she knew whose it was. She would know it anywhere. If she had heard it once, she had heard it a hundred times. Even after all the years, that high-pitched nasally voice reverberated in her nightmares. "You nigger-loving bitch . . ."

He had used it to torture her, but in Clarendon County, he had used it to foment violence. Impassioned by his fiery rhetoric, his followers unleashed a reign of terror with the intention of starting a "race war" that was supposed to ultimately result in the destruction of blacks and other minorities in America. As it turned out, the only destruction King and his followers brought about was their own.

BOOK TWO

SEVENTEEN

We're Watching You

For an area that would eventually draw national media attention in July 1998, Clarendon County appeared fairly unremarkable. The majority of it was either covered by thick forests or used as farmland. The largest town was the county seat, Manning, which had a population of about five thousand.

Even if they had heard of Clarendon, many South Carolinians in other sections of the state would be hard-pressed to say exactly where it was. Of those who did, they knew of it mainly because Lake Marion set within its borders. The exceptional quantity of largemouth bass, striped bass, catfish, crappies, and other fish in the freshwater lake made it a favorite place for anglers to enjoy the day.

It was sadly ironic that Clarendon was either overlooked altogether or known only for Lake Marion when events that took place there helped change America. During the 1940s, black children in the county had to walk nine miles one way to attend schools with no indoor plumbing, running water, or electricity. Rev. Joseph A. DeLaine, an AME minister and schoolteacher, led black parents in petitioning for publicly funded school buses so that their children could ride to school like white children. In response to their 1948 petition, R. W. Elliott, school board chairman for Clarendon District 26, replied, "We ain't got no money to buy a bus for your nigger children." The parents scraped together enough money to purchase a used school bus, but the school district refused to supply gasoline.

In 1949, Reverend DeLaine went before the state NAACP for help. With the assistance of a young Thurgood Marshall, two dozen black parents—including navy veteran Harry Briggs and his wife, Eliza—sued, challenging the basic premise of "separate but equal."

Briggs v. *Elliott* set the stage for vicious retaliation against the black plaintiffs. They were shot at, had their houses and churches firebombed, were run off roads, were fired from jobs without reason, and were evicted from homes without notice. Assailants firebombed Reverend DeLaine's church in nearby Lake City and shot at him in his house. He fired back, apparently hitting one of the men in the car. Aware that retribution waited for him from police as well as local white supremacists, he and his wife had to flee the state in the dead of night, knowing they could never return.

Nevertheless, the plaintiffs persevered with the lawsuit that eventually became part of *Brown* v. *Board of Education of Topeka*, one of the cornerstones of the Civil Rights movement.

In 1994, Clarendon once again became the stage for a landmark court decision, one that the Ku Klux Klan and other hate groups would not forget. The catalyst was when a man named Ed "Duke" Garvin arrived in the county.

It was almost impossible not to notice him. He didn't have any arms. Without prompting, he told anyone he met that he had lost his arms in a job-related electrical accident. The county sheriff, Hoyt Collins, never forgot the first time he laid eyes on him. Collins was having lunch at the Downtown Deli, a restaurant in Manning. Located across the street from the courthouse, the deli was a popular gathering spot for locals, and Collins went frequently, partly because his son worked there. While looking across a few tables, he saw the unusual man who had a woman sitting with him—Collins later learned she was Garvin's wife. She had to feed him like a baby.

Almost as if to compensate for his disability, Garvin had a very outgoing personality, striking up conversations with strangers with ease. Collins saw him around Manning quite a bit and shot the breeze with him on a few occasions about nothing in particular. He found that though Garvin was very friendly, he was vague about where he was from or what had brought him to Clarendon County.

His arrival led to many conversations at the Downtown Deli and other casual meeting places to include, "Have you met that poor fellow without any arms?" Like the sheriff, folks couldn't help feeling sorry for him.

Jesse Young, a sergeant in Collins's department, felt the same way after he met him. He talked with Garvin several times in Manning, and on one afternoon, Garvin had someone drive him out to Young's home, located out in a sparsely populated area of the county known as Bloomville. Pleasantly surprised, the African-American lawman invited the disabled man in.

Taking a seat at the kitchen table, Garvin said, "You know me and my wife really like it around here. I'm looking for a place to live, somewhere we could put a house up. Do you know of where we could buy some land?"

Thinking for a moment, Jesse said, "Well, there are a few places around here that are for sale, including one piece of land with about six acres."

"Six acres?" Garvin appeared impressed.

"Yeah, maybe a little more than that. You're only about two miles away from it. It's right behind my church, Macedonia Baptist."

Garvin bought the land and came to Jesse for more advice. "I've got a single-wide trailer, but I'd like to get someone to put an addition onto it, kind of make it into a double-wide. I don't know anyone who does that kind of work, so I figured I ought to come to you. Do you know any good carpenters, Jesse?"

"We've got a couple of guys at church who do carpentry. I'll talk with them about it and see what they can do."

"Man, I'd sure appreciate it."

Jesse got the carpenters he knew from Macedonia in contact with Garvin, and the men did the work, but Garvin didn't fully pay them. Feeling sorry for him like everyone else in Clarendon, they let the matter drop, figuring he was in a bad way financially with his only income being Social Security disability. Jesse understood. Had he had been them, he would have forgiven the debt, too.

Within about a month after Garvin's arrival, he noticed flyers appearing all over the place—on pay phones, telephone poles, stop signs, trees. His mouth dropped open when he read one for the first time. The bold lettered headline proudly announced—KKK RALLY!

KKK? He could hardly believe his own eyes. The very initials hit him like a shotgun pellets. But what he held in his hands gave witness to the fact that the hate group refused to lurk only in his childhood memories—they were determined to force their way into the present, as well—and into Clarendon County. Why Clarendon? With nearly 60 percent of its residents being African Americans, it was one of the most non-white counties in the entire state. Though racism existed in it like everywhere else, it had been decades since folks had seen any real Klan activity in the area.

The flyer listed the date and directions to where the rally would be. Jesse's shock intensified. The location of the rally was Ed Garvin's place.

For years, people living around Bloomville felt that the rural area was so quiet and safe that few bothered to lock their doors at night, and they often left car keys in ignitions. Kids played freely without fear, and folks took evening strolls alongside the two-lane blacktop. All that changed when the flyers appeared. Fear set in like cancer, especially amongst elderly African Americans who were still haunted by ghastly memories of charred bodies hanging from tree limbs shrouded with Spanish moss.

Jesse talked the situation over with Sheriff Collins and the other officers in the department.

"If the Klan wants to have a rally, they're going to have to go somewhere else," the sheriff said firmly. "I'm not putting up with that kind of thing around here. Nothing but trouble's going to come of it. I've got enough to deal with as it is."

A phone call to Robert Stewart, who was SLED's director, ruined Collins's hopes of stopping the rally. Chief Stewart told him that the Klan's First Amendment rights entitled them to hold a rally. As long as they obeyed the law, there was nothing Collins or anyone else could do about it.

Collins spoke with Dean Williams about the matter, as well. Williams was an informant whom SLED paid to glean information about what the Klan was doing. The white supremacist organization was aware of Williams's ties to SLED, but still allowed him to attend rallies and marches. However, they weren't stupid enough to let him in on anything that could get them into trouble. Through him, they were able to relay any information, or misinformation, that they wanted SLED and other law enforcement agencies to hear.

What the Klan told Williams was frequently padded with lies. Nevertheless, he often knew a great deal about what the group was up to. In Clarendon's case, he discovered that Ed Garvin was tied in with Horace King, and so far, their core recruits were members of the Haley family.

Locals called them as the "Burning Haleys" to differentiate them from another set of Haleys in the area who had the misfortune of sharing the same last name. A listing of all the arson, drug trafficking, thefts, assaults, and murders that the Burning Haleys had been either convicted of, arrested for, or suspected of was enough to melt down a computer's hard drive.

The most notorious of them were three brothers: Lester, Arthur, and Romeo. They had grown up down in Bloomville along with five sisters. They endured a punishing childhood marked by poverty, violence, and alcoholism. After their parents' marriage broke up, their father burned down the home they shared with their mother. The torching of the house seared a lesson into the children: The best way to strike back, to control people, to instill terror was through fire.

Though they were linked or suspected of being behind a variety of crimes, arson became known as their calling card. Even one of their younger sisters, Sue Nell Haley Rowell Way Hinkle, had been convicted of third-degree arson along with other charges. Whenever a suspicious fire occurred, which was frequently, folks automatically figured that one of the Burning Haleys was behind it. If not one of them, then Hubert "Herbert" Rowell, who might as well have been a Haley since he was constantly hanging out with the family and often spent nights at Arthur's, even though his marriage to Sue Nell had fallen apart.

Though Horace King was a functionally illiterate sixth-grade dropout, he was a genius when it came to picking out people like the Haleys—people on the fringes of society who felt that success and status had been unfairly denied them, people who were constantly on the lookout for scapegoats to blame for their disappointing lives, people who were easy to manipulate by playing to their anger and insecurities.

Since Sheriff Collins couldn't prevent King and Garvin from staging the rally behind Macedonia, he decided to have a massive show of police force. He had SLED agents there, highway patrolmen, game wardens from the Department of Natural Resources, and as many of his deputies as possible. He even got a helicopter to monitor from above. If the Klansmen so much as jaywalked, he planned to be on top of them like white on rice.

The large turnout of law enforcement officers nearly matched that of Klansmen and their supporters, many of whom neither Collins, Jesse Young, nor any of the other local officers had seen before. Pickups and cars lining the road bore license plates from Georgia, North Carolina, and other southeastern states, but North Carolina plates predominated. A few, however, had South Carolina plates.

The rally itself resembled a warped, surreal tent revival. Outfitted in a bright, Kermit-the-frog-green silky robe and pointed hood that was open in the front to reveal his sharp, thin face, Horace King thundered with the fervor of a hell-and-brimstone country preacher. He nasally screeched about the need for white Christians to start standing up to reclaim America from all the niggers and Jews.

He, Ed Garvin, and other speakers, including a guy from North Carolina, Charles Beasley, who claimed to be a minister, used Biblical passages out of context to justify white supremacy. Periodically, old-timey gospel songs poured out from King's speakers that he had unloaded from a battered white van. Like a commercial van boldly advertising a local plumbing service, "KKK" blazed across the side of King's vehicle in clumsily spray-painted, two-foot-tall black lettering. Off to the side of where speakers addressed the crowd was a tent where people bought baseball caps, T-shirts, pocketknives, and trinkets bearing the Klan logo.

The Haleys acted as if they were having the time of their lives. Curiously, Romeo wasn't around, but Arthur, Lester, and Herbert Rowell walked around, each with a fresh swagger to his gait as if newly elected to county council. For most of their lives, they had been treated like poor white trash, but at the rally, it appeared they finally found somewhere they could be looked up to. The sheriff saw a few more in attendance who had made frequent handcuffed appearances at the jail for one reason or another. Losers, the whole lot of them. King knew it. That's why he was there.

If spouting reprehensible nonsense was a crime, Collins and the other officers could have filled the county jail within an hour, but as it happened, all they could do was watch. At the end of the rally, King sent word to the lawmen by Dean Williams that the rally was a one-time event. Now that the Klan had had it, they were packing up and going somewhere else.

The news brought a wave of relief. Finally, things would get back to normal.

A woman called into the sheriff's department with a complaint about Ed Garvin. Jesse Young went out to talk with her about it. He discovered she was Garvin's ex-wife. She had two teenage children by him—a boy and a girl—and the three of them had a lot to say about the county's mysterious newcomer.

"He's been making our lives miserable," the woman told Young. "I've been trying to get away from him so me and the kids can have a decent life, but wherever I move, he follows me. He stalks me all over the place, even though he went and married someone else. On top of that, he's forever trying to get me in trouble with the law so he can get custody of the kids."

"And he beats us up, too," one of the kids said. "He ain't got no arms, but he'll kick at us."

The other child spoke up. "Daddy's got a machine gun. He's got bombs and automatic weapons. He keeps them all locked up in a room in his trailer."

That information caught the sergeant by surprise. Garvin's ex-wife confirmed it.

"He's got a stockpile of all kinds of weapons. You name it—

he's got it. He wants to get a race war started. That's about all he talks about. He's dangerous. That man put the *e* in *evil.*"

"Aw, Jesse, none of that's true," Garvin drawled when Young questioned him about it. "I don't have any kind of stuff like that. That's all illegal." Striking an affable pose, Garvin tried to turn the tables on his ex, accusing her of abusing their children and generally being up to no good.

In the rash of charges and countercharges that subsequently flew back and forth between the battling ex-couple, Jesse and the guys at the sheriff's department wondered if there was anything to what either said or if the allegations were merely an extension of a bitter divorce that refused to end despite a judge's decree. Both Garvins denied any wrongdoing. With only the word of an ex-wife, who possibly had an ax to grind, and kids who were on their mother's side one day, then their father's the next, there was scant justification for a judge to grant the department a search warrant for Ed Garvin's trailer.

In the meantime, new KKK flyers fluttered on anything stationary. The Klan was having another rally in Bloomville.

Sheriff Collins's shock gave way to disgust. King had told Dean Williams they were leaving. Obviously, his word wasn't worth a damn.

At first glance, Manuel Leroy Thompson didn't notice anything out of the ordinary when he arrived at his job on an early October morning. He managed Clarendon County's recycling center, located in Bloomville, where area residents dropped off things like piles of old newspaper and empty soda cans. But before he entered the maintenance shed that doubled as his office, he saw something tacked on a light pole.

He snatched the paper down and read it: "KKK. We're watching you." Below the words was a picture of a Klansman outfitted in a robe and hood and pointing at the reader.

As an African American, the words and picture made his blood run cold. He tore the flyer down, but within a few days, another one took its place. He tore that one down, too. He was leaving the center one day when he noticed Arthur Haley turning into it with a ladder in the back of his pickup. When Thompson returned a little later, Arthur was gone, but another flyer was tacked to the light pole. It had been posted so high that someone had to have used a ladder to put it there with the clear intent of placing it beyond Thompson's reach. That told him exactly who had been tacking up the flyers. He got his ladder and ripped it down.

While in Manning a short while afterward, he caught sight of Arthur and his wife, Tammy, and Herbert Rowell together. He walked over to where they were parked and asked them to quit putting the flyers up at the recycling center.

"Why, why?" Arthur demanded. "We gonna—"

"You gonna do what you got to do, Arthur, regardless, and I'll tear them down."

"Who's been tearin' 'em down?"

"Me."

"Why? You ain't got no business tearin' 'em down. You know that, don't you?"

Thompson didn't flinch. "It's against the law to put those up on county property."

"No the hell it ain't," Arthur snapped.

"I ain't got to lie to you."

"You don't know who you're messin' with," Rowell said ominously to Thompson.

Thompson came to work one day not long after the run-in. He was so bone-tired after finishing a shift at his second job that it took a few moments for what he was looking at to sink in.

His office had been burned to the ground.

The Burning Haleys. A chill flashed through him and strangely left him even more resolved. He was not going to back down. If they put up another flyer, he'd rip it down and he'd keep ripping them down.

One day, someone fired shots toward his home. He and his wife quit allowing their children to play in the yard. He kept coming to work. With the maintenance shed in ashes, he worked out of his car and kept it pointed toward the road so he could leave quickly if need be. He also positioned it opposite a large metal recycling bin that could serve as a shield. He kept his gun handy. He had to be prepared for anything. When it came to the Haleys, he knew he had to be, or else.

Sheriff Collins felt like he was sitting on a tinderbox on the verge of explosion. The Haleys were sinking into the Klan's control deeper by the day. Their torching of Thompson's workplace simply because he took down their flyers was proof of that. As bad as the Haleys had been, King and the KKK made them worse because they helped turn the Haleys into something no one had ever accused them of being before—racists.

That was what struck everyone so strangely. For all their faults, the Haleys had always gotten along well with blacks. They had grown up playing with African-American kids and counted many among their friends after becoming adults. If asked who would be most likely to join the Klan, folks would have put the Haleys at the bottom of the list.

State Senator John Land was among the many who were shocked about their sudden conversion to the ultraright. In addition to being a longtime Democratic power broker in the senate, he was a lawyer specializing in workman's comp cases. The Haleys had been frequent clients because they primarily made their living from construction, and their dangerous work conditions often resulted in injury, especially for Sue Nell and Arthur, who were welders. He had represented Haleys on a range of cases ever since the early 1970s. With the passage of

the decades, he saw them so much he developed a casual friendship with them.

Shortly before discovering their involvement in the Klan, he
happened to be driving by Sue Nell's house, which was down in
the southern end of the county near Lake Marion. She was
having a party. People spilled across her front yard chatting and
laughing with each other. What made Senator Land do a double
take was that Sue Nell had decorated the place with Confederate
flags and Republican signs.

He turned around and pulled up into the yard behind some
other cars.

"Sue!" he exclaimed, smiling at her while motioning to the
Confederate and Republican displays. "Are you a damn Republican now?"

"I certainly am," she said coldly.

Despite their years of friendship, there was a meanness in
her that he had never seen before.

He tried to take it lightheartedly. Laughing, he said, "Damn,
things sure have changed around here. You—a Republican."

He got back in his car and left.

Though they had been racially tolerant before, now the
Haleys acted like the sun rose and set on Horace King. By giving them various leadership responsibilities, he bestowed upon
them a status they had never enjoyed before. They carried on
about his speeches as if they were sermons from the Mount, and
they set out spreading his twisted gospel to others to recruit
more people into the KKK.

The sheriff learned that two more newcomers had showed
up in Bloomville and moved in with Arthur and Tammy Haley.
Originally from Virginia, the two young men—Gary Christopher
"Chris" Cox and Gary Harris—were in their early twenties. Collins couldn't help becoming aware of them: almost as soon as
they arrived, they got arrested. They stole some four-wheelers,
including one belonging to Ferrell Cothran, the county prosecutor. Harris made himself scarce after striking a deal for probation, but Cox, who also received probation, stayed on with

Arthur and Tammy and they brought him to Klan activities. Upon learning that fact, Collins grimaced. No doubt Cox had joined, too. The growth of the Clarendon Klan chapter could only spell more trouble.

However, the Christmas season of 1994 brought the sheriff's department an unexpected present. Ed Garvin left town suddenly with no apparent intention of ever returning. Judging from the tidbits of information the department received, Garvin left in disgust with the nascent chapter. He grumbled that they were more interested in running around having illicit affairs with one another and then fist-fighting about it than they were in getting a race war started. He announced he was going up to Virginia, where people were serious about starting race wars. To hell with everyone in Clarendon.

Despite Garvin's declaration of moving to Virginia, Jesse found out that the man actually moved down to Charleston, South Carolina. Whatever. At least he was Charleston County's to deal with now.

In any case, Garvin's assessment of the chapter appeared to be right on target. All sorts of lurid stories buzzed around about the sexual shenanigans amongst the Klansmen and -women. The chapter was in shambles, and its members decided to call it quits instead of letting meetings keep dissolving into slugging matches.

Then King returned. He convinced them to regroup, and Lester Haley took over the leadership, becoming the Exalted Cyclops. Shortly afterward, Manuel Leroy Thompson's car was firebombed in front of his house, and shots were fired across his yard.

The Klan was back in business in Clarendon County.

As a construction worker, Wanda Mitchum frequently worked out of state for months at a time, and when she left the county

several months earlier, she hoped the Klan would be long gone
by the time she returned. She remembered her father's fear-
some stories of how they had terrorized the small Mississippi
town where he'd grown up. They posted signs about town that
said things like, NIGGERS, DON'T LET THE SUNDOWN CATCH YOU
OUT. Although he was white, her dad had been as frightened as
his African-American friends and neighbors. His anxiety
mounted after he fell in love with and married a full-blooded
Native American. Through her Cherokee mother and Black
Foot father, Wanda's mom inherited a complexion so dark she
nearly looked black. The mixed marriage didn't sit well with
many whites in Mississippi or in Bloomville, where they eventually settled. Perhaps because of that, the majority of their friends
in Bloomville were black, including Anna Bell Carter, who was
best friends with Wanda's mom.

The thought of the Klan being in Bloomville was bad
enough, but the idea of them having rallies within a stone's
throw from Macedonia Baptist Church and some of its members
disturbed Wanda even more. Of special concern was an elderly
black woman who had attended Macedonia throughout her
ninety-three years—Effie Cantey.

She had helped Wanda raise her kids, and they all called her
Aunt Effie. She had been a rock for Wanda, as well as for nearly
everyone else in the area. It didn't matter if someone was black,
white, brown, or purple, Aunt Effie helped anybody who came
along and asked. If anyone suffered a house fire or other dis-
aster and needed clothing, a place to sleep, or food—they knew
she would find a way to help them, even though she was barely
managing herself and had to heat her home with an old woodstove.

After discovering the Klan held their rallies close enough to
Aunt Effie's home to practically be in her yard, Wanda went over
to see her. Pointing to Ed Garvin's place, Wanda asked, "Do you
know that the Klan is back there?"

"Baby, they've been back there for a while," the old woman
said patiently. "I can hear them from here in the house."

Wanda's mouth dropped open. But Aunt Effie seemed to be taking it all with a remarkable calmness.

Macedonia's pastor, Rev. Jonathan Mouzon, had a similar reaction. "They have a right to have their rallies," he said. "As long as they don't disturb us or anyone else, they've got a right to hold rallies as often as they want."

He explained that the rallies tended to be weekend events— starting on Friday nights and winding down on Sundays. At first law enforcement swarmed all over them. The sheriff even had a helicopter brought in. But Klan members appeared to feed off all the attention, going around bragging they were so big and bad that a virtual SWAT brigade had to be called in on them. Recently only a light detail of officers monitored the rallies. Apparently, Sheriff Collins's idea was to show them they couldn't rattle people's cages so easily anymore.

From what Reverend Mouzon picked up, the people coming to the rallies seemed to be bothering one another more than anyone else. They mainly got drunk and then got to slugging one another about one thing to the next. He didn't think much would come of them, and with any luck, the whole thing would fizzle out soon.

It didn't, though it had come close to doing so following Ed Garvin's abrupt departure during December. Later in the following spring, Wanda was home for a while. She and her son, Timothy, went fishing one day off a bridge near I-95.

"Momma," Tim said, "I've been hearing some stuff about the Klan that's made me wonder if they've got a bad rap they don't deserve."

At first, she couldn't believe what she had heard. This was her own son talking, a young man she had raised to treat people the same regardless of their color, someone who had been raised among African Americans just as she had. What the hell was going on? Was this some strange nightmare?

Struggling to keep control, she said, "Son, we don't need no

Klan around here, and I'd better not be catching you near them."

"But they're against wife-beating. They want to stand up for women and children. That's a good thing, ain't it?"

His question hit her directly in her Achilles' heel. She and Aaron Mitchum had been together for nearly twenty-three years, although they didn't actually marry until 1990. When he was sober, she couldn't have asked for a better man, but when he was drunk or high from cocaine or other drugs, he was something out of a bad dream. A slender blonde, Wanda had lived her life harder and tougher than most men, but despite her toughness, Aaron had beaten her up more times than she could count. On some occasions, she had fled to the woods behind their house and hidden amidst trees until he passed out.

There were always apologies—heartfelt, teary ones—that continually kept her giving their relationship another chance. She did it although she realized she should know better, if not for her own good then for her children and his, too, who she raised as her own. Sometimes the kids, especially Tim, got hurt when they jumped in trying to protect her.

But the Klan wasn't the answer to that, and she told Tim so.

She had barely left town for another construction job when he joined the Klan. Like the majority of those who joined it, Tim had tasted success in very few things. School certainly hadn't been one of them. He dropped out in the tenth grade. He suffered from epilepsy severe enough to keep him from driving safely, and he drifted from one job to the next. In addition to their supposed belief in protecting women from abusive husbands and boyfriends, the Klan attracted him by offering a safe haven for his battered self-esteem.

He quickly made friends with Chris Cox. The two men had a lot in common. They were close in age—Tim was twenty-three, and Chris, twenty-two. They both loved fishing during the summer, and they dated two young women who were close friends.

Both of them also exhibited a bravado that thinly disguised their need to win the approval of those they looked up to.

King quickly sought them out, and soon the young men savored the belief that they were part of the Grand Dragon's exclusive inner circle. Chris's fervor for the Invisible Empire was even more white-hot than Tim's. Basking in the responsibility he was given to work security at Klan meetings, he guarded the door, checked membership cards, and made sure anyone entering knew the current secret password.

Whether at the meetings or hanging out with the Haleys, Rowell, or any of the other dozen or so people involved with the KKK in Clarendon, Tim and Chris were fed a steady diet of hate. The more they heard that blacks were evil, nonhuman creatures whose sole goal in life was to take whatever God-fearing whites had gained through honest, hard work, the more they believed it. It conveniently explained why their short lives had been one disappointing series of wrong turns and dead ends after another. Before the enlightenment, they had been ignorant enough to believe that it had been their fault, their own poor choices. Now they knew The Truth.

The Great Race War would make everything right, and it could start in South Carolina. Why not? The state had been the birthplace of the War of Northern Aggression. With this war, things would end the way they should have 130 years ago. The only thing that was needed was a triggering event, something that would get blacks so riled up, they would take to the streets. That was when the fun would begin.

Tim and Chris did the prep work for one of the rallies. They spruced up the yard, built the cross that was to be burned, set up a tent, rigged up the electrical wiring, and put out tables and chairs. Despite threatening clouds, King came, and he attracted the couple dozen Clarendon Klansmen and -women, as well as an array of people from nearby states. Once again, that included a strong contingent from North Carolina.

Tammy Haley whipped out her video camera to capture King addressing all of them, and with his portable sound system cranked it up to stratospheric decibels, King preached his fiery sermon of hate:

"It's time, people, to wake and shape up and say, 'This is our county, white people. Take it back.' Anyone that don't like it—politicians, the laws, or whatever—then let him, them go to the next county. Get the hell out of this county. This is a white man's county.

"And if the niggers don't like it, put them on a rowboat. Send 'em back to Africa to swing from coconut trees and eat one another like when we brought 'em over here. That's includin' the law that's goin' around with a badge on 'em, calling them a cop. They still a bubble head, kinky-headed nigger."

Inside Macedonia Baptist, Reverend Mouzon and some of the congregation had assembled for a Saturday meeting. Among those sitting on the plain but sturdy wooden pews was Jesse Young, who had attended the church his entire life, chaired its trustee board, and sang in the choir. But as soon as King started shrieking venom into the loudspeaker, he was so loud that it was as if he were inside the church and screaming at them at the top of his lungs. They could practically hear his every word.

Jesse immediately got in touch with Sheriff Collins, who told his sergeant not to confront King, but to let him do it. Though Jesse Young could go up against anyone, he and his wife and their two daughters—aged six and one—lived only a couple of miles away, in the rural, isolated area. So just to be on the safe side, the sheriff wanted Jesse to keep a low profile.

So while Collins and a chief deputy were en route to the rally, Jesse, Reverend Mouzon, and the others inside the church couldn't help listening to King's continued ranting.

"My friends," the Grand Dragon screeched on, "I have no respect on the highway for nigger cops. If they want to be a nigger cop, send him over to Nigger-town where he belongs. No nigger should have a badge on him out arresting white people.

I'm drivin' that white van right over there. Why don't a nigger try to pull me over? I'll kick his damn taillights out if they stop me 'cause I ain't got no use for 'em."

The crowd whooped in response. King's silky green robe fluttered behind him as he paced from one side to the next like a caged panther. Chris and Tim sat mesmerized. The power and energy from the thin, robed man astounded them despite that how he spoke called notice to the fact that he was a sixth-grade dropout.

"Time to wake up, people! You're losing. But it's your fault. It's not the nigger's. Don't blame it on the nigger. Blame it on Mr. and Mrs. White for sittin' back and givin' it to 'em. I tell you one thing, the county I live in and the neighborhood I live in, they ain't no bubble-headed niggers livin' in it. And as long as I can breathe breath, where if I get in a wheelchair with a motor on it, there will not be none. If you've got niggers livin' 'side of you, it's your fault. Get him out."

Thunder rumbled ominously from a distance, and an occasional drop of rain fell from above, but Chris or Tim hardly noticed.

His robe billowing in the strengthening wind, King clutched the microphone. "Why is it the laws do not want y'all here in Clarendon County? Why does the sheriff's department not want you here in this county? Because the niggers is controlling the laws in this county, people. It's time for you to wake up and control 'em for a while. And you can do it and you shall do it."

He played the crowd like a master puppeteer.

"My friend, don't tell me that you do not control your enemy. If you do not destroy, then they will destroy you."

Tim and Chris drank in each word.

Accompanied by a deputy, the sheriff walked up to King as Klan members looked on menacingly. Though they shot poison with their stares, all of them knew better than to do anything then, especially when they could bide their time and strike when it was least expected.

"Turn that noise down," Collins told King.

"I don't appreciate you coming over and picking on me for no reason," King whined.

"I didn't come over to hear that. I've come to tell you to turn those speakers down."

He and King glared at each other.

Then King flinched. "Okay." He twisted the knob of the system from its highest setting to nearly its lowest.

After Collins and the deputy left, Collins drove over to Macedonia and filled in Jesse, Reverend Mouzon, and the others on what happened. On the surface, the problem appeared resolved, but the sheriff had a nagging feeling that it hadn't reached its end.

King and his followers drew together away from the prying eyes and ears of the law. None of them needed to see the sheriff going over Macedonia to figure out where the complaint had come from. Nearly from the chapter's inception, some members had voiced worry that the church would bring them trouble. It was too close. And in Jesse Young, they had a damned police sergeant within earshot, not to mention bunches of others who were only too eager to clue in on what they were up to.

Something had to be done, especially after King revealed more of his truths to them—nigger churches were evil, he declared. Niggers worshiped the devil in them. When they went into them, they were taught how to get free cheese, food stamps, and such from the government, and what was worse, they also learned how to plot the destruction of the entire white race.

Whites like Sheriff Collins and Senator John Land were "wiggers." That meant they were whites who visited nigger churches. Wiggers were worse than niggers because God had given them the good sense to stay away from niggers, but they mingled with them, anyway. They deserved to be shot. If any Klansman spotted a wigger going into a nigger church, he should throw a grenade or a bomb inside the place.

Niggers were the enemy. They were readying a plan to destroy the white race. The only good nigger was a dead nigger. They should be piled up and burned.

If a Klansman met one at the Wal-Mart or some such place, he wasn't to go around him, he was to barrel straight into the nigger to force him out of the way. If they caught a nigger tearing down a Klan sign, they were to take a two-by-four and thrash the hell out of him. If they caught one walking alongside the road, and no witnesses were around, they were to grab a bat, stick, or whatever and kill him.

The race war was inevitable. What niggers wanted to do was to throw little white children in concentration camps. They were plotting the destruction of the white race.

Whites had to prepare for the war.

But Horace King would protect them. They didn't have to worry about how. All they needed to know was that he would take care of them. If the law ever picked them up, they wouldn't spend a day in jail. If the law got them, he'd have them out before the damned cops could close the cell door.

Niggers were the enemy.

EIGHTEEN

Fire in the Night

KKK IS WATCHING YOU.

Those words assaulted Reverend Mouzon and Jesse Young as they looked at them emblazoned across a flyer one of the deacons had found tacked on the church's front door earlier that morning. Manuel Leroy Thompson had received such a warning before someone burned down his office, firebombed his car, and shot at his home. They knew they had to take it seriously. Jesse left to take the flyer to police headquarters.

Jonathan Mouzon drew in an even breath. He was not someone spoiling for a fight. He was no activist looking for a cause. He was simply a minister wanting to lead his small church in serving God. He had a right to do that, just as his congregation had a right to worship in peace. They weren't trying to trample on anyone's rights, and no one should trample on theirs.

The Klan's emergence showed that some area whites' acceptance of integration and the advances blacks had made since the sixties was about as deep and lasting as a dusting of snow in late spring. He had lived in Clarendon nearly all his life, and he thought back to the resentful glares he and other blacks faced at the start of integration when they ate at white-owned diners in Manning. The restaurant staff knew they couldn't deny them service, but after they finished eating, white waitresses took their empty plates and smashed them on the floor to show the restaurant's refusal to wash plates from which blacks had eaten.

Court-ordered school desegregation went no easier. He remembered how a white principal declared that before his school was integrated, blood would run down the streets of Manning. In an ironic twist of fate, the same day the principal uttered that statement, he went home and choked to death while eating a steak dinner.

And given that the county was the birthplace to one of the watershed cases leading to school integration—*Briggs* v. *Elliott*—it was a sad irony that Clarendon saw a mass exodus of white children from public schools to all-white private academies following the seminal ruling. The legacy of racism lingered as county schools approached the new millennium still essentially segregated with white children attending well-funded academies and black children going to perennially cash-starved public schools that consistently ranked among the state's lowest in scholastic achievement and performance.

Reverend Mouzon looked at the door, where the flyer had been placed. Clarendon had a long way to go.

The race war wasn't far off, KKK members agreed, and one of the triggering events would be the destruction of some nigger churches, especially that troublesome one down the road—

Macedonia Baptist. But they couldn't move too quickly or it would be too easy for the law to piece things together. No. They had to wait until the time was right.

While they lay in wait, Tim Welch and Chris Cox passed the time fishing. One of their favorite fishing spots was Wilson's Landing, near St. Stephens, a small community down in Berkeley County, southeast of Clarendon.

Their treks on back roads often paralleled the routes of rural transit authority buses. With the lack of work inland, many blacks had to travel toward the coast for work, and they stood in isolated, sporadic clusters along roadsides to board buses that carried them to low-paying service jobs miles from home. Some had to go only as far as Moncks Corner, about twenty miles to the southeast. Others had to keep riding to Goose Creek or farther down into Hanahan. Some had to go all the way into Charleston or ritzy beach resorts near the historic city, like Isle of Palm, where they cleaned hotel rooms and maintained golf courses that would cost them a day's wages to play on.

Traveling back and forth from Wilson's Landing, the two Klansmen noticed one of the blacks waiting for the bus. What drew their attention toward the middle-aged black man was that he appeared to have Down's syndrome. They saw him nearly every trip into Berkeley County, standing beside Highway 45, a two-lane blacktop stretching the width of Berkeley County, almost parallel to the Santee River slightly north. Their instructions from King resounded in their minds: *If a Klansman caught a nigger walking alongside the road, and no witnesses were around, he was to grab a bat, stick, or whatever and kill him.*

The man's mental retardation made him easy prey. The only thing they needed was to catch him alone.

Accompanied by a fellow Klansman, Arthur Haley ventured over into Greeleyville. Locals took advantage of the warm, sunny day to visit the small downtown and go by the post office, shop at the few existing stores, complete other errands, or gossip with friends over blue-plate specials at the diner. Walking down the sidewalk, the two Klansmen saw a smartly dressed young black fellow emerge from a bank and start down the sidewalk toward them.

As the distance between the men lessened, the realization grew that the sidewalk wasn't wide enough for three of them to pass by at the same time. Either the black guy had to step off onto the grass or one of the Klansmen had to, or fall back behind the other and walk by single file.

If a Klansman met a nigger at the Wal-Mart or some such place, he wasn't to go around him, he was to barrel straight into the nigger to force him out of the way.

They stopped for a moment and stared at him. The man was short, but he had the muscular, compact build of a running back.

The man stared back and then said, "Well, can I pass?"

"Sure," Haley told him. "Get on the grass."

"No, on the sidewalk." The younger man, who appeared to be in his thirties, stood his ground. "I've got all day, guys. I've got nothing to do but stand here and look at you, but I will not walk on the grass to get by."

The Klansmen glanced around—witnesses everywhere. Some women at the corner chatting and laughing. People going in and out of the bank. Two older ladies coming out of a store. A man waiting in a parked car. A mother directing her kids toward the post office. A police officer swinging his squad car into a parking space across the street.

They stepped onto the grass, muttering at him, "Nigger."

"When I find one, I'll tell him you're looking for him," he shot back.

Rev. Terrance Mackey watched the two white men skulk over to a parked pickup, climb in, and take off. If the elderly members of his congregation learned of what had happened, he knew what their reaction would be. As usual, they would shake their heads and warn him about his militant, outsider ways. They would say, "You just don't understand how things are around here."

In the four years he had been assigned to their small church—Mt. Zion African Methodist Episcopal—they had done their best to drill him on the carefully choreographed dance between the blacks and whites in Williamsburg County. The social minuet included blacks not using specific roads, not appearing certain places after sunset, and not going into the grocery store during early afternoon because that was when white housewives preferred to shop.

He had not accepted that way of life in Williamsburg County any more than he had growing up in segregated Fort Pierce, Florida. As a boy, he chafed under his parents' warnings to stay out of the section of town referred to as "white town," where a wrong look or word could be fatal. At the height of civil rights tension, a contingent of Black Panthers moved into the area. He found himself attracted to them, not only for their snazzy black berets and leather jackets and gloves, but also for their defiance, especially against white cops who came into "black town" to harass young men. He became a member when he was only thirteen, and despite the local branch of the group disintegrating from police infiltration soon after, their ideals stayed with him.

Over the following years, Terrance's adherence to Black Panthers' principles got him labeled as being everything from a troublemaker to a racist. Many in Williamsburg County didn't quite know what to make of him. He didn't quite know what to make of Williamsburg County. As in Clarendon, African Americans were the majority, yet they wielded little political or economic power. Indeed, most black families lived in shocking poverty. He commuted there several times each week from Charleston, where he worked a second job at a manufacturing plant and lived with his wife and children.

The bishop for the AME church appointed him to Mt. Zion, located near Greeleyville. The church was originally started about eighty years earlier by African Americans who worked the large surrounding plantation. The land was heavily populated by deer, rabbit, and other wildlife. Except for Mt. Zion's property, most of it had been converted into a private hunting reserve. A small, squat structure, Mt. Zion was tucked amidst it and was accessible only by a rutted dirt road.

Tim Welch and Chris Cox drove near Mt. Zion AME each time they went down to Wilson's Landing.

On June 16, 1995, after a day of fishing, the young men were traveling down Highway 45 when they saw the mentally retarded black man again. He stood alone. The bus was nowhere in sight. Chris shot a glance toward Tim. "You know, we ought to just beat him."

"Yeah, we could do that." Tim smirked.

Chris maneuvered the car onto the shoulder of the isolated stretch of road.

They got out of the car and approached the lone man, pretending to need directions. They asked him, "Do you know where Allyap Street is?"

They had made up the street name while in the car. Allyap— All you a plan. For some reason, it struck them as hilarious, and they grinned at each other about their cleverness.

Arthur Mulligan looked at them blankly. "Uh-uh."

He wished he could help them. He liked helping people. He lived with his aunt, who couldn't walk anymore. He worked at Wal-Mart in Moncks Corner. They paid him to push shopping carts. He had never heard of Allyup Street.

The two men charged at him. "You're going to die, nigger," he heard one of them say.

Cox got to him first. His first punch staggered Mulligan. The second knocked him to the ground. Then Welch took over—stomping and kicking him. When Mulligan grabbed Welch's legs, Welch yanked a switchblade out and brought it down deeply into his back several times. Dazed and bleeding heavily, he released Welch, who jumped into the sports sedan with Cox. The two men sped off, leaving their victim for dead.

Arthur Haley was asleep when Chris returned home. Chris woke him up and told him what had happened.

"Did anyone see you?" Arthur asked.

Miraculously, Arthur Mulligan was still alive when the rural transit bus came upon him. The driver took him to the county hospital, but the man's wounds were so severe that he had to be transferred down to Charleston's Medical University of South Carolina. He didn't remember much about the two white men who tried to kill him for no reason.

Tim and Chris savored all the attention and approval they received from other Klan members after the attack. The person whose approval they valued above all was Horace King. Following his instructions, they had scored the equivalent of a home run, and not a soul had seen them—except their victim, who they assumed was dead. That whetted their appetites to carry out more of his instructions—to start setting fire to black churches. They knew exactly which ones to start with.

Nigger churches were evil. Niggers worshiped the devil in them. When they went into them, they were taught how to plot the destruction of the entire white race.

The two young Klansmen were soldiers, willing and able to go to battle. When Arthur Haley openly hinted of his worry that they would chicken out and Herbert questioned their arson skills, that only steeled their determination. Committing the arsons would not only prove that they were for real, it would also catapult them into more prominence within the Christian Knights of the Ku Klux Klan. The national leader of the group was a North Carolinian named Virgil Griffin. After leaving the United Klans of America, Horace King joined the Christian Knights and established it in South Carolina in 1985. After the last rally, he told all of them to wait a few weeks before doing anything so as not to bring the law down on them.

Nearly three weeks had passed. Enough. Chris and Tim couldn't wait to see the look of pride on King's face.

In the predawn hours of June 20, 1995 they were returning from Wilson's Landing. Four days had passed since they had beaten and stabbed Arthur Mulligan. Chris slowed the car as they approached Mt. Zion AME. Turning to Tim, he said, "It's about time, don't you think?"

"Yeah, let's do it," Tim agreed.

He and Tim walked up to the cinder-block building and, taking turns, kicked the front door until it gave way. Once inside, Chris knelt down and put his Bic lighter to the carpet while Tim created a pyre of hymnals, paper, wicker collection baskets, and wooden chairs. Tim set fire to the pile. Nourished by the materials atop it, flames jumped higher on the carpet and spread out like a wave. Chris noticed some insulation hanging down from the ceiling near the pulpit. Apparently, the church had been undergoing some repair or renovation. He climbed up on a pew and held his lighter beneath the material until it smoldered and sparked to life, too.

Within only a few minutes, they had succeeded in sending fire across the floor to lick at the furniture, drapes, and walls. Above, flames stretched toward the roof.

Tim and Chris backed out of the church, but not before stealing an amplifier and—of all things—the church's fire extinguisher.

Laughing, they dumped the stolen items into the trunk and climbed into the car.

"There's going to be a bunch of sad niggers standing out here Sunday morning," Tim said.

Later that morning, Reverend Mackey got a call at his daytime job at the Bosch plant in Charleston. He took off for the hour's drive to Greeleyville. A fire? It was probably something small that would be a chore to clean up, but nothing more. Still, he needed to be there.

When he arrived and saw what had happened, it was as if he had just found one of his four children murdered. Resisting the efforts of the firefighters who encircled it, fire still raged within what had been the sanctuary. Through acrid black smoke and ashen haze, Mackey saw that nearly the entire church had been reduced to charred rubble.

Some of his congregation ringed the edge of the property out of the way of firefighters trying to bring the blaze under control. He went to them and as they held one another, tears streamed down their faces, mixing with the ash and soot drifting down from thick smoke.

"Pastor, what are we going to do now?" one of them asked.

"We're going to have to rebuild this church," he answered, and then wondered how on earth they could do that. How could he lead them in it? He didn't know how to go about building a church. He would have to learn. They would have to learn together.

In their grief, they were barely aware of the occasional car or truck that passed by, so they didn't see a silver Ford F-150 rolling past. Inside the pickup, Chris Cox pointed out his and Tim's handiwork for Arthur Haley's inspection.

"You did good," Arthur told him. "That'll get the sons of bitches."

They laughed at the sight of the weeping church members and kept on down the road.

Reverend Mackey tried to figure out what started the catastrophe. Although Mt. Zion had been founded eighty years earlier, the current structure had been built only twenty years ago and had been renovated several times, not including some work on the ceiling under way at the time of the fire. Structurally, the building had been in fairly sound shape.

He thought back to the sporadic vandalism they had had over the past few years. Mainly, folks broke in and stole things that could be easily pawned. Despite Williamsburg being very rural, crack and other drugs had swept in like a wildfire and caused all kinds of crime just like everywhere else. Had someone set the place on fire to cover up a robbery? Or had some homeless crack addict come in search of a place to sleep and accidentally started a fire?

Something else nagged at him, too—several in the church had told him that his presence at Mt. Zion wasn't going over well with some whites in the area. "Stirring up trouble" was how one of his members heard someone refer to him. And what about that run-in he had had with those two guys outside of the bank? Had someone done this to get back at him? To try to put him in his place?

One of the investigators came over to him. Reverend Mackey hoped he had answers. "What happened?" he asked.

"It looks like it was electrical."

"Electrical?"

"Yes, must have been a power surge that came through the wiring, then set the place on fire."

"But that can't be. We turn the power off at the breaker box at the end of each Sunday. Every Sunday. I was the last one to leave church last Sunday and I know I did it."

The investigator tried again. "What happened was a surge of—"

"That's not what happened," Mackey cut him off. "Something

else happened to this church, and I want to find out what it was. If I don't, it'll happen again."

With Mt. Zion out of the way from the day before, the Klansmen turned their attention to Macedonia.

"That's the one I want you to do," Arthur told Tim and Chris as they gathered in his home along with Herbert Rowell. "But if you're scared, you know, you don't really have to do it."

Bristling at his remark, both young men assured him they were up to the crime and, in fact, would do it later that night.

And though Arthur had been satisfied with their work at Mt. Zion, Rowell wasn't. He thought they could have gotten the fire started quicker by using flammable liquid instead of holding cigarette lighters to hymnals, wicker baskets, and other material.

With Tim, Chris, and Arthur trailing him, Rowell had Chris dig out an empty plastic milk container from a garbage can. He mixed up gasoline and chain-saw oil in it and gave it to Chris and Tim along with directions on how to commit arson better: Once inside the church, they were to go to the middle of it and pour the liquid on the floor near the pulpit and pews and continue pouring while walking back to the door. After returning to the door, they should set fire to the end of the trail of accelerant and throw the jug into the center of the sanctuary, where it would be among the first things to disintegrate. The melting of the plastic container would not only eliminate their fingerprints, but also help destroy evidence pointing to the cause of the fire. Upon leaving, they were to pull the door to within a few inches of being shut. That way, enough oxygen could still get in to feed the fire, but the partially closed door blocked flames from leaping back at them as they made their getaway.

He went on to tell them where to park the car so as to be out of view from passing motorists and which side door to kick in. Arthur told them that as soon as they set Macedonia on fire, they should immediately go to one of the convenience stores in order to establish an alibi should the police question them later.

Taking Chris's girlfriend's car, the two Klansmen rode to Macedonia. Tim easily remembered how to get there, even in the dead of night. He had spent so much time there as a boy. He used to climb up in a large tree near the front door and wait for the end of services for one of Aunt Effie's grandsons to emerge from the sanctuary so they could go off fishing together. While he waited in the tree, he used to love listening to the soul-stirring gospel music emanating from inside the church.

He shook those distant memories away. That all had happened before he learned The Truth from Horace King.

Nigger churches were evil. Niggers worshiped the devil in them. When they went into them, they were taught how to plot the destruction of the entire white race.

Tim remained at the door to serve as lookout while Chris poured the gas mixture around on the floor in accordance with Herbert's instructions. Darting out of the doorway, he asked Tim to light the trail. As Tim lit it, the darkened church suddenly blazed to light. It was as if he had flipped all of its lights on at once.

In her home next door to Macedonia, Lorraine Kenney watched late night TV. Her husband, David, had just returned home after working the second shift at the Georgia Pacific plant.

Lorraine sat up. "Hey, I smell smoke."

"Me, too," David said.

A quick search of the house revealed nothing, but when David looked in the direction of Macedonia, he saw flames through one of its windows.

"Call nine-one-one!" he yelled as he flew outside and climbed over the fence separating his property from Macedonia's and tried to put out the raging fire with water from his garden hose.

The church and its pastor were special to him and his wife. Although they were white, when Reverend Mouzon and his congregation learned that they wanted to marry but were struggling financially, he and the rest of the church arranged a complete wedding ceremony for them, and he officiated their exchange of vows.

Exploding from intense heat, fragments from window panes shot at David like a spray of bullets, forcing him to back away, and flames jetted up through the roof, lighting up the night's sky.

Reverend Mouzon was still awake, but only barely, when he got the call from Lorraine Kenney after she called 911. He had returned home a short time earlier after delivering a guest sermon at an area church's revival.

Similar to Reverend Mackey, Reverend Mouzon's initial thought was that the fire was probably something small. But when he was still a mile away from Macedonia, a numbness descended over him. In the distance, he could see the sky lit up as if by powerfully bright stadium lights. Then, he knew.

The ringing phone woke Jesse Young from his sleep. It was one of the dispatchers. "We've got a report of a fire at Macedonia. I know that's your church, so I wanted to let you know."

The sergeant quickly got to his feet. A fire? The first thing that came to his mind was that about a month or so earlier, they had an electrician do some repair work. Had something gone wrong? Or had one of the violent electrical storms—so common during the summer—suddenly swept through, throwing a bolt of lightning at the church?

He lived about two miles from Macedonia. Within a short distance, he looked up into the night. It was nearly as bright as sunlight. Dawn was more than four hours away.

Reverend Mouzon, Jesse Young, the Kenneys, and dozens of others who learned of the fire could only stand helplessly as the roof collapsed in a fiery crash and the walls buckled, then fell. The roar that the fire made sounded like horses' hooves hammering the scorched ground. The eerie sound was joined by cries of anguish and sobbing. It was the funeral of a loved one none of them had been prepared for. The church had been there for nearly a century. In only a few hours, it was gone.

Sheriff Collins had raced to the scene along with others from his department, SLED officers, and firefighters. Even before smoldering debris cooled enough by daybreak for arson investigators to sift through for clues, he had a hunch that the fire had not been accidental. And when it came to arson in Clarendon County—that almost always pointed to the Burning Haleys.

The county's chief arson investigator immediately noted something suspicious. The concentration of the damage showed that the fire had started in the center of the church. Had it been accidental, a more likely point of origin would have been a place like the kitchen where there were many electrical appliances, or around the heat pump or a closet containing combustible cleaning supplies. Neither the kitchen, heat pump, storage area for cleaning supplies, nor any other possible safety hazard was close to the center of the sanctuary.

Once the ashes cooled down totally, specially trained dogs confirmed the investigator and Sheriff Collins's suspicions—the dogs instantly detected accelerants.

Collins took in the blackened ruins of Macedonia. He knew what happened and had a good idea of who was behind it. Now the question was how to prove it.

He was in his office two days later, June 23, when Ray Chandler called him. Chandler was a local attorney who handled a lot of defense cases, and while the Haleys used Senator Land's firm whenever they got hurt on the job or were in car accidents, they turned to Chandler whenever they ran up against the police.

As they exchanged pleasantries, Collins leaned back in his chair. His deputies had picked up Romeo and Sue Nell earlier that month on charges of blackmarketing Xanax, a prescription narcotic used as a sedative. Romeo was already a two-time felon, having been convicted of arson and assault and battery. He was out on bail awaiting trial, but should he be convicted of this third felony, he faced serious jail time.

"Do you want to talk to Romeo?" Chandler asked. Although he didn't say what about, Sheriff Collins thought he had a good idea.

"Sure, I'll talk to him."

"We're on our way."

The sheriff placed the phone back in its cradle. Romeo wasn't quite as easy to pigeonhole as the other Haleys, despite his proclivity for crime. For one thing, he had been noticeably absent from Klan activities. While working surveillance, agents had seen him attend the first rally, but he left after only fifteen minutes.

"Hey, Romeo, leaving so soon?" one of the SLED agents called out to him as he walked back to his truck.

Gesturing in a dismissive way toward the crowd that included his two brothers and a number of other relatives, Romeo said, "Man, they too crazy for me."

From all reports, he refused to become a Klansman, and this was becoming an increasing source of family conflict.

Romeo Haley and Ray Chandler came into Collins's office.

"Sheriff," Romeo said after taking a seat, "I want to talk with you about Sue Nell. She's found the Lord, and she has turned her life around."

"That's good," Collins said, and then waited for Romeo's next move.

Sue Nell had a lengthy rap sheet of her own. Charges that had been filed against her ranged from writing bad checks to third-degree arson, but Collins doubted that Romeo had come simply out of brotherly concern. If she received any latitude on the prescription drug charges, he would eventually request the same.

"I'm asking that you ask the judge to go light on her."

"I'll see what I can do."

" 'Preciate your time, Sheriff." Romeo stood up to leave and had opened the door when Collins asked, "Did you know that Macedonia, Jesse Young's church, burnt down?"

Romeo froze for a moment, and then turned to face him. "It did?"

"Yeah, a couple of nights ago. You know anything about it?"

"Uh, hold on a minute."

Romeo summoned his attorney out into the hallway, and they whispered for a few minutes. Before stepping back into the office, Romeo glanced in the direction of Jesse Young, who was behind a nearby counter. In spite of his run-ins with police, Romeo made no secret of the fact that he thought the sergeant was a great guy. Like many others in the county, he appreciated Young's easy demeanor and willingness to help anyone, no matter who they were or what color their skin was.

Quickly looking at the lawman again, he stepped back into Collins's office with Chandler following him. The two men sat back down.

Romeo said to Collins, "Everything I tell you has to stay confidential—"

By the time Romeo finished talking, Collins found out that in addition to burning Macedonia, Chris Cox and Tim Welch had destroyed another black church in Williamsburg County and had beaten and stabbed a black man down in Berkeley County, but Romeo didn't know the man's identity.

Although Romeo did not link the two men to the Klan, his allegations suggested that the crimes were not random acts by young hotheads with too many beers under their belts, but instead were part of an orchestrated campaign of terror against African Americans. Collins placed a call to the FBI.

"Why should we get involved?" an agent asked after Collins told him of the arsons and assault.

"I think we've got a civil rights violation here."

Upon being told that two agents would be assigned to the matter, Collins got one of his detectives, Glen Barron, to start working the case up along with Gary Martin, a SLED agent who covered Clarendon.

The two investigators decided to begin with Chris Cox. He agreed to go down to the sheriff's department with them, but denied having anything to do with any church burnings or assaulting anybody.

Barron and Martin came at him from every direction with questions in an effort to undercut his claims of innocence. Unless they could get him to crack, they had nothing but the word of a recalcitrant felon to build a case on. After a barrage of more questions, Chris turned to Martin. "Can I go smoke a cigarette?"

"Sure, go ahead." Martin motioned to Barron. "Glen, walk out there with him."

Standing outside with Glen Barron in the summer's heat, Chris shook a cigarette from a pack. He pulled a deep drag from it, and as he exhaled a cloud of smoke he said, "You know I'm about to tell you something, don't you?"

———

Returning inside, he gave a statement placing all the blame on Tim. They had been coming back from a fishing trip at Wilson's Landing, he told the agents, when they stopped at a convenience store to buy soft drinks. Tim spotted a retarded-looking black fellow standing near the drink machines, and before Chris realized what was going on, Tim ruthlessly attacked the guy with a three-inch bladed knife.

He went on to say that a few days later, they were coming back from another trip to Wilson's Landing when Tim asked him to pull over into the deserted churchyard of Mt. Zion, saying he needed to "take a piss." Sitting in the car, he watched Tim kick in the door. He followed him inside at which point he saw Tim steal a black Radio Shack amplifier. He decided to steal a red fire extinguisher. Later, when they returned to Tim's trailer, Tim told them he had started a fire inside the church using some wicker collection plates.

The next day, they were coming back from another day of fishing when Tim talked him into driving to Macedonia.

"Whatever you're gonna do, hurry up," Chris recounted saying before Tim dashed across the street into the building.

Chris claimed he stayed in the car, but smelled smoke after Tim scrambled back into the passenger seat.

"Go!" Tim yelled at him.

"What the fuck did you do, Timmy?"

"All I did was torch a flag."

Not realizing his friend had betrayed him, Tim played the innocent when Barron and Martin, accompanied by two FBI agents, picked him up later that day—he didn't know what they were talking about.

The first place Wanda Mitchum went to upon returning to Clarendon from her out-of-state construction job was Tim's trailer.

She listened in shock while his roommate informed her of Tim's arrest. Jumping back into her pickup, she sped off to the jail to see him. As she drove, her shock gave way to rage at her son for letting himself get duped into joining the Klan.

But her anger at him was far surpassed by her fury at the Klan for using him to do its dirty work. And it had to be the Klan behind it all. There was no way Tim would have done something that hateful and vicious on his own, especially to Macedonia.

The more she thought about it, the more furious she grew. The idea of grabbing one of her pistols and using it on local Klan leaders crossed her mind.

At the sight of Tim in a cinder-block jail cell, Wanda nearly lost control. How could he have let himself get sucked into something like this?

Leaning over him with her palms planted on the scarred table, she yelled, "Boy! What the fuck have you been doing? Have you lost your fucking mind? I know you did it! Son, I want the truth. I don't want you to play any damn games with me. I want the fucking truth!"

Tim could barely look her in the eye, but in a quiet but firm voice, he said, "We did burn the church and we did stab that man on the side of the road."

She collapsed in the chair. "Oh, Lord have mercy."

This couldn't be happening. Yet, she knew it was.

"I think it was Romeo who turned us in."

"Who put you up to this? Arthur? Herbert? If they did or anybody else from the Klan, I swear to God—"

"Nobody had anything to do with it but us."

"I don't believe you. I told you, son, I want the damned truth."

"I'm telling it to you!"

He was holding back on her. Why? Why was he protecting them?

Her voice cracked as anguish overpowered her rage. "Son,

do you realize what you've done? Do you know how many people you've hurt? Do you realize how you've hurt the people you were raised with? You hurt Aunt Effie. You hurt your grandmomma, your granddaddy. You hurt me. Do you know the hell they're gonna have to live through? The hell I'll have to live through? You've damn well put our whole family in the spotlight for being a bunch of damn bigots."

His eyes turned shiny from tears that refused to fall. "Momma, I'm sorry. That's all I can say—I'm sorry."

"Well, I guess this is one time in your life when 'sorry' isn't good enough."

Jesse tapped on the door and stepped in. She and Tim had known him for years and thought the world of him. Figuring Tim would open up to him, she had asked Jesse to come in after giving her a few minutes with Tim first.

"Tell Jesse everything," Wanda commanded.

Sliding into a chair across from Tim, Jesse looked at him and wondered what had gotten him so offtrack. He had been a good kid. He had practically grown up at Miss Effie's and Macedonia.

"What happened, man?" he asked Tim gently.

"Jesse, you know Aunt Effie?"

"Sure."

"I used to go out playing and fishing with her grandson when he'd spend nights with her. On Sundays, I'd climb up in that big tree and wait for him to come out of church so we could go off in the woods."

Jesse folded his hands together. "Yeah, I remember."

Tim fished around in his pocket and pulled out something. He slid it across the table to Jesse. "This thing here, it's nothing but trouble. I want you to take it and get rid of it."

Jesse picked it up. It was Tim's Klan membership card.

NINETEEN

A Season for Justice

Tim gave a detailed account of how he and Chris set fire to the churches and attacked Mulligan. But he continued to deny they had acted under Klan orders. Chris changed his story, and his new statement revealed not only his guilt, but his role as the ringleader in what they had done. The more each of them talked over the course of the week, the clearer it became that Tim was a follower, participating after being prompted by Chris.

"Look," Wanda told them, "you two are going down for a whole lot of years for shit that you didn't think up. Somebody else thought it up. You need to tell the truth. Y'all gonna go down in a big way unless you drop a dime on whoever's behind this."

But neither appeared concerned.

"Aw, we're gonna be out of here before you know it," Chris said.

"What makes you think that?" she asked.

He shrugged nonchalantly.

"Things are just gonna work out okay, Momma." Tim tilted his chair back and dangled one of his legs. "You'll see."

"Y'all think the Klan's gonna cover y'all's asses? They're the ones who got you in here."

"I've already told you—" Tim said.

"You're a goddamned liar!" she snapped. "I know fucking well that Arthur and Herbert and the rest of them sons of bitches put you up to this. When you boys gonna wake up and smell the damned coffee? Y'all getting set up to take the fall. I want you to name names, not some of them—every fucking one of them!"

For all the reaction she was getting from them, she may as well have been talking to stones.

She went to Collins with her suspicions that the boys were covering for someone. Despite being often put off by Wanda's coarse language and behavior, Collins couldn't discount her suspicions. Neither Tim nor Chris was the type to do something like this on their own. The question was how to find out who was behind them. Another question was which judicial branch should take the lead. The decision to go state or federal with the case depended on finding proof that the crimes were not random acts of violence but part of a systematic campaign to violate citizens' civil rights because of their race. If they were able to do that, the federal route offered the stiffest penalties through laws and statutes ushered in during the height of the Civil Rights movement. That both men admitted to being KKK members and had membership cards on them when arrested was indicative of, but not irrefutable proof that the Klan masterminded the crimes as part of an organized campaign.

In addition to the FBI's involvement, the Bureau of Alcohol,

Tobacco and Firearms indicated they might want to take part in the investigation. ATF agent Scott Etheridge had first come to Clarendon back when Ed Garvin was around, and the ATF had received an anonymous complaint by a resident who said he heard machine gunfire at Garvin's place during Klan rallies. Etheridge's investigation hadn't turned up anything so far, but he still came to monitor the situation and stay abreast of how the case progressed against Tim and Chris in the event they had violated federal laws.

Whether or not the two defendants faced a state prosecutor or a federal one, their arrests appeared to have dealt a fatal blow to their KKK chapter. Obviously fearful of being linked to the crimes, the group disbanded immediately after the arrests, and former members appeared nervous as jackrabbits during hunting season. Arthur put on a big show of bringing in the stolen fire extinguisher when Tim and Chris were taken into custody. Supposedly wanting to assist in the investigation, he claimed innocence to any involvement. He went on to say that Chris had boasted to him and Tammy of having "beaten up a colored guy" and set a church on fire, but they thought he was joking around, as he often did.

At least publicly, former Klansmen and -women put the word out that the two men had been rogue members—loudmouthed hotheads who constantly broke Klan rules and were under consideration for expulsion prior to their arrests because of their recalcitrance. However, as late June ebbed into July, among Tim and Chris's frequent visitors was a member of the Klan, and after nearly each visit, Tim and Chris had a fresh supply of petty cash and revived spirits.

The effects of the visits proved temporary. The next few months were hard on Tim and Chris. They were beaten up several times after African-American inmates learned the reasons for their arrests. Following Wanda's complaints about it, the two young men were moved to another jail. Despite that, she noticed the confidence they used to exude about a quick release was sagging.

One afternoon she noted that Tim was more quiet than usual, but it wasn't because there had been more trouble with fellow inmates.

"You know, Momma, there's this black lady preacher who comes over here to the jail a lot to talk to anybody locked up about God and Jesus and all. She's real nice. It don't matter what color somebody is. She talks to all of us. She told me everybody can be forgiven, no matter what they have gone and done. That's what she said—everybody can be forgiven. Isn't that something?"

Folding his hands together, he turned his face toward sunlight streaming through the window.

On his way from his day job as a shift supervisor for a security company, Reverend Mouzon stopped to see how construction was progressing in the rebuilding of Macedonia. After the fire he discovered the church had been severely underinsured. They had only $85,000 of coverage: $80,000 after meeting their $5,000 deductible. Because they owed the bank $15,000 on renovations done shortly before the fire, they were left with only $65,000. The best bid they received to rebuild Macedonia was $180,000.

The congregation consisted of only about one hundred members, and most of them struggled financially. It would probably take years to pay off the loan.

He took some consolation from seeing that construction was moving along at a steady pace. With any luck, it would be finished by late May of 1996. Until then, another church—Holly Hill Baptist—was graciously allowing them to hold services in their building.

Upon arriving home, Mouzon was surprised to receive a phone call from Tom Turnipseed. The two of them had never met, but like many South Carolinians, Reverend Mouzon had seen him on TV and in the newspapers over the years expressing his strong support of various civil rights issues, some of which, like payment of reparations to descendants of slaves, were considered fairly radical.

Tom didn't take long in getting to the reason for his call. "I've got a cousin in Alabama who has been very active in fighting against the Klan. He's a real good guy. I told him about what they did to your church and the one over in Greeleyville, and he wants to see what he can do to help y'all hold the Klan accountable. Would you be interested in talking with him?"

"I most certainly would."

"Great. I'm sure he'll be in touch with you soon. His name is Morris Dees."

Morris Dees—no name on earth was more feared and reviled by members of the Klan and other white supremacist groups. Their hatred of him grew each time he won record-breaking judgments against them and each time their attempts to assassinate him failed. They had torched his office in downtown Montgomery and had fired shots into his home as he shielded his young daughter. Law enforcement officials had uncovered five assassination plots against him, one of which involved the collaboration of a North Carolina Klan faction and members of another hate group called the White Patriot Party. One of the Klansmen was in the army, and the group planned to steal rockets, plastic explosives, and M-16 rifles from an armory in Wadesboro, North Carolina, then travel to Alabama, and kill Dees.

Given the family history that he shared with Tom Turnipseed, who was his first cousin, Morris Dees was an ironic target for white supremacist organizations' abhorrence. Although Dees' parents were fairly progressive in their racial views, relative to the times—his dad once whipped him for calling a field hand a nigger—on the whole they did not question a system that denied African Americans the most basic of human rights, and initially, their son was the same way.

However, the killing of Emmett Till—a fourteen-year-old black teenager lynched by a Mississippi mob in 1955 for speaking to a white woman—forced him to begin questioning a society that fostered such a heinous crime. The murders of Addie Collins, Denise McNair, Carole Robertson, and Cynthia Wesley— the four girls attending services at the Sixteenth Street Baptist Church in Birmingham—as well as the assassination of Medgar Evers and other civil rights advocates fueled more questions.

Finally, in 1971, he decided to start the Southern Poverty Law Center with another lawyer, Joe Levin, to fight against racism and its proponents who manifested their hatred through violence.

Using his expertise in direct-mail advertising to raise funds, he spearheaded SPLC's growth into an organization that employed sixty-five people and had an annual budget of $17 million. He was able to raise millions each year because of his successful, unorthodox approach toward combating violent racist groups—to hold such groups financially liable for their conduct just as if they were businesses that knowingly injured and killed innocent people. His first victory was against the United Klans of America. He bankrupted the group, winning a $7 million judgment against it for Beulah Mae Donald of Mobile, Alabama, whose nineteen-year-old son, Michael, was lynched by UKA members in 1981. The verdict was a harsh blow to the Klan faction that once had about thirty thousand members at its height in the early 1960s. The members' beating of Freedom Riders, bombing of the Sixteenth Street Baptist Church, and murdering Viola Liuzzo helped galvanize the Civil Rights movement. When Dees faced the UKA in court in 1987, investigative officials estimated its dues-paying members, who were spread over thirty states, had fallen to only a few thousand. By the time Dees finished with it, United Klans couldn't meet in its own national headquarters in Tuscaloosa, Alabama. It was forced to give the property to Mrs. Donald.

In the following years, Dees fought hate groups in court-rooms across the country. He forced the White Patriot Party to disband, and when its leader—a former Green Beret named Glenn Miller—tried to reorganize it, Dees returned to court and had him imprisoned for violating the judge's order.

In another case, on November 13, 1988, young members of a white supremacist group called White Aryan Resistance (WAR) beat to death Mulugeta Seraw, an Ethiopian who had immi-grated to Portland, Oregon, to attend college. Police discovered the murderers had carried out the crime after being told by their leader, Tom Metzger, to go out and beat and kill blacks. Taking on Metzger and WAR, Dees got an Oregon jury to return a $12.5 million verdict against them.

And in the aftermath of a 1993 lawsuit against a KKK faction called the Invisible Empire—Knights of the Ku Klux Klan, Chief U.S. Magistrate Allen L. Chancy Jr. forced the group to give up all its assets and disband. He even stripped it of the right to its name. His court order prohibited members using "Invisible Empire—Knights of the Ku Klux Klan" in any fashion, including on T-shirts, bumper stickers, and jewelry. He also ordered that they cease publication of their magazine, *Klansman*, which had previously gone out to 11,000 subscribers. He meted out the punishment to them because of their assault on marchers who were in Forsyth County, Georgia, protesting against racism in the county. James Farrands, Imperial Wizard of the group, had to pay marchers $37,500 personally after SPLC investigators re-vealed he used Invisible Empire money to finance his farm. The previous wizard, Edward Stephens, was made to pay $26,000. The victory against this group was an especially sweet one for Dees because the Invisible Empire was purported to be the larg-est of the Klan factions and one of the oldest.

Because of death threats and recurrent assassination at-tempts, Dees lived under security tight enough to befit a head of state. With armed patrols and surveillance cameras, both his home and SPLC's office building on Dexter Avenue—on the same block as Dexter Avenue Baptist Church, once pastored by

Dr. Martin Luther King—were veritable fortresses. He traveled in a Jeep with a bevy of heavily armed guards.

His exploits against hate groups had garnered him celebrity status. National and international media covered the trials he argued, and his memoir, *A Season for Justice*, became a best-seller. *Hate on Trial: The Case against America's Most Dangerous Neo-Nazi*, a book in which he recounted the suit against Tom Metzger and WAR, was also a commercial and critical success, as was his third book, *Gathering Storm: America's Militia Threat.*

But the fact that Dees was a celebrated, acclaimed civil rights attorney was not what impressed Reverend Mouzon when Dees came down to Clarendon within days of Tom's initial phone call. What impressed him was that he could see the sincerity in Dees's eyes and hear the compassion in his voice. The lawyer wanted to help; more specifically, he wanted to help them send a clear message to the Klan and other like-minded groups that the days of their being able to getting away with hate crimes were over.

Initially, he, Tom Turnipseed, and a SPLC investigator met Reverend Mouzon at the plant where he worked security. Shortly afterward, Reverend Mouzon arranged for Dees, Tom Turnipseed, Senator John Land, and his daughter, Ricci Land Welch (who was an attorney in her dad's law office), to meet with everyone at Macedonia. In the same plainly spoken language he used whether standing in front of a judge or sitting with friends at a backyard barbecue, Dees began by telling the people of Macedonia about Beulah Mae Donald.

At the time of her son's murder, Donald was sixty-four and worked as a cleaning woman. She used to beam with pride that her son was in college and had all the makings of a bright, successful future lying ahead of him. Instead, his life was viciously ended by two young Klansmen who kidnapped him from off the street, beat him, and strangled him to death, then hung him from a tree in downtown Mobile because United Klans of America leader, Robert Shelton, had promoted violence against blacks. It was not vengeance or money that she asked Morris Dees to help her get—it was justice for her son. And that's exactly what he convinced an all-white jury to give her.

When UKA claimed destitution, SPLC investigators and researchers uncovered shell businesses that Shelton's underlings had created to disguise the UKA's ownership of their headquarters, a 7,200-square-foot, two-story building set on a 6.5-acre lot. When they had to turn it over to Mrs. Donald, she sold it and used the proceeds to buy a home—the first one she had ever owned in her life. Several years after the case, a defeated Robert Shelton was quoted as saying, "The Klan is gone. It will never return." In aiming squarely at its leadership and command post, Dees had neutralized the UKA and its ability to wage war against minorities.

He neither had asked Mrs. Donald for money nor would have accepted any from her. The same would be the case for Macedonia should it decide to sue the Christian Knights of the Ku Klux Klan. SPLC had an endowment of nearly $90 million. Income from that as well as the millions that poured in annually from private donors would cover all of his and SPLC's expenses. Tom Turnipseed and Senator Land added that their law firms would work on the case for free, too. They would assist in doing the local legwork to prepare the case for trial and generally serve as co-counsel to Dees.

Even before taking a vote amongst his deacon board and congregation, Reverend Mouzon had already made up his mind— Macedonia should file the lawsuit against the Christian Knights of the Ku Klux Klan. It was not about money. From what he could see, the Christian Knights Klansmen had none to speak of. The point was to stand up to them, to tell them that African Americans would not let their violent attacks go unchallenged.

He realized the potential trouble. Things had been fairly quiet since the church burning, but all of that could—and probably would—change if they went ahead with the suit. As pastor, he could expect the lion's share of the retributions.

One of his dad's favorite sayings entered his mind: "If you don't have something in this life that you're willing to die for, then you really don't have anything to live for." Then he thought of Macedonia. Yes. He was willing to live—and die—for it.

Reverend Mackey had a similar reaction after talking with Tom and meeting with two SPLC attorneys. It wasn't enough to only punish the two losers who actually did the Klan's dirty work; the whole organization and its leaders had to pay, too.

Before he could confer with his congregation, news of Dees's visit to Macedonia and the two other SPLC attorneys' visit to Mt. Zion spread through the area. Almost immediately afterward, Reverend Mackey detected fear on the faces of members of Mt. Zion's congregation, especially among the elderly women who were widowed and lived alone. He soon found out why—they had received threatening calls, warnings of what would happen to them and Mt. Zion if they agreed to join the lawsuit.

One of them said something that cut him to the quick. "Pastor, after services, you leave and go home to Charleston. We're here. We have to stay here and they know where we live."

Her words told him what the decision had to be.

TWENTY

A Lesson from Galatians

In December of 1996, Tim and Chris asked for Scott Etheridge. The ATF agent came immediately, and the two young men told him what everyone had suspected all along—that Klan leaders had ordered them to attack blacks and torch black churches and, more specifically, Arthur Haley and Herbert Rowell actively participated in the burning of Macedonia. Wanda's continuous exhortations and the visits of the female minister had pushed them toward revealing the truth, but what pushed them over the edge was a visit from Tammy Haley. She had come to deliver a message from Horace King—they had to be the fall guys. King couldn't keep his promise to protect them, to get them out after they had carried out his orders. They had to take whatever sentences they received. He hoped they would understand.

They did understand. They understood too clearly that King had used them to commit crimes he was too much of a coward to do himself, and now they were expendable. Neither could believe how stupid he had been.

Armed with a search warrant, ATF agents raided Arthur's home on February 28, 1996. A search of Arthur's house turned up videos Tammy had made of Klan rallies and other activities, a Klan robe, Klan statues, and thirteen guns, including a Mini-14 rifle. Like his brother, Arthur was a felon—he had been convicted of grand larceny twenty years earlier. He claimed that the weapons weren't his. He said some belonged to one of his nephews and Tammy had gotten him to buy the assault rifle for her during a Klan rally because she liked the way it looked.

That he wasn't immediately arrested on gun charges evidently did little to ease Arthur's mind. A federal grand jury was being convened in Charleston later in the spring, and he was convinced they would indict him. He was overheard telling someone that agents weren't going to take him off to jail without a fight. In making his last stand, he'd dig a moat around his house and fill it with gasoline.

However, Herbert Rowell didn't appear so rattled. Many years ago, he and Wanda had been lovers, but now she loathed him. As much as she despised him, she tried to maintain a rapport with him in hopes that he would say or do something incriminating. One day later in the spring, she saw him parked on the roadside. She pulled over to chat. When he made a comment about Tim and Chris's treatment by fellow inmates, she remarked, "I think they ought to be let out. Instead of sitting around in jail doing nothing, they ought to be made to get back here and rebuild those churches, starting with Macedonia. You know—put their asses to work building up what they tore down."

"Well, if they rebuild it, we're going to burn it down again."

His audacity temporarily stunned her. Her child was locked up for a crime Rowell had helped convince him to commit. Yet he had the gall to say that to her. He had to know she would immediately report what he said. What kind of games was he playing?

A few weeks afterward, Reverend Mackey received an unexpected letter. It was an invitation from the United States House of Representatives' Judiciary Committee chaired by Henry Hyde. The committee had a hearing scheduled on May 21 concerning church fires, and it wanted him to speak about how the crisis had impacted him and Mt. Zion.

Like most of the other ministers at the hearing, it had only been recently that he realized the enormity of the problem. He had thought what had happened to Mt. Zion and neighboring Macedonia had been isolated incidents. Knowledge that nearly thirty African-American churches had been destroyed within just the last eighteen months both saddened him and lessened his sense of isolation.

It was almost surreal to sit in front of people he had seen so many times on the news, but he refused to allow himself to get nervous. After Rev. Dr. Joseph Lowery with the Southern Christian Leadership Conference spoke, Mackey recounted the emotions he and his congregation had upon seeing flames disintegrate their place of worship and upon the capture of the two Klansmen.

He told the congressional panel, "To see the church burned was sad to me, but to learn that the church was burned by hideous acts of others crushed my heart. To know that in 1995 people still have that much hate in their hearts for others—I said to myself, 'Are we going forward or are we going backward in this country?' "

After he spoke, Rep. Sheila Jackson-Lee (D-TX) minced no words in telling him and the others at the hearing that, when it came to church burnings, she had no intention of turning the other cheek.

". . . I'm a good person, and I'm going to do the best I can, and respect everybody, but I'm not going to love my enemy. I'm not going to pray for him. I'm going to pray that my enemy is apprehended. When they burn your church, I'm going to pray that the racism in America is eliminated through some of the work that I'm going to do. So I want you to know, so that we're very clear on that.

"Reverend Mackey, I feel your pain, and I see the pain in your face, and I want you to know that I'm going to help you get that enemy. I'm going to do everything that I can. And you probably can pray a lot better than I can, and you do that, because I'm going to use all my power and my influence to put him in jail. . . ."

Reverend Mackey returned the next month to attend the conference sponsored by the National Council of Churches. Ironically, it took traveling more than five hundred miles to the nation's capital for him to first meet Ammie Murray and Pat Lowman, although Mt. Zion was only about seventy miles from St. John. Given the hectic pace of the meetings, they barely had a chance to talk but promised to stay in touch upon returning home.

Like Ammie, he quickly developed a deep admiration for Rev. Dr. Mac Charles Jones, who headed up NCC's Office for Racial Justice, and he was in awe of how adept the older minister was at talking with reporters from national news programs. He was a bit astonished when Reverend Jones asked him to participate in some of the interviews with him.

"Me? Why me? There are dozens of other ministers here."

"Your story is more compelling because they arrested the Ku Klux Klan," Jones explained.

The interviews proved to be as heady an experience as had testifying before the House Judiciary Committee. It was all very exciting, but he looked forward to returning home and overseeing the finishing touches on the church's reconstruction. The rededication ceremony was scheduled for the following weekend.

After a whirlwind of meetings, he went back to his hotel room to recover from the exhausting day. No sooner had he walked in the room than he received a call from the NCC with a message that President Clinton wanted him to come to the White House the next morning to stand beside him while he read his weekly radio address, which would focus on the fires.

His immediate reaction had been the same as when Reverend Jones asked him to participate in national interviews. Of all the people there, why did the president select him? He tried to beg off. "Look, right now, all I want to do is to go back home and be with my church. Can't somebody else do it?"

"No, he wants you there," the NCC staff person said. "He read your testimony from the House Judiciary Committee hearing, and he wants you there."

At ten the next morning, White House staff members ushered Reverend Mackey into the Oval Office. Amidst the crowd, he spotted Rev. Mac Charles Jones and Rev. Dr. Joan Brown Campbell of the NCC. Several DOJ officials accompanied Janet Reno. Robert Rubin, who headed the Treasury Department, was present, too, as well as ATF and FBI officials.

Reverend Mackey was following the instructions given to him—about where to stand and what to do when President Clinton entered the room—so intently that he didn't have time to be nervous. As news cameras whirled, he and Rev. Al Anderson, another African-American minister whose church in Tennessee had been torched, stood next to President Clinton as he read his weekly address while seated at his desk. The grin on Reverend Mackey's face broadened even more as the president came toward the conclusion of his address:

> Religious freedom is one of the founding principles of our democracy, and the black church has historically been the center of worship, self-help, and community life for millions of families in our country.

That's why it was so hard for Reverend Terrance Mackey to break the news to his daughter last June when they woke to find an ash-scarred field in the spot where only the day before stood their church home, Mt. Zion AME Church in Greeleyville, South Carolina. Reverend Mackey reassured his daughter in these words—he told her, "They didn't burn down the church. They burned down the building in which we hold church. The church is still inside all of us."

On June fifteenth, Reverend Mackey, his daughter, and his congregation will march from the site of the old church to a brand-new building. And all Americans will march with them in spirit.

We must all do our part to end this rash of violence. America is a great country because for more than two hundred years we have striven to honor the religious convictions, the freedom, the extraordinary religious diversity of our people. The only way we can succeed in the twenty-first century is if we unleash the full power of those convictions in that diversity and refuse to let anything divide or defeat us.

Following the address, those assembled moved over to the presidential seal for photos. As the president shook his hand, Reverend Mackey said, "Mr. President, we'd like to invite you to the rededication ceremony on the fifteenth."

"I'll see what I can do and let you know," Clinton said jovially before moving to the next person.

"Yeah, right," Reverend Mackey thought as he was ushered out. Still, the morning had been one of the highlights of his life, something he would tell his grandchildren about, and it left no doubt in his mind that the nation's leader was genuinely concerned about what had happened to Mt. Zion and dozens of other churches.

He joined Reverend Jones, Reverend Campbell, and other NCC staff for lunch at the NCC's Washington office. While he was eating, a call came in for him from the White House.

"The president asked me to call you," one of Clinton's office staff persons explained. "He said he's sorry, but he can't make it to the rededication on the fifteenth because he'll be out of the country, but he can make it on the twelfth."

"The twelfth! The church won't be ready by then. We don't have the carpet down yet, and we've still got some other things that need to be done."

"That's not a problem. He said he can make it on the twelfth, but he'll come only if you say it's okay."

He laughed. "How can I tell the president he can't come someplace? Sure, it's okay."

Despite blistering temperatures, thousands crowded in front of Mt. Zion and the road leading to it on the morning of June 12, 1996, to greet Clinton. Rev. Jesse Jackson, Janet Reno, Sen. Fritz Hollings, Rep. James Clyburn, Rep. Bob Inglis, and Charlie Condon, South Carolina's attorney general, came also. Before traveling to where Mt. Zion had been reconstructed, Clinton and Mackey went briefly to the church's original site. Mackey explained that he had convinced the congregation to rebuild a few miles away in a more visible location.

As they drove through the wooded land around where the church had stood for nearly one hundred years, Mackey noticed the president's expression turn wistful as he gazed out the window. "This reminds me of my home church in Arkansas when I was a kid," he said to Mackey. "To get to it, you'd come down a dirt road with trees like these."

They made it to the new church that faced a state road and, accompanied by AME bishop John Hurst Adams, Clinton and Mackey went into the new Mt. Zion to pray. They reemerged after a few minutes to the delight of the huge crowd who shielded their faces from the sun with wide-brimmed hats, paper fans, and newspaper.

"This will probably be the only time I get to say this, but I'd like to introduce to you the president of the United States," Reverend Mackey said from the podium, drawing some laughter before the crowd burst out in loud applause for Clinton.

Clearly in his element and amidst a crowd representing his most ardent supporters, Clinton thanked Reverend Mackey for the invitation and spoke of his administration's commitment to stopping church fires and helping churches rebuild. The all-out fight against church arsonists included the assignment of more than two hundred federal agents to investigate the crimes. In addition, he was lobbying for additional funds to enable HUD to provide loans to affected churches. He also praised recent House and Senate legislation that toughened federal penalties regarding church arsons and made it easier for arson cases to be prosecuted in federal court.

As he drew his speech to a close, he issued a challenge to everyone in the country. "I want to ask every citizen of America, as we stand on this hallowed ground together, to help rebuild our churches, to restore hope, to show the forces of hatred they cannot win."

Both his words and his visit cheered Reverend Mouzon, who stood in the crowd. That the leader of the free world would travel to tiny Greeleyville and visit Mt. Zion spoke volumes. Reverend Mouzon had long admired Clinton, but his visit to the church increased the president's standing in his eyes.

With all the demands of finishing Macedonia's rebuilding, he had not been able to go to the NCC meetings in Washington. However, he had accepted an invitation from the White House to attend a breakfast with the president on June 26 to discuss church arsons. Thirty-six other black ministers would be there, as well. Not only would he get to personally meet Clinton, but he would also have the opportunity to talk with others who had been through what he had.

Of course, Macedonia's case was somewhat unique. In addition to criminally prosecuting their attackers, they were suing them. The SPLC had filed the lawsuit earlier that month. The Christian Knights of the Ku Klux Klan, Horace King, and Tim and Chris constituted the defendants so far, but Arthur Haley and Herbert Rowell would be added if the feds charged them, too.

Already, crank calls had started. Reverend Mouzon tried to brush them off. He and his church had come too far to turn back now. They had to stay focused.

Reverend Mouzon flew up to D.C. on June 25, and that night had a chance to meet Dr. Joan Brown Campbell, Dr. Mac Charles Jones, the thirty-six other ministers, and several Russian Christian evangelists. The next morning, he went to the White House. Every few moments, he wondered if it were all a fantastic dream. Here he was, a working-class black man from Clarendon County, South Carolina, talking with one of the most powerful men in the world.

Clinton asked his opinion about the factors leading to the crisis.

Clearing his throat and mustering up his courage, he replied, "In my opinion, Mr. President, I believe it all comes down to a degree of poverty. The reason I'm saying that is because in Clarendon County, blacks and whites grew up together, played together and everything, but when blacks started to excel, to get good jobs and a college education and all that, that's when the Klan faction came in. Poor whites got the idea that blacks have done something to them or taken something away from them. But if everyone was on the same level, we wouldn't have this kind of thing."

Reverend Mouzon had planned to fly home that afternoon, but he accepted an invitation from a staff person with the Senate

Judiciary Committee, who asked him to stay over through the next day to testify before the committee. He was moved by Rev. Mac Charles Jones, who spoke shortly before he did:

> . . . fire can destroy, or it can galvanize and purify. The burning bush in the story of Exodus in the Hebrew scriptures was not consumed, but rather was a prelude to liberation. The site of the burning bush became holy ground, the initiation of a movement. This prompts us to recall another image of the refiner who sends precious metals through the fires to burn away the impurities and leave that which is most valuable.
>
> Is it possible that these fires can galvanize this nation and initiate a movement that will mobilize us against racism, white supremacy, and hatred in all of its forms? Is it possible that these burned sites can become our holy ground on which we build and restore community? Is it possible that these fires are moral demands that we submit ourselves to the painful process of honest and truthful engagement in communities, hamlets, towns, cities, and rural countrysides until we are purged of our intolerance and of all attitudes of superiority? Yes, we believe all of the above to be possible, and we trust that the good people of this country will respond in such a way that we will turn tragedy into triumph.

Reverend Mouzon had decided against reading from prepared remarks. Instead, he opted to speak from his heart. Facing a panel that included Senators Joe Biden, Edward Kennedy, Fred Thompson, Patrick Leahy, and the committee's chair, Orrin Hatch, he said:

> Last night when I was told that I may have to witness here, I thought of sitting down and trying to write out some type of speech, but I want to give you a sense of what it is for a pastor to lose a black church. If I could take you down a country road in the rural South, there is a wooden building that sits on about

an acre of land. The building itself is not worth much to maybe those of you here, but it means a great deal to those who own that building.

This building is where we teach our children to do the right thing. This is where we teach our children that you are worth something. This is the place where we tell our young men to work hard and be productive. This is all we have, and we work for six, seven, eight dollars an hour and over a period of years, we pay for and we own this building. This is ours, and in one night, because somebody hates us because of who we are, this is taken from us. We are left with nothing. Now, we are faced with rebuilding, and because this is all that we have, we are even forced to mortgage the land that this building is on. So not only has our building been taken, but our land is also gone.

I am going to close with—I was trying to comfort and counsel the members of my church, and I was asked two questions that have stayed with me. I was asked by one of our youth, "Pastor, does this mean that God is no longer on our side?" And then one of our older parishioners asked, "Pastor, are we allowed to own anything?"

With that said, he thanked the committee for allowing him to testify.

Upon assuring Reverend Mouzon that Macedonia and other burned churches meant a great deal to them and that the Senate was determined to help solve the problem, Orrin Hatch yielded the floor to Joe Biden. The senator from Delaware said, "Reverend, words attributed to John Locke several hundred years ago went like this—he said, 'He spoke words that wept and shed tears that spoke.' I think your testimony was as close to that as I have heard in a long time here, so my advice to you is don't write anything down. Just continue to speak from your heart."

Two months after he returned to Clarendon, ATF agents managed to uncover enough evidence through questioning numerous people to indict Arthur Haley and Herbert Rowell. They were arrested and charged with being co-conspirators to the burning of Macedonia and they were hit with other charges related to firebombing Manuel Leroy Thompson's office and car, destroying a migrant camp, gun running, and other crimes. Morris Dees added them as defendants to the lawsuit.

On November 15, 1996, Tim and Chris pleaded guilty to the federal charges of torching Mt. Zion and Macedonia and beating and stabbing Arthur Mulligan. Chris received nineteen and a half years, and Tim, eighteen.

Wanda tried to find solace in the knowledge that Arthur Haley and Herbert Rowell faced lengthy sentences, too, and Horace King stood in jeopardy of losing everything he had. But in the midst of all the destruction and broken lives, what solace she found was scant. By the time Tim got out of the federal pen, he would have spent nearly half his life behind bars. And if the knife that he plunged into Mulligan's back over and over again had lanced the black man's heart, perhaps Tim would be on death row instead of a regular prison cell.

She hoped some degree of healing came. Perhaps it had already started. The fires had jolted the country out of complacency and into stark realization that racism still existed and was as vicious as ever. As a result, millions of people, from the president on down, responded to the call to action. She watched television newscasts showing thousands of volunteers streaming in from across America to help affected congregations. Major corporations, private foundations, and religious organizations had raised millions toward reconstruction. More important, she took heart that the news programs showed people coming together—not as whites or blacks or whatever, but people wanting to work together to make things different, better. She had heard old folks say something good could come out of the worst situations. Maybe they were right, even considering what had happened in Clarendon. Time would tell.

The next year, Arthur Haley pleaded guilty, but within months, he tried to withdraw the plea, claiming he was so spaced out because of going through withdrawals from Xanax that he didn't know what he was doing. He also claimed his lawyer was in cahoots with the ATF. Throwing out the claims, a federal judge sentenced him to twenty-one and a half years.

Herbert Rowell, who also pleaded guilty, received fifteen. Romeo had already begun serving a fifteen-year sentence. He clung to hope that in exchange for his testimony, prosecutors would convince a federal judge to let him out soon.

In mid-July of 1998, Tim and Chris's sentences were reduced because of their continued cooperation with federal investigators. Tim's sentence was cut from eighteen years to twelve; and Chris's, from nineteen and a half years to fourteen.

The next week, on Monday, July 20, the eyes of the country were riveted upon the Clarendon County Courthouse in Manning. Mammoth news trucks from the three major networks, CNN, and Fox ringed the squat neoclassical building that had a concrete obelisk in front of it paying homage to the area's Confederate soldiers with the inscription, OUR HEROES, at its base. Camera crews, reporters, uniformed and undercover police, and crowds of onlookers jammed the main square. Inside, Court TV set up cameras to cover the entire trial that was anticipated to last through the end of the week.

What had been a small, sleepy downtown had turned into a media maelstrom almost overnight. Suddenly, if locals were lucky enough to find spots at the Downtown Deli that weren't taken by some out-of-town strangers, they couldn't enjoy a cup of coffee without reporters shoving microphones in their faces and asking them their opinion about the imminent trial. More than a few townsfolk grumbled that the trial was putting Clarendon County, indeed the whole state, in a negative light. But others, especially many African Americans, believed that the trial was an important new chapter in the long-running fight for civil rights and that national media should cover it.

Reverend Mouzon arrived at the courtroom early that morning, along with his family, members from Macedonia, and various supporters, including Reverend Mackey and members from Mt. Zion. Although Mt. Zion could not be a partner in the lawsuit, the congregation wanted to show its support, and Reverend Mouzon appreciated that. He entered with a sense of peace after spending many of the preceding days with Dees and other members of the legal team. They had briefed him extensively about what the strategy would be, which witnesses would be called, and what evidence would be presented. He and the congregation had complete confidence in them. However, regardless of whether they won or lost, they were taking a stand against Horace King and the people he convinced to carry out acts of racial hatred, and that alone was a victory.

As people packed into the courtroom, he watched Horace King accompany his attorney from Columbia, Gary White, into the room. Immediately, Reverend Mouzon picked up on King's strategy. The Grand Dragon shuffled and limped to the defense table as if he had been dragged off his deathbed. Upon making it to one of the chairs lining the table, he sank into it like he couldn't have taken another step. Playing the sympathy card. Hoping jurors would see him as just a sick, broken-down old man, completely incapable of rallying a cell of domestic terrorists to burn and destroy. Reverend Mouzon prayed jurors wouldn't fall for it. He folded his hands and waited for the trial to begin.

"About three years ago," Morris Dees began his opening argument to the predominately African-American jury panel seated to the side of the packed courtroom, "almost to the day, as the sun was beginning to come up about twenty miles from here on the county line of Williamsburg County, flames shot up through Mt. Zion Church, reaching nearly two hundred feet in the air. The fire trucks got there too late to do any good."

His Alabama accent gave rhythm to his words. "And after the charred timbers, the ruins of that church, cooled that afternoon, a group of members of the church gathered; sad—some crying. In fact, they probably didn't hear the gray pickup truck driving down that gravel road that led in front of that church. They didn't see the two white men in that truck lower the windows. They weren't crying. They were laughing. One slapped the other on the back and said, 'Good job.' They were members of the Christian Knights of the Ku Klux Klan, and they were carrying out Klan business, a plan to burn churches in the area.

"It started before that church was burned. In 1994, this man who's sitting over here—" He motioned to King, who glared at him from the defense table. "—he's the Grand Dragon of the Christian Knights of the Ku Klux Klan of South Carolina. He came into Clarendon County to establish a base for his organization."

King's granitelike expression didn't change as Dees described his actions.

"He preached hate. He preached hate for Americans of African descent. And he didn't call them that. He called them niggers. He told his people in meetings big and small that the only good nigger was a dead nigger; that they should all be killed, put into a pile, and burned. He said, 'If you catch a nigger walkin' along the street and nobody's watchin', you just hit him over the head and kill him if you have to.' And he said a lot more."

Dees told of how King used his persuasive skills to manipulate vulnerable whites into believing a race war was imminent and how black churches should be destroyed because blacks met in them to plot how best to get government aid and to kill whites. And over the next half hour, he described the brutal chain of events that occurred as a result of Christian Knight Klansmen carrying out their leader's orders, ending with the destruction of Mt. Zion and Macedonia.

He went on to describe how arson investigators found Macedonia's partially destroyed Bible while sifting through the rubble for clues. "They took photographs of the burned pages of that Bible. And the portion of a page burned around the edges was from Ecclesiastes: 'For everything there is a season, a season to love, a season to build up, a season to tear down.' And it goes on. I know you know it. It goes on and says, 'There shall be a time to speak.' And now we're here—a time to speak, to speak the truth."

And in closing he said, "You'll see that this is not some fire set by a couple of drunk teenagers running around trying to steal something from churches. You'll hear witnesses that come from that witness stand, a large number, who'll say that Mr. King's hand was in this all, in it all. And now it's time to do justice. Now it's time to put an end to this racial hatred."

In defense of King and the Christian Knights, Gary White denied that King or any other Klan leaders had either called for or sanctioned violence. In spite of its reputation, he claimed the Christian Knights was a law-abiding organization that did not tolerate members stepping out of bounds. He went on to launch a preemptive strike against Tim and Chris's credibility, telling the jury that the two young men bore complete responsibility for the arsons but were now trying to shift the blame in order to get lighter sentences. They also were trying to get back at King and the Christian Knights for their expulsion from the organization after they were caught breaking the law.

Admitting that his clients' views were racist and reprehensible, White stated they were still protected under the First Amendment. In any case, these were the harmless rantings of

King, a feeble old man too sick and elderly to harm anyone. White also claimed that even if King and the Klan lost, they were so dirt poor that any attempts to collect damages would be an exercise in futility. Worse yet, a victory for Macedonia would only inflame racial tension because it would make whites in fringe groups feel there were no nonviolent alternatives in dealing with their sense of alienation and vulnerability.

Dees put King on the stand the next day. Stumbling to the witness stand, King grasped the wooden railing for support. Virgil Griffin, the national Imperial Wizard for the Christian Knights, sat at the defense table, trying to look just as pathetic.

"Are you Mr. Horace King?" Dees asked.

"Yes, I am."

"Do you reside in Pelion, South Carolina?"

"Say that again?" King said, acting as if he had to strain to hear.

When Dees repeated the question, he confirmed he lived in Pelion, and Dees asked him what was the correct pronunciation of Pelion.

"I don't know. I don't have much education."

Reverend Mouzon, Jesse Young, and others with Macedonia suppressed grins. So now not only was King sick and on the verge of death, he was supposed to be ignorant, too.

In a series of detailed questions, Dees inextricably tied King and the Christian Knights together so that the fate of one was the fate of both. King admitted he ran the organization in South Carolina, intermingled its money with his own, kept a portion of the dues paid by all state members, and had used $25,000 of Klan money to construct a building on his property to hold Klan meetings.

With that groundwork set in place, Dees moved on. "When blacks give you trouble, isn't it kind of your policy or your philosophy to try to run them out or burn them out?"

"No, sir."

Dees directed his and the court's attention to a copy of a video capturing King speaking at a KKK rally in Washington, D.C.

"We're coming back!" the video showed King screeching to a small crowd of Klansmen. "We are strong believers. We are going to take Washington, D.C., away from the niggers. That time is coming, if we have to whip every damn nigger in the state of Washington."

Marching back and forth, gripping the microphone, he railed on, "The taxpayers in the South is what's feeding them bums laying, you see laying on the street. Twenty miles of nothin' but niggers."

A reporter stopped him to ask him his name.

"Horace King," he replied proudly. "Grand Dragon, state of South Carolina. If we had this garbage in South Carolina, we would burn the bastards out or run them out of town!"

Dees clicked off the VCR. "Mr. King, have you forgotten? When I took your deposition, did you forget about that?"

King had no response.

He didn't have much more to say when Dees showed the video confiscated by ATF that Tammy Haley had made of the Klan rally in Clarendon County a few weeks before Macedonia burned. As if to mock his efforts at appearing weak and in poor health, the video showed him pumping his fists and delivering his message of hate with all the fervor of a country preacher fired up to deliver the true gospel.

"Time to wake up, people! You're losing! But it's your fault, it's not the nigger's. Don't blame it on the nigger, blame it on Mr. and Mrs. White for sittin' back and givin' it to 'em. I tell you one thing, the county I live in and the neighborhood I live in, they ain't no bubble-headed niggers livin' in it. And as long as I can breathe breath, where if I get in a wheelchair with a motor on it, there will not be none. If you've got niggers livin' 'side of you, it's your fault. Get him out!"

During the rest of his testimony, King discovered his own words coming back to strike him. Video clip after video clip showed him spewing hate and exhorting his followers to violence. As if that weren't enough, he realized that he had submitted evidence against himself, including a flyer showing a Klansman holding a noose.

Armed guards escorted Tim and Chris from prison to testify. They added to the damning evidence by saying that King had told them to attack blacks and burn their churches. Both spoke of their continuing remorse for allowing King and the Klan to use them. "I feel bad what I did to my family, to those families I messed up," Chris said. "The church—I don't even know those people, none of 'em. I didn't know none of 'em."

And despite being an almost hostile witness for the plaintiffs, Arthur, brought in from a federal prison in Virginia, confirmed that King had called for violence against blacks and subsequently that became the underlying policy for the Christian Knights. Even people who testified for King and the Klan didn't help. King's bodyguard, Rufus Drury, tried to claim that Klansmen weren't racist but kept slipping up and calling African Americans "niggers" while testifying.

By Friday morning, the trial drew to a conclusion. During his closing argument, Dees called King "a yellow-bellied coward" who manipulated young people to do his dirty work and then left them to twist in the wind. King was guilty of everything Macedonia Baptist accused him of being, the civil rights attorney argued. So was Christian Knights. Now it was time for them to pay.

Jurors listened with rapt attention as he spoke to them. "In America, you have a right to speak, and it can be nasty, because in America, you have the right to hate, but you don't have the right to hurt. When you cross that line, that's when you," he motioned toward them, "come into play. That's where justice comes into play."

In appealing to jurors' sense of magnanimity, White argued that a judgment for Macedonia was not justice, but vengeance. "You can't answer prejudice with prejudice. That's not the answer. You just become the same thing that you're fighting. You can't fight hatred with hatred because you become hatred." He reiterated his argument that all the people who testified against King were lying criminals scouting for sentence reductions, and that the only thing King and the Christian Knights were guilty of was holding unpopular opinions.

Before jurors were ushered out for deliberations, Sen. John Land was allowed to make an additional closing argument. "Macedonia Baptist Church now rests in your hands," he told jurors. "It's a big responsibility. No one else now has any control over this case after the judge charges you, but you. And you have the choice and the chance to right this wrong, to balance these scales for what's right."

Everyone from the courtroom was still milling around inside the courthouse or outside on the square when word came that the jury had reached a decision. People checked their watches. The jury had deliberated for only about forty-five minutes.

"The jury rules for the plaintiff," Judge Howard King (no relation to Horace King) announced. Gasps filled the courtroom when he announced the judgment: $22 million in punitive damages against Christian Knights, $15 million in punitive damages from King, and $800,000 collectively in punitive and actual damages against Herbert Rowell, Arthur Haley, Chris Cox, and Tim Welch.

Jubilation erupted amidst Macedonia's legal team, and everyone from the church as reality began sinking in about how successful the verdict was, $12 million more than they had asked for. In fact it was the largest verdict against a hate group in U.S. history. After throwing his arms around his wife, Reverend Mouzon hugged Morris Dees, and they all celebrated with Senator Land, Tom Turnipseed, Ricci Land Welch, Richard Cohen, Jessie Young, and other trustees and deacons of Macedonia, along with other members and supporters. Some of them smiled and laughed as tears of joy ran down their faces.

A reporter fought through the celebrating crowd for interviews. "This is an overwhelming repudiation for the action of these people," Dees told her over the din of talk and laughter from their side of the courtroom. "This verdict is going to speak loud and clear around the nation. I liken this as a day of reckoning."

"This is vindication for Clarendon County," Reverend Mouzon said to her. "It shows the world that residents here are standing up against racism. We're standing up for our rights. That's what this was about all along. And this helps us have some closure."

When Reverend Mouzon saw Horace King marching angrily out of the courtroom alongside his lawyer, he reached out to shake King's hand. The Grand Dragon glowered momentarily at Mouzon's slender, dark hand with pure contempt and kept walking. The reporter caught up with him, asking if he had anything to say, "I'd rather talk when my mind is more settled," he told her stonily before shoving open the exit door and storming away.

Shortly afterward, King made a hollow effort at apologizing to Macedonia by allowing Gary White to send a letter to Dees on his behalf that stated, "The senseless destruction of God's house was wrong. I am sorry that anyone who ever had anything to do with the Christian Knights played any part in it." However, he continued to deny any responsibility for anything that had hap-

pened and refused to renounce racism. White expressed hope
that the letter would be sufficient to convince the church to
drop its claim on his client's property.

It was not. Reverend Mouzon explained that while he and
the church forgave King, their forgiveness did not free King
from the consequences of his behavior. He quoted Galatians
6:7: "Do not be deceived; God is not mocked, for you reap whatever you sow." King had no choice but to turn over the deed to
his property which consisted of his home, the 2,400-square-foot
building paid for with Klan money, and seven acres of land.
SPLC investigators announced that if the Christian Knights had
anything else of value either now or in the future, they would
secure it for Macedonia until the $22 million judgment was paid
in full.

With its leader bankrupted and exposed as a shameful coward
and with a long roster of its members behind bars, the KKK
crumbled throughout the state. If it wasn't completely dead, it
was certainly comatose, especially in Clarendon County.

Once they sold King's property, Macedonia's congregation
decided to donate the proceeds to a charity such as the United
Negro College Fund, thus transforming a legacy of hate into
something positive. The bountiful donations they received gave
them that option. As had Mt. Zion, Macedonia received large
contributions from various organizations that helped pay for the
rebuilding. Both churches received five-figure donations from
NCC and Kenneth Copeland Ministries. However, Macedonia's
largest contributor was none other than Morris Dees and SPLC,
who gave them fifty thousand dollars, as if what they had done
for Macedonia had not been generous enough. Combined with
the $65,000 insurance payment and donations from NCC, Ken-
neth Copeland Ministries, and other organizations and individuals, Macedonia was able to pay off its mortgage with money left
over for savings.

The growing congregation signaled a bright future also. At

the time of the fire, the church had about ninety members, but by July 1998, nearly fifty others had joined. Although all the new members were special, one of them held particular significance—Wanda Mitchum. Reverend Mouzon, Jessie Young, Effie Cantey, and everyone at Macedonia welcomed her with open arms.

BOOK THREE

TWENTY-ONE

Saying Good-bye

When Court TV televised the verdict in Clarendon County, Ammie cheered out loud, startling her dog, Casey Baby, who barked excitedly in her lap. Considering the insurmountable case Dees and others on his legal team presented, she never doubted Macedonia would win, but she had not expected them to win a record-breaking judgment. She wished she could have been there in the courtroom to celebrate with them. She wished she could have stared straight into Horace King's bony, craggy face the moment he learned he was going to lose what he had worked a lifetime to gain.

She didn't feel a bit sorry for him. If anything, he deserved far worse than what he got. After former Klansman Clayton Spires testified against him, Spires's attorney, Bill Nettles, said that with all of the evidence accumulated against King, he thought federal agents were negligent in not indicting him. "That guy is a one-man hate machine," he told reporters. King deserved to be thrown in prison along with all the men he duped and then turned his back on. They were the ones Ammie felt some sympathy for. Their lives were ruined, especially those two young men, Chris Cox and Tim Welch. And all for a mealy-mouthed, low-down, back-stabbing skunk.

Had James Brenner been one of King's pawns, too? According to the informant who called in the tip leading to his arrest, he had bragged about being a Klansman and had given her a KKK membership application. However, her information remained uncorroborated, and he denied ever having had anything to do with the white supremacy group. Unable to post bail, he was still in jail. The Emersons were out on bail and signaled to prosecutors that they would plead guilty and testify against Brenner. Neither their trial nor his had been scheduled yet.

In the meantime, Ammie had a daughter to help nurse back to health and a church that needed finishing. After being settled in a convalescent home, Betsy was holding her own, but when Al Hoelscher left, it seemed the momentum to rebuild St. John left with him. Not much had been done since his departure. He had served as the general contractor for the project, making sure everyone followed blueprints and building codes, delegating tasks, identifying what materials and supplies were needed, and generally supervising construction. Without him, St. John was drifting like a boat without a rudder, and no one else appeared capable of taking his place. Perhaps if Matt were in better health or if Willie didn't have to spend nearly all his time at the steel mill or if she didn't need to be with Betsy so much, one of the three of them might have been able to do it, but they couldn't. Unless they did something, the church might remain a shell of a building.

With input from the congregation, they decided to ask Al if he was willing to return. Although they certainly couldn't afford to pay him what he normally earned, they could pay him at least enough to squeak by on. That also went for any of his employees he was able to talk into coming with him.

Al was sorry that no one had been able to pick up where he left off, but at the same time, he was excited by the opportunity to come back. Considering that Mandy had to return to school soon, neither she nor Linda could make the trip, and most of the crew had to stay in Texas also in order to finish up other jobs. However, Mike Garcia and Roland Vega agreed to go. Al estimated the roofing business could spare the three of them for about a month or so. With luck, that would be enough time to get the church completed.

Thankfully, Al, Mike, and Roland's trip back to Dixiana in Al's truck was uneventful, and they arrived the second week in August. About two weeks had passed since they left in July. Ammie, Matt, Willie, and nearly a dozen others welcomed them as they pulled into the churchyard. Ammie hugged each of them fiercely as they climbed out of the pickup. "Man, am I glad to see y'all. I don't know what we would have done if y'all couldn't have come back."

Looking at St. John, they understood what she meant. What little that had been done during their absence had been done wrong. Before being told not to come back, a novice volunteer, who had a fairly abrasive personality and swore he was an experienced construction worker, insisted on doing some of the interior millwork. His work was shoddy and uneven. All of it needed to be redone. They hoped at least to be able to salvage the lumber he used.

When Ammie helped Emmala deliver dinner the next day, Al, Mike, Roland, and a crew of volunteers were working like a well-oiled machine. Some were busy shingling the roof, others were building a front porch while others were inside putting up plasterboard. Despite having had a recent hip replacement, Warren was there, climbing up and down a ladder to work on the roof. Of all the volunteers involved in the recent rebuilding, he had been among the most faithful. As far as Ammie knew, he had not missed a single day—always showing up at the crack of dawn and going on until nightfall. Al had to nag him constantly to take breaks so he wouldn't get overheated under the brutal summer sun.

"I want the people here at this church to know that all whites aren't bad," Warren explained simply. He spoke of how earlier that day a couple of the church's elderly members had someone bring them over to see how things were going and to offer thanks. "Oh, my God," one of the ladies told them as tears streamed down her face, "I can't believe y'all are doing this for us."

"That's why I'm going to keep working until we get this thing finished," Warren said.

That made Al think about Bessie Mae Jackson. She had been the lady who told Linda her only remaining wish was to be buried at St. John. When he asked about her, Matt answered that she was still alive, but her health worsened by the day. Al hoped they could finish the church before she died.

Jim Spearman and Jay Wedeking from Emmala's church came after putting in full days at their regular jobs and worked until nightfall. Jay had been contracted to do a construction project that he would complete by the end of the week. After that, he planned on joining Warren in volunteering full-time at St. John. He didn't know how many days he could take off from his business, but he would do so as long as possible. Luckily, his wife, a nursing administrator, and their two teenage daughters had grown accustomed to the time he devoted to volunteer projects. They understood he was a man who believed in putting his deep spiritual faith into relentless action. In addition to holding various leadership positions at St. David's, he served on the board of a local Christian service agency.

Despite having other volunteer commitments, from the moment he first got involved with the church, it and its people became special to him. He remembered that first day. Al, Linda, their two children, and the four other Texans had arrived only a few hours earlier. Toward the end of the afternoon, everyone joined hands and formed a circle to bless the site. Something moved him to say, "This is a circle that no one is going to break because the spirit of God is here with us. No one can break us. We are going to finish this church."

Jim's career in state government wasn't as flexible as Jay's, so he couldn't volunteer full-time, but he felt sure he could put in several hours each weeknight and work all day on Saturdays. Several other fellows from St. David's Episcopal, including Mike Jensen and Steve Hatten, said the same as did Willie and Tommy Lee Guess. A friend of theirs, an African American named A. C. Howell, was between jobs and wanted to pitch in, too.

Matt more than made up for his inability to do manual labor by working his contacts to come up with donations of expensive supplies, materials, and services. If he couldn't get people to donate things outright, he could almost always talk them into selling things or providing services at heavily discounted rates. With the exterior brickwork waiting to get started, he was working on getting a company to give them the necessary bricks.

As bad as the heat had been in July, it was even worse in August. After sunrise, temperatures climbed into the eighties, and by afternoon, they broke into triple digits. That added to the discomfort that Al, Mike, and Roland felt at being more than a thousand miles away from home in a cramped trailer that was so small, they could barely turn around without bumping into one another. When they weren't busy working, thoughts of home weighed on their minds. Constructing St. John was separating Roland from his girlfriend, Mike from his wife and their new baby, and Al from Linda and their children, not to mention his elderly parents who lived near their home. The three men called home every night, but hearing the voices of loved ones made them miss them all the more.

Everyone working at the church was bowled over when Tri-City Heat and Air donated a heating and air-conditioning system valued at over twenty thousand dollars. Not only did they donate and install it, but employees hauled over a large grill and prepared steak dinners for everybody, as well. Richtex Brick donated all the needed brick, and Pete Goldston, an African-American masonry subcontractor, did the bricklaying at a reduced rate.

Work was temporarily halted when Bessie Mae Jackson died. Though the initial hope had been for her funeral services to take place inside her beloved church, what occurred was as good. A graveside service was held for her amidst the serenity and beauty of the churchyard. Al and some of the other men rigged up a temporary bell that they rang as her casket was lowered into the ground. And just as she had wanted and in accordance with ancient West African traditions, a family member laid her favorite piece of china atop her grave.

Later the next week, Ammie made her daily pilgrimage to the site. With the brickwork and shingling complete, it looked like a real church, not simply a framed-up structure. She marveled at how much they had accomplished.

Al met her at her car. "You're not going to believe who's in there working."

"Who?"

"Horace King's son."

For a moment, she was so astonished, she could only stare at him. "You've got to be kidding."

"I'm dead serious. He's been here all day working on the ceiling. From what he's said, he feels bad about what his daddy's done, and he wants to try to do something to help make up for it. When he told me who he was, he said, 'I guess you're going to be angry with me.' I told him, 'No, I'm not. You haven't done anything to me.' Go on in and meet him for yourself."

Walking into the church, Ammie couldn't help wondering if they were being set up, but that didn't make sense. Why would King send his son to work an entire day in blistering, merciless heat without getting paid a dime only to turn around and destroy what he had done? And yet, how could Horace King, of all people, have a son who wanted to help an African-American church?

She discovered the answer to that question when she met Vernon King.

"I love my daddy, but I don't believe like him," he told her plainly. As to why he had chosen such a completely opposite path, he didn't say. However, he did allude to the heartache his father's actions were causing their family. Recently, his daughter had been in school when the subject of the Ku Klux Klan came up. Her teacher singled her out. "Why don't you talk about that? I'm sure you know all about the subject considering your grandfather is the Grand Dragon."

Burning with shame, the young girl fled the room, sobbing.

"That teacher had no right to embarrass that child like that," Ammie said. "She's got no control over who her granddaddy is or what he does."

"It really upset her," Vernon King replied, getting back to work. "And it tore me up to see her hurting like that."

She felt for him and his daughter, too, as well as the rest of their family. They all lived in the shadow of Horace King's notoriety and had to prove constantly that they were not racists.

She wondered how it must feel to be torn between sharply divided emotions—to love someone and yet be against what they stood for. "I love my daddy . . ." Was it possible for a man who harbored such racial hatred to have been a good and loving father? Apparently so. Perhaps it was true that even the most evil people had some redemptive quality in them. Even Horace King.

When the building inspector came to make his periodic visit, he gave them what at first seemed like catastrophic news. The building could not pass inspection with its current flooring. He said the floor joists weren't strong enough, and after listening to him, Al and the rest of the crew pieced together what had gone wrong. It wasn't so much one mistake as a combination of several. For starters, the lumberyard apparently had mixed some yellow pine into the load trucked over. The pine had not been pretreated to resist rot, and it was too pliable to use given the church's structural design. Another problem was that the joists were spaced too far apart. With most of their experience concentrated in roofing, not to mention their zeal to get started, the errors had escaped the notice of the Texans.

However, the problem was solved as quickly as it had emerged. The owner of a construction firm indicated his company could donate the extra materials and complete the needed repairs at no charge. From the looks of it, all that was needed was some additional bracing to fortify the existing joints. Some of the firm's men could come out before the building inspector was due to make another visit.

With the issue resolved, the men worked on, but the weeks away from home and their families were taking their toll on Roland and Mike, especially on Mike, who had barely gotten to spend time with his infant before returning to South Carolina. The two cousins decided to go back to Texas. Everyone thanked them for what they had done. Their reasons for needing to return were perfectly understandable. One of the volunteers from St. David's Episcopal had a lot of frequent-flier miles, and he donated some to Mike and Roland. After a warm send-off, the pair boarded a westward flight.

Al had to admit that the strain was wearing on him, too. He missed Linda and their family. There was his company to consider, too. He could handle only so much by phone and through delegating tasks to Linda, who already had Mandy and her disabled mother to care for. Each additional week he stayed in South Carolina meant another week he wasn't home lining up other projects to keep payroll going. He figured he could hold out another week or so before having to follow Roland and Mike.

Fortunately, the most difficult stages of the construction were accomplished. Mainly what remained was "finish work," which included putting in the cabinetry, shelving, and interior and exterior railings; installing bathroom and kitchen fixtures; and laying down linoleum and carpeting.

Despite knowing he was leaving a nearly finished project in more than capable hands, Al had a difficult time leaving. "Go," Matt told him, his command tempered with affection. "We can take it from here. You need to be back home."

"Matt's right," Ammie said. "I don't want to hear any back talk. Now when you get home, give Linda and Mandy a big hug and a kiss for us and tell everyone else that we send our love. We couldn't have done all this without y'all. And call me as soon as you get home so I'll know you made it in safely." She kissed him on the cheek.

Fighting back tears, Al jammed his fists into the pockets of his faded jeans and kicked into the parched ground. Maybe someday it would be easy saying good-bye to St. John and its people, knowing he would return.

After seeing Al off that morning, Ammie returned to Betsy. Her second stay at the rehabilitation hospital had gone even worse than the first. Shortly after she was transferred there, her condition drastically regressed, and her vital signs grew unstable. She had been put back in the hospital and began suffering seizures. They came one after another, despite the different medications her doctor prescribed. Each time Betsy had a seizure, Ammie felt as if her own heart was being wrenched from her chest. All throughout her life, she had been able to overpower problems, and yet now, when her child lay in front of her suffering so horribly, she felt helpless.

As the day dragged on, Betsy's breathing became more labored, and her vitals deteriorated precipitously. By nightfall, she hovered between life and death. Ammie, Christy, Emmala, Steve, Scott, Shannon, Betsy Dyches, and other close friends and family members did their best to support her and one another in the face of the inevitable. They were with her when it came the next day—Monday, September 14, 1998. She died encircled by those who loved her the most, including her mother, who kissed her good-bye as she drew her final breath.

TWENTY-TWO

An Expression of God

Ammie hadn't realized how unprepared she had been for Betsy's death. But it was impossible to adequately prepare for such an event, especially when each additional day Betsy survived gave strength to Ammie's hope that she would get better.

The loss of that hope left her feeling numb and hollow.

As bad as the hollow numbness felt, it was nothing compared to the grief she felt as the brutal realization set in that she would never, ever see her daughter on earth again. It came when she least expected it. She was driving down to St. John one afternoon when suddenly, it struck her from out of the blue, forcing her to pull off the road and sob uncontrollably. Her grief was unbearable, but somehow she had to figure out a way to go on with her life. Somehow.

Given the shape her sister was in, Emmala wanted to take as much pressure off Ammie as possible, including arranging for someone to take Al's place to oversee completion of the finish work. Once Emmala conferred with Willie and Matt, she asked Jay if he was willing to do the job. She added that, unfortunately, the Save St. John Baptist Church Committee couldn't afford to pay him any more than they had Al.

But had they not been able to pay him anything, Jay still would have accepted. He was as committed to seeing the project through in part because of the deep friendships he had formed with Al, Linda, Matt, Willie, Warren, and all the other dozens of volunteers who had worked themselves raw for the church. And he wanted to do it for Ammie. She had been through so much. After they had said good-bye to Al, he and Warren accompanied her back to the hospital and spent most of the day with her, Emmala, and the rest of their family and close friends in what turned into a death vigil. Jay had helped take care of his only sibling, his younger brother, who lost his battle with mouth and throat cancer at the age of forty-one. That gave Jay an inkling of the anguish Ammie was feeling. There was no way he could turn his back on her now.

Construction at the church had reached the point that it was time to put down the carpet, but Jay wanted to get the floor joists repaired first. He didn't want to chance having carpet put down only to discover that all the repairs couldn't be done from underneath the floorboard. So before he asked Ammie to order the carpet, he made some calls to find out when workers planned to install the joist reinforcements. He felt his mouth go dry when he heard the answer—there weren't going to be any workers. The man who thought he could have the repairs done wasn't going to be able to do it after all. St. John was on its own. Sorry.

Jay asked the architect to come out the next morning and meet with him and Warren to figure out what to do. He didn't sleep the entire night for worrying. He had been working on another job when the flooring was done, so he had no clue what lay underneath the plywood covering. How bad was the problem? What had to be done to correct it? Could they do it?

This complication couldn't have come at a worse time. They had practically finished—or so they thought. Many of the final touches had been completed—the trim work, the molding, the painting. Ammie, Willie, Matt, and the congregation had already started planning the dedication ceremony, scheduled for November 8.

The hours inched by until nascent sunlight tinted his bedroom window. He headed over to the church and met Warren, who looked as bleary-eyed as he did.

"Man, did you get any sleep at all?" Jay asked him.

"Not a wink. I kept wondering what we're going to do. How in the world are we going to get this fixed? I mean, if we can't, we're just stuck."

"That's about the size of it."

While they waited for the architect, they opened up a big enough section of the floor to drop down into the crawl space and inspect the structural underpinning. The architect arrived not long after they got the space open.

As the three of them examined the joists, Jay's heart sank further and further. The more they looked, the more it became evident that the only feasible way to fix the problem was to pull up the entire plywood covering, remove all the joists within the sanctuary and foyer, and put new ones in.

It was worse than anything he had imagined. He didn't know if they could do it, but they had no choice but to try. The building wasn't structurally sound enough to be safely used. It couldn't pass inspection. It would sit empty and useless after people had made incredible sacrifices for it. As if that weren't nightmarish enough, the building permit was good for only another few weeks. Even if they managed to figure out a way to do it, they might not finish in time.

Another worry was the cost. They were on a shoestring budget as it was. Jay usually spent most of his salary getting supplies, buying meals for volunteers, and providing gas money for those who came from far away. Warren spent a lot of his own money on supplies, too, refusing reimbursement. They might not be able to afford all the extra lumber, especially if they couldn't salvage the expensive sheets of plywood that had to come up. It seemed as if they had been thrown into a maze with failure waiting at the end of each turn.

For Ammie, the news was like salt on an open wound. Were even the heavens conspiring against St. John? At times it felt like they couldn't win for losing. And now that they were so close to finishing, they had run smack into a brick wall. It seemed impossible to take out an entire floor without tearing up the building.

She went down to the church to meet with Matt, Willie, Jay, Warren, and the rest of the crew. Jay explained the plan as they followed him into the sanctuary. "We'll start over here." Jay motioned to one side of the large room. "First we'll take up the plywood, marking each sheet so we know how to place it back when we finish. We're going to try and save every sheet possible to save money. Then we'll take the old joists out from above and put the new ones in spacing them only twelve inches apart instead of twenty-four like they are now. When we finish the joists, we'll put the plywood back on. Once we finish that side, we do the other and get the sanctuary finished. Now in the foyer, we're not going to be able to remove the joists from above because there's not enough room to maneuver. We'll have to use hydraulic jacks to lift the floor a fraction of an inch up, so we can slip the joists out from below and then insert new ones."

"Good God, that is an awful lot of work," Ammie sighed, looking down into gaping hole where Jay, Warren, and the architect had stood. She could make out the sandy ground about two feet below. The work would be hard enough from above, but it would be brutal from within that cramped crawl space. Anyone working down there would have to do it flat on their back because there wasn't enough room to sit up.

"Yep," Warren responded. "But we've got no choice. We've got to at least give it our best shot."

Before she drove away, Ammie looked back at St. John. It looked beautiful. Its red brick walls, white vinyl trim, gleaming windows, and sturdy porch all indicated a completely sound structure. It was hard to imagine it had such a catastrophic flaw. Dispirited, she took out the letter from Pete "The Greek" Critsimilios, although she knew it by heart. She had kept it in her purse ever since she received it. ". . . Take heart, Mrs. Murray. We stand with you." It was just like the old stump. Although it didn't make her problems go away, it did help her to put them into perspective so that they weren't as overwhelming.

It might very well be impossible for the guys to redo the floor. But on the other hand, St. John was a place where the impossible came true.

The men started painstakingly dismantling the floor. Ammie couldn't get over the sight of the sanctuary. On one side, it looked nearly complete; on the other side, the floor was gone, as if someone had come in with a giant saw and cut it out. There was nothing but sandy ground and concrete pilings.

Successfully installing the first new joist boosted everyone's spirits. It was exhausting and exacting, but possible. The crew literally worked from sunup to sundown, and within a week, the new floor was finished in the sanctuary, and they turned to the smaller floor in the foyer.

No one looked forward to tackling it. Even with flashlights and lights at the end of drop cords, the space between the ground and flooring was claustrophobic, not to mention dank and dusty. Lying on their backs, they had to move around in the dirt to pull out the old joists and put in new ones. They spent hours down there at a stretch, and when they emerged, they were covered from head to toe in dirt.

One afternoon, Warren climbed out to get a little fresh air. Glancing down, he noticed his arms and torso had turned totally black. It took him an instant to comprehend that the blackness was thousands of ants. He had obviously positioned himself onto a colony of them while working. In the next instant, they attacked, and it felt like his whole body exploded. Jerking off his shirt, he used it to flail away at them.

Noticing his frantic movements, the others ran over to help. Once the last ant had been beaten off, they tried to talk him into going to the hospital.

"Man, you could go into toxic shock or something from all these bites," Jim Spearman said. "You need to go and get checked out."

Warren shook his head, although he was already feeling nauseated and had started seeing stars. "Naw, I'll be all right. I just need to rest awhile here under the tree." He sat down only long enough for his stomach to stop flip-flopping and his vision to return to normal; then he got up and went back to work.

They finished all the repairs within two weeks. Ammie was amazed. Another miracle.

In order to spare the men from having to go back underneath the church and spending days installing the needed insulation, she arranged for a group of volunteers to come over from City Year, an AmeriCorps-funded program that matched college-age people with community service projects. Many in the City Year group were young women, and though they were wary of snakes and rats, they got down underneath the building. They had to pass batting from one to another to get it in place, and despite using protective covering, the fiberglass made their skin itch like mad. Warren went down there to help and at the end of the day, he felt almost as awful as he had when he had been bitten by ants. However, they finished all the insulation in one day.

That left getting the carpet down as the last major task. Ammie got a carpet wholesaler to donate the carpet, and she found a man in West Columbia, David Hunter, to install it for free. Jay had never seen someone put down carpet so fast and effectively. But what was more astonishing about David Hunter was something he did two years earlier that ended up capturing national media attention.

His actions were triggered by a notorious occurence in the town of Laurens, a small town about eighty miles northwest of Dixiana. Laurens was the base for the Keystone Klan of the Ku Klux Klan, the other active Klan faction in the state. Two Keystone Klansmen, Mike Burden and John Howard, took the town's former theater and turned it into a Klan museum and gift shop. Naming it the Redneck Shop, they sold various Klan trinkets such as pens, T-shirts, key chains, and belt buckles. In the back of the building, they had a Klan robe and hood. For ten dollars, patrons could put on the outfit and get photographed.

The opening of the Redneck Shop created a storm of controversy, and within months, CNN and other national news media did stories about it. A local African-American minister, Rev. David Kennedy, organized marches and demonstrations against the shop, and hundreds of townsfolk, white and black, participated. Rev. Jesse Jackson attended one of the rallies and called for the Justice Department to investigate the store's owners for civil rights violations.

Driven by fury at the existence of such an outrageously racist business, David Hunter, who was white, decided to take a more direct stand against it. He traveled up to Laurens and rammed his van right into the place. Crushing and shattering nearly everything inside, he rammed the van into it several more times before jumping out with a stick, climbing on top of his van, and attacking the shop's marquee. His destruction of the building and his subsequent arrest for it garnered as much media interest as the shop's opening.

He considered what he did to be an act of civil disobedience and spoke about it with pride as he laid down the carpet. "I did it because the Redneck Shop was wrong," he told Jay. "I couldn't deal with it. I knew I had to do something about it, and that was what I decided to do."

Not long afterward, the fate of the Redneck Shop took an ironic twist. Because of surprising compassion from Rev. David Kennedy and the love of a woman who opposed the Klan, Mike Burden ended up renouncing the KKK and deeding the Redneck Shop over to Kennedy's church.

To Ammie, what happened with the shop was more evidence of the power of courageous love and spiritual faith. Though its victories did not always come quickly, they did come, and in the end, that was what mattered most.

And so it was with St. John. Now valued at $235,000, it had 4,250 square feet—six and a half times larger than before. The majority of the labor had been volunteered, and most of the materials and supplies donated. It was paid for, free and clear, with savings left over to pay insurance premiums. The congregation was growing, too. For the first time in years, young children accounted for some of its members. Their presence helped to ensure St. John would live on.

On Sunday, November 8, 1998, the dedication ceremony felt like a reunion of a large multiracial, multigenerational family. Ammie was thrilled to see Rick Meyer again. He had flown in to do a follow-up story for the *Los Angeles Times*. Rita Reif came down from New York. She was an arts reporter for the *New York Times*. After reading Bob Herbert's op-ed column in the *Times*, she had contacted Ammie. She and a number of others, including renowned authors Tom Cahill and Sister Helen Prejean, had formed a group to promote social justice, and one of the causes they wanted to make a donation to that year was St. John. In the course of doing that, Rita and Ammie developed a close friendship, phoning each other often.

Al, Linda, and Mandy flew in also, to everyone's delight, although Linda vowed she was never going to fly again as long as she lived. During part of their journey, they had to ride a small commuter plane. Calling it a "puddle-jumping, crop-dusting piece of shit," she said the ride in it was so rocky she was certain they wouldn't make it out of the thing alive. But the sight of the completed church erased thoughts of the horrible flight from her mind and caused tears to cascade down her cheeks. The last time she saw it, it was a mere shell. Now it looked like a regular house of worship, just as she had envisioned when she came four months earlier.

Al had phoned every two to three days since he had left two months ago, and Ammie, Matt, Jay, Warren, and Willie had given him updates, but nothing took the place of being able to view the church with his own eyes. He wouldn't have traded the time he spent on it for anything. The only thing he wished he could change were the mistakes made with the floors—not having the joists spaced close enough and not catching that the wrong wood had been delivered—but the errors had been more than ably corrected, so there was no sense dwelling on it. Now was the time to enjoy their trip there because it might be months, perhaps years, before they were able to return again.

A standing-room-only crowd packed into the church. Jerry Bellune, Stick Harris, Bulldog Yarborough, Sheriff Metts, Tom and Judy Turnipseed, and Matt were among the people there who had been involved since the early days while Al, Linda, Mandy, Jay, Warren, Tommy Lee, Jim, and Al Browder were some whose involvement began within the past few months. Camera crews and reporters from local news stations worked their way through the crowd to cover the event, which began with Willie saying a prayer and Pat pumping out an energetic gospel song on the organ.

Ammie wanted to clap along with everyone else, but a bulky cast ensconced her left wrist and arm. She had fallen a few days before, and her broken arm still throbbed, but she used her good hand to pat her knee to the beat of the music.

Before she came to the podium to give remarks, a long line of people gave theirs. Had it not been for her, each person said, St. John would have never been rebuilt. At the mention of her name, everyone applauded loudly. Ammie sat, soaking in all the love within the crowded sanctuary. She wished Barbara were with her. That's how it all began. Barbara and her.

And that's what she talked about once it was her time to speak. She started the story from the beginning—how Barbara had led her down to St. John nearly fourteen years earlier—and she recounted everything that had happened since. When she said Betsy's name, emotion overwhelmed her, and she broke down and sobbed. Emmala put a comforting arm around her, and after a few minutes that helped her to regain her composure, she finished what she wanted to say. She stepped down to cheering applause.

Rev. Isaac Heyward gave the main address. He used much of it to pay homage to all the volunteers who had worked at the church, but especially to Ammie. "Thank you!" he shouted. "Thank you! Thank you!" He pointed at her as she beamed back at him. "This little powerhouse of a woman! This is God's spiritual and special servant. You are an angel. You are an expression of God. Everywhere you go, a light will shine."

Everyone got to their feet, giving her another standing ovation. Ammie cried again, but this time her tears came from joy.

TWENTY-THREE

There's a Rainbow Waiting

At first, media coverage surrounding St. John had barely registered with me, but it caught the attention of my dad, George Johnson. Like Linda and Al, he and my mom had watched the PBS show *Not in Our Town*. A short while afterward, he read an article in *The State* newspaper about how a tall white Texan was coming from more than a thousand miles away with his family and an interracial crew to help rebuild the church.

Upon finishing the article, Dad couldn't get St. John off his mind or the Texan who was making such a sacrifice. He fell asleep that evening only to wake up with a start about one o'clock the next morning. A dream—a vision—came to him in the night about how he had to help. He woke Mom. "Mary, Mary, get up. We've got to help that church."

"What?" she asked in sleepy confusion.

"That church down in Dixiana—St. John."

Dad went on tell Mom that if a white man was willing to come all the way from Texas to help the black church, surely they could do something. St. John was only about fifteen miles from their house. In addition, Dad was president of the Columbia Travelers at the time, and the club was still in search of a community service project for the year. He was sure other club members would want to help the church, too.

At daylight, he called *The State.* The reporter who wrote the article about Al's arrival gave Dad Ammie's phone number. After mentioning that helping the church would be a great community service project for the Columbia Travelers, he asked Ammie, "What is there left that we might be able to do? We're not a big organization, and we don't have a lot of money. We're just campers, but we'd like to contribute to St. John in any way we can."

She said that there were still a number of things they needed. For one thing, they didn't have any paint or anyone to do the painting.

He responded that he thought the club could buy the paint and volunteer to help with some of the painting. Ammie expressed her thanks over and over and suggested that he contact Al.

After meeting with Al, my father met Ammie for the first time and told her that not only had the Columbia Travelers enthusiastically agreed to buy all the paint, but they also wanted to do every bit of the painting, both the interior and exterior work.

I live only a few miles from my parents, so I frequently drop by to see them. I showed up shortly after Dad returned from St. John one afternoon, and he told me about what a great time they were having volunteering down there. I had often seen him volunteering on various community service projects, but I had never seen him so excited about it before. The camaraderie he and Mom shared with the other volunteers—especially Ammie and Al—created his extraordinary enthusiasm.

He and Mom spoke about painting the church with fellow

Columbia Travelers members as if the work was something they would be willing to pay to do. One of the couples from the club, Ansol and Doris Graham, went so far as to drive their RV to the church and spend the night there so they could start painting the first thing the next morning. Another member, Ernest Curry, helped, although his diabetes had worsened to the point that he was on a waiting list for a kidney transplant. All of that convinced me to spend a day down there, as well. Mom, Dad, Mr. Curry, and his wife, Vernell, and I painted while other volunteers worked outside. Ignorance about what St. John had endured made it appear like just a simple country church in need of volunteers. After spending the day there, I didn't think much about it until a month later when Dad invited me to go to the dedication ceremony with him and Mom.

It was during that ceremony on November 8, 1998, that I finally got to meet Ammie, Al, Linda, Willie, Matt, Jay, Warren, Tom, Judy, and a host of others who had sacrificed money, time, sweat, and tears. I was able to talk to Ammie and the others for only a few minutes, but an idea struck me that St. John's triumph had the makings of a good magazine article.

A week or so following the rededication, I called Ammie, explaining I was George and Mary's daughter and—

"Oh, I love your parents!" she cut in, her voice ragged from what sounded like a bad cold. "They are just the most precious people in the world, and the way they came down to help like they did. I'm just crazy about them."

That took some of the edge off my nervousness. Writing was more of a hobby than a profession at the time, so I wasn't used to calling people for interviews, but Ammie greeted my request with excitement, voicing hope that a magazine article could bring in more help that the church still needed. With the leftover money earmarked for paying the critical insurance premiums, St. John didn't have enough money to buy new pews, among other things. During the ceremony on November 8, we had to sit on mismatched folding metal chairs.

She said that she would have to call me back to arrange a time for the interview once she had gotten over whatever kind of infection she had. She went on to say that the shock of her daughter's death had apparently dealt a severe blow to her immune system. There didn't seem to be a cold or flu virus around that she didn't catch, and once she had it, it was hell shaking it off.

A month passed before she felt well enough for us to meet. Because it was so warm that January day, we carried outside two metal chairs from the sanctuary.

For the next four hours, she told me St. John's story. She had been interviewed on countless occasions, and yet she told the story as if it were the first time. She took me through the horror, anger, fear, joy, sorrows, disappointment, and delight that they had all experienced.

Before we left, she showed me Deacon Roscoe Sulton's grave and the old stump that she loved so dearly. Because of the constant vandalism, almost all the headstones were gone. A sheriff's deputy had found one thrown in the mud alongside the bank of the Congaree, and no one was sure which grave it had come from, so they left it propped against the rear of the church. Most graves were marked with small, unmarked wooden white crosses that Emmala helped to make. Their stark anonymity struck me as both beautiful and sad.

The setting sun took away the last of the afternoon's warmth, and we reluctantly prepared to leave. I stood outside while she reset the church's alarm system and locked up the doors.

We moved down to the wrought-iron gates near the road, and as she struggled to get the padlock back onto them, a truck approached, throwing up a cloud of dust in its wake. Through the dimming light, I made out a scruffy-looking white man at the wheel and felt my mouth go dry. Looking at Ammie, I saw her still fiddling with the gate lock. "I can't get this thing right. I thought it went like this, but—"

"Ammie," I said, trying to remember if I had told anyone where I would be that afternoon and wishing she would hurry up so we could get the hell out of there.

"There!" she said, locking the gates and giving them a satisfied tug, not noticing the relief that washed over me as the truck sped past, the driver barely glancing our way.

She stood upright, and we held each other tight before getting in our cars.

"I love you," Ammie said, kissing me on the cheek.

Normally, I'm a cynic when it comes to people telling me they love me after knowing me for such a brief time, but with her, I knew it was real.

"I love you, too." I was choked by emotion that I didn't understand, but it dissipated after she got into her car and gave me a cheerful wave good-bye.

I worked on the article for several weeks and was disappointed when a magazine that had initially expressed interest in it rejected it. *Reader's Digest* had just run a condensed version of Rick Meyer's 8,200-word piece from the *Los Angeles Times*. That ruined the timing for my article.

I hated to add my news to Ammie's recent disappointment—only a couple of weeks earlier, on April 29, 1999, James Brenner was acquitted of all charges and set free. With no physical evidence linking him to the crime, the prosecutor was forced to build his case around the conflicting testimonies from Roger and Bobby Emerson, who pleaded guilty to reduced charges (accessory after the fact of arson and accessory after the fact of burglary) in exchange for light sentences. The jury, which included an African-American forewoman and two other African Americans, reached the not guilty verdict in about two hours.

I regained some determination once I realized that despite all the TV interviews and newspaper and magazine articles, most of St. John's story still had not been told and never would be except through a full-length book.

Despite Ammie's faltering health, she shared my excitement about the book and helped set up interviews for me. One of the most critical people I needed to contact was Barbara, and yet we couldn't find her. A year and a half had passed since Ammie had last seen her. Knowledge of Barbara and Michael's whereabouts still eluded Willie, as well. Since the caustic divorce, he had had only indirect contact with her and their youngest son through her dad, who accepted Willie's child-support payments and routed them to her.

My search for her resulted in several dead ends, including one at a local high school where someone told me that her youngest son, Michael, attended. Ammie and Willie gave me hope that perhaps one of Barbara's sisters could help me to connect with Barbara. I finally met the sister, Carolyn Summers, during one of my visits to the church, but Carolyn hadn't seen Barbara since their mother's funeral several years earlier. Even at that sad event, fallout from Jonathan's troubles had created so much family discord that Barbara and Carolyn barely spoke to each other.

I continued my search and worried that I would have to finish the book without Barbara's input. Meanwhile, the local PBS affiliate contacted Ammie to participate in a televised audience discussion of the PBS documentary about hate crimes called *Seeking Solutions*. Rev. Jonathan Mouzon and Jesse Young weren't able to come, but Ammie did meet Wanda Mitchum and Sen. John Land at the taping. Tom Turnipseed came, as well. The documentary highlighted how communities in different parts of the country fought against intolerance and hate crime.

The studio audience for the program broke into loud applause when Ammie spoke of St. John and the volunteers who rebuilt it. "The church was founded by slaves, but volunteers came together from all different races and backgrounds. We put aside our differences to work together for the greater good. We all decided that silence is acceptance, and we were not going to be silent anymore. I think that's a big problem in this country—

wc keep our mouths shut and say, 'We can't do anything.' Well, by God, we can!"

Several months after *Seeking Solutions* aired, Ammie called me one evening and barely let me answer the phone before she said, "God, Sandra, I'm so excited, I'm shaking like a leaf. You'll never believe who called me."

"Who?"

"One of the producers for Oprah! They want me to come on the show!"

She didn't have much time to prepare and rushed around in a frenzy to get all the photos and other things the producer needed for a preliminary taping. She had been fighting one of her recurrent colds. It grew worse as her scheduled flight to Chicago drew near, even though she had gone in for medical treatment nearly every day. None of the medicines she tried seemed to be taking hold.

A few days before her scheduled flight, her doctor diagnosed her with pneumonia and told her there was no way she could go anywhere, and indeed, she needed to be hospitalized.

Ammie told him she was determined to go to Chicago and was sure the antibiotic he just prescribed would make her well enough to function.

I asked if there was anything I could do to help, and she asked me to meet her at the airport on the day of her flight to help her with her luggage.

Of course, I agreed, but when I arrived at the airport that day, I couldn't find her. I checked at the baggage counter, then the terminal. No Ammie. I waited at the terminal as the flight began boarding. The ticket agent assured me that although she was booked for the flight, she hadn't checked in.

They finished boarding; then the plane took off.

Worry seized me. The pneumonia—I envisioned her passed out on the bathroom floor of her home. I knew she wouldn't miss going on the show. It would be one of the highlights of her life. I tried calling but only got her answering machine. The only thing I could do was to return home.

I was walking back through the airport when I saw her. Sweat streamed down her face, mixed with her makeup, and dripped onto her jacket. I ran to her, full of relief. She told me how she had lost track of time gathering pictures for the show, and when she arrived, they told her she had missed the flight. Luckily, the airline found her another flight to Chicago that actually put her into the city earlier.

She collapsed on one of the chairs in the terminal, still sick and exhausted from struggling with her suitcase. But no sooner had I helped her dab off her jacket than the flight started boarding.

"I guess you've got to go now," I told her.

"No, I don't. My flight doesn't leave for another hour."

"That's your flight boarding now."

She looked at her watch in confusion. "It can't be. It's only eleven o'clock."

"No, it's twelve."

"Sandra, it's eleven. Look at my watch." She held out her wrist for me to see it.

"You forgot to set back the time!"

The time had changed the day before, but in her rush, Ammie had forgotten about it.

As she realized this, her mouth dropped open, and she looked at me in amazement. "Well, I'll be doggone. I could have missed this flight, too. My Lord, it's a miracle I'm here!"

I helped her up, and she started off toward the ticket counter, but then I remembered something.

"Hold on, Ammie." I took my camera out. "Let me get your picture."

Although she had endured a frantic morning and felt like hell, she turned and smiled. I had never seen her look more beautiful.

Her appearance on the show completely amazed me. She and Oprah sat side by side onstage talking as if they were longtime next-door neighbors. After viewing a taped segment that dramatically highlighted Ammie's role in St. John's resurrection, Oprah said to Ammie, "I heard you tell the producer that your feet wanted you to leave, but your heart wouldn't let you."

"That's true, Oprah." Ammie nodded in emphasis.

"What makes you keep getting up when you often feel so defeated?"

"I had to. There was no choice. You know, we can sit around and say how sad something is that these things happen and wish something could be done about it, but each of us in our own way can do something. I didn't know how to rebuild a church, but I darn well knew how to raise some Cain and to make some phone calls and a few other things. I had to keep going. I just had to."

She screamed in delighted surprise when Oprah revealed that the show had flown in Pete Critsimilios, the Brooklyn firefighter whose letter and gift of one hundred Bibles meant so much to her. Although they had spoken by phone, they had never met. He descended from his seat into her outstretched arms as the audience gave them a standing ovation. Clutching him with one arm, Ammie used her other hand to wipe away joyful tears.

"I just want the world to know how proud I am that I'm your friend," Pete told her once they sat down. "You're a shining example of what's good and decent and right in this world, and you've inspired me and a lot of other people to look inside and say, 'What do I stand for? What can I do?' I'm just proud to be here with you. God bless you."

The show ended with BeBe Winans performing a song titled "Stand" to Ammie and other guests who spoke about people standing up courageously for what they believe in. I couldn't think of any song more appropriate for Ammie.

———

Her being on the show was a dream come true for Ammie, me, and everyone else involved with St. John. Calls flooded in to her, some from complete strangers, some from people too moved to speak—they just cried uncontrollably. I hoped one of the calls would be from Barbara, as we had not been able to find her. But none of them were.

Still miserably sick, Ammie went from one medical appointment to another for examinations and more tests to determine why she hadn't recovered.

Upon arriving home one day, I received a call from Viola Robinson—wife of St. John's pastor, Roosevelt Robinson. She told me Ammie had been rushed to the hospital earlier that afternoon. Further tests revealed lung cancer and a tumor lodged in her heart.

I found her in a room across from the nurses' station. She looked so small in the hospital bed, like a little girl lying on her parents' bed. Her hair that she always meticulously styled now hung limply about her face.

"Hey, Sandra," she greeted me as I walked in and reached out to hug her. "I've got a dramatic new ending for the book—" A cough rattled through her; then she slowly swept her hand across from left to right as if underscoring a large news headline that materialized in front of her. "—Ammie dies."

"Don't you say that." I embraced her. "You're like a cat with nine lives, and you've still got a few lives left in reserve. Look what you've already come through. The doctors don't have the last word. Only God does."

"Well, you're right about that," Ammie said, and sat up straighter in the hospital bed.

It struck me that more of the fight was coming back to her. She told me the specialists would determine what kind of treatment she needed after doing more tests, but she suspected that she would have to go through chemotherapy and radiation. She planned to move in with Emmala until she was well enough to return home. Her hairdresser and best friend, Doris Nelson, had already said she would check her mail and feed her beloved little dog, Casey Baby.

Doris arrived about an hour after I had. "How's my bestest friend in the whole wide world?" she asked. That drew a bit of a smile from Ammie and from me, too. Doris cherished her friendship with Ammie so much that she even frequently introduced herself to complete strangers as "Ammie's bestest friend in the whole wide world."

She had joined St. John because of Ammie. Although several other whites had become members, Doris was the only one who regularly attended. She had been elected church treasurer and was an usher along with Mrs. Rosa Bell Eleazar. I found it heartening that Doris had been the first person baptized at the church after it was rebuilt in 1998.

As the weeks passed, Ammie's illness took her and all of us who loved her on a roller-coaster ride. One day she would be sitting up in bed relishing her copy of the premier edition of Oprah's *O* magazine, cracking jokes, and drinking milkshakes people brought in; the next day she was barely able to catch her breath and too weak to stand without help.

Mom, Dad, and I traveled to Texas so I could interview Al and Linda. While at the Hoelschers' home, I called Ammie, and over the din of laughter and talking in her hospital room, she told me the aggressive regimen of chemotherapy and radiation she had started was taking effect. The oncologist told Emmala and Christy earlier that day that one of the tumors had nearly disappeared and another one was shrinking. She would probably be discharged before we made it back home.

As if that weren't good enough, Ammie had more good news. "I saw Barbara. She and Robin came by the hospital today."

"You're kidding!"

"I told her how we've been looking for her and how you needed to talk to her. She said she wants us to get together once I'm out of the hospital."

She did not find out much about where Barbara had been or what had been going on with her, but that all fell to the wayside at the joy of seeing her old friend.

When we returned to Columbia, Ammie was still hospitalized but was released a few days later and went to Emmala's. The first time we visited her there, Ammie gave us all a big laugh when she insisted on modeling her new wig, even though radiation hadn't affected her hair much. I teased her about looking like one of those big-haired country divas, but she just patted the thing, saying she was going to wear it after she got well because all she had to do was swish it around in the sink, shake it dry, put it on, and go.

She arranged for Barbara and me to meet her at Emmala's.

When I picked Barbara up, she apologized over and over about being so hard to track down, though no apology was necessary. She said that she had only recently returned from North Carolina. It was through a chance meeting with an acquaintance that she learned Ammie was sick and in the hospital.

The three of us spent the afternoon on Emmala's screen patio overlooking a serene lake. It was only after Barbara vividly described her years at St. John that I could fully appreciate how important it had been to find her. She filled in gaps in the overall story that I hadn't realized existed, especially concerning the years leading up to the involvement of Ammie and the other volunteers.

Ammie insisted on sitting up with us, though her health had grown worse over the last few days, and she was occasionally seized by fits of coughing. Barbara and I cautioned her against wearing herself out. The love the two women had for each other was palpable, and they reminded me of two elderly sisters who had never spent a day apart. At times, they even finished each other's sentences.

As the sun began its descent toward the horizon, we all looked at the lake, taking in its quiet beauty and remarking on what a lovely day it had been. Barbara turned back to her friend. "We're sisters, Miss Ammie, you and me. We're like salt and pepper. We season each other."

Returning her loving gaze, Ammie said, "You're right about that, Barbara."

A few weeks after our afternoon together, Emmala and Christy had a cookout at the house. The reason for it was more purposeful than simple entertainment. Emmala needed to go out of town for a week, and Christy had to return to her home in Texas for about two weeks. Ammie was too ill to remain alone. Emmala and Christy asked everyone willing to volunteer to care for Ammie to come to the cookout so that a round-the-clock respite schedule could be worked out.

So many of us came that some people had to sit cross-legged on the floor. When I didn't spot Ammie amongst the crowd, Mom told me she wanted to stay in her bedroom to work on something while we arranged the schedule and got instructions from Christy as to what medications her mom was on, how to give them, who to call in case of an emergency, and so on.

Ammie emerged from her bedroom, wobbling slightly as she walked over to us. Her breathing had deteriorated to where she required an oxygen tank and the clear plastic tubing feeding the oxygen into her nostrils trailed her like a long umbilical cord. She clutched some papers. We gathered around her on the patio after she said she wanted to tell us something.

"I was in the doctor's office when I saw this on the wall," she said, indicating one of the colored papers she held. "I thought it was so good and I asked the receptionist if she would make me a copy, and she did. I wanted each of y'all to have one as some way for me to thank you for what you're doing for me—" Her voice broke, and she leaned against her grandson, Scott, who was now a college freshman and stood more than a foot taller than she did. "Oh, God, I swore I wouldn't start crying," she said as tears seeped out.

We all offered words of comfort and told her go ahead and have a good cry.

But she didn't. She wiped the tears away and read from the paper:

Lessons from Noah
Much of what you really need to know about life is in the story of Noah's Ark:

1. Don't miss the boat.
2. Don't forget we're all in the same boat.
3. Plan ahead. It wasn't raining when Noah built the Ark.
4. Stay fit. When you're six hundred years old, someone may ask you to do something really big.
5. Don't listen to critics. Just get on with what has to be done.
6. For safety's sake, travel in pairs.
7. Two heads are better than one.
8. Build your future on high ground.
9. Speed isn't always an advantage. After all, the snails were on the same Ark with the cheetahs.
10. When you're stressed, float awhile.
11. Remember the Ark was built by amateurs. The *Titanic* was built by professionals.
12. Remember the woodpeckers inside are a larger threat than the storm outside.
13. No matter the storm, there's a rainbow waiting.

She appeared to feel better with each item she read, and by the time she finished, she was laughing along with us, her good spirits restored. She passed copies to us, and at the bottom of each one, she wrote: "You have my eternal love and gratitude.

Regardless of the trials and tribulations which may lie ahead—please remember this and keep the thirteenth lesson from Noah in your heart always!!!"

After Emmala returned, she and her daughters and their children took Ammie down to the beach, where they had a rented condo. They stayed for a week, and Ammie called me the night she got back in town. She sounded awful. Each time she took a breath, it sounded like air leaking from a tire. I thought she should call her home health nurse, but she said she was just exhausted from the trip and needed rest. She didn't protest, however, when I told her I would call the next night to check up on her.

I called her the following night but got no answer. Doris phoned a couple of hours later to say they had admitted Ammie back in the hospital right after she had spoken to me the night before.

The next day, Mom and I found her in her hospital room watching the *Antiques Road Show* with Emmala and speculating about whether any of the things they had gathering dust were actually valuable treasures.

Glancing at the TV for the next appraisal, she took a sip from her milkshake, one of her favorite foods. Although her face was splotchy, her breathing was steady and she spoke with ease.

I knew she was feeling better when she good-naturedly fussed with her nurse and complained that her oxygen mask was uncomfortable, but moments later she spoke about her life as if little of it remained.

Mom took her hand and held it in both of hers. "You've had a good life, Ammie."

"I've went through some tough times," she said, looking up at my mother.

"And you'll come through this, too."

"I don't know, Mary." A wistful look clouded her face. "You get tired sometimes."

I came down with a bad cold the next day, and I called Ammie and told her that I would visit as soon as I was sure it wouldn't spread to her. She expressed worry about me, but I felt more alarmed for her as she spoke. Once again, her breath sounded ragged and wheezy. We spoke for only another minute before I told her I didn't want to tire her with too much talk and that she needed to get some rest.

"I love you," I told her before we hung up.

"I love you, too, darlin'."

My cold symptoms eased up enough for a trip to the grocery store, and I planned to go to the hospital later that afternoon. I was in the middle of the cereal aisle when my pager went off. It was Emmala. In a shaky voice, she said, "Things aren't looking too good here in the hospital. If you want to say good-bye to Ammie Jean, you'd better hurry."

As I sped down the highway, I tried to get into an argument with God, but He wasn't having any of it. "Why?" I questioned. "Why does it have to be Ammie? Why does she have to die at sixty-seven when a racist like Horace King gets to live to be a hundred?"

From somewhere, I didn't so much hear, but feel a response. "If Horace King lives to be one hundred, he'll still never know the love she experienced. He'll still die a bitter and angry man."

Another answer came. Perhaps Ammie had lived a hundred years; she had simply packed them all into sixty-seven.

I worried that I wouldn't make it to the hospital in time. I had taken about two minutes to call my parents' home. Dad answered saying Mom was out running errands but that he would leave for the hospital immediately. I hated that Mom would probably get the news too late—she loved Ammie as much as Dad and I did.

I found a parking space right in front of the hospital, bolted from my car, and ran through the main corridor into one of the elevators. The seconds that felt like hours passed and the elevator doors opened onto the eighth floor—the oncology floor. I burst out of the elevator and raced down the hallways, but slowed as I got to Ammie's room—I heard more than a dozen people reciting the Lord's prayer in unison. The way they were saying it made me feel that I was too late, and I had barely walked in when a lady I didn't know leaned back and whispered to me what I thought sounded like, "She's gone."

"Oh, God," I moaned, and leaned over onto a closet door, but the different angle gave me a clearer view to see that, though she was barely hanging on, she was still alive. Within the crowded room, I was amazed to see my mom and wondered how she had known to come then. I was even more amazed that after Mom made her way through several people to reach Ammie and a tearful Christy said, "Mom, look, Mary's here," Ammie replied slowly, "Hey, Mary."

Her voice came out strangely gurgled, as if coming from the bottom of a well, but I could understand her perfectly and could barely believe that as she lay on her deathbed, she was still conscious.

Taking Ammie's hand between hers the way she always did, Mom told her that she loved her. I noticed people softly crying and passing around a box of tissue as I weaved through the crowd to Ammie's bedside and stood beside Mom.

Christy, nearly overcome with grief, told Ammie, "And here's Sandra, too."

I stroked her thinning hair, something I had never done before, and was surprised by how soft it was. I suddenly felt at a loss for words with someone that I used to talk with for hours on end. The only thing I could think of to say was, "Ammie, I love you more than you'll ever know."

I didn't understand how I could say it without crying as everyone else in the room was. Her eyes remained closed, and her breathing came out in ragged gurgles as her small chest rose and fell. Warren Smith shook his head as he turned toward the window and wiped his eyes. "She's not going to be able to last much longer," he whispered to me and Mom.

But when Dad made it to the room a few moments later and Christy announced his presence to Ammie, she distinctly said, "Hey, George." Her voice came from farther away this time, and the rise and fall of her chest were further apart. Removing his cap and gently kissing her forehead, Dad told her he loved her and then moved back against the wall.

Rita Reif, the *New York Times* reporter, stood at the foot of her bed as if she were a sentinel. She had arrived straight from the airport only an hour or so earlier, and her suitcase was set at her feet. I was grateful that she had not taken time to check in at a hotel first.

I doubted if anyone had been able to get in touch with Barbara. She didn't have an answering machine and was normally away from home during the day. For a moment, sadness fell over me because she wasn't there to say good-bye, but then I realized that in her own special way, she had done so that afternoon on Emmala's patio.

Emmala took Ammie's hands, which were turning a light shade of blue, into her own. Ammie opened her eyes for the first time that I had seen that day and looked intently into those of her younger sister.

Just when I thought Ammie had taken her last breath, she took another one. We watched Christy exchange places with Emmala so that she could look directly at Ammie. "Momma, I love you," she said, struggling for enough composure to speak. "Tell Betsy "hi" for me when you see her. Tell her I love her."

The tears that I wondered why I had not shed now poured down. I found myself standing beside Jim Spearman, who had helped build St. John. Although we didn't know each other well, he put an arm around me, and we held each other as we cried.

It struck me that Ammie was holding on for those on their way to the hospital. Doris, who had been at work when she got the call, was the next to the last one to come in. "I'm here, Ammie, your bestest friend in the whole wide world."

I gathered enough strength to let go of Jim and join Mom as she moved over to Dad, who leaned against the wall in silence. As I huddled against the wall with my parents, our arms wrapped around one another, I pressed the side of my face against Dad's chest, thankful for his steady heartbeat and the strong rhythm of his breathing.

Ammie's breathing suddenly grew rapid and shallow, as if she were panting. Rev. Jeff Lewis entered the room and reached her bedside. A tall African-American man with warm brown eyes and a rich voice filled with compassion, he had gotten to know Ammie through his wife, who had been one of Ammie's physicians. In the course of his visits with her, he had helped her prepare spiritually for what was to come. He told us that Ammie had confided to him that while she felt at peace about dying, she worried about how all of us who she had to leave behind would cope.

"But she can go in peace now and know that we will be okay. We have assurance that she will be with God and that through faith, we will see her again." He opened his Bible and read Psalm 46:

God is our refuge and strength, an ever-present help in trouble. Therefore we will not fear, though the earth give way and the mountains fall into the heart of the sea, though its waters roar and foam and the mountains quake with their surging.

There is a river whose streams make glad the city of God, the holy place where the Most High dwells. God is within her, and she will not fall; God will help her at break of day. Nations are in uproar, kingdoms fall; he lifts his voice, the earth melts.

The Lord Almighty is with us; the God of Jacob is our fortress.

Come and see the works of the Lord, the desolations he had brought on the earth. He makes wars cease to the ends of the earth; he breaks and shatters the spears, he burns the shields with fire. Be still and know that I am God; I will be exalted among the nations, I will be exalted in the earth. The Lord Almighty is with us; the God of Jacob is our fortress.

After he closed his Bible, Ammie took in her last breath. On that warm summer day—August 5, 2000—she died as she lived, surrounded by young and old, rich and poor, black and white. Her love for us—and ours for her—had made us one.

After her funeral, a memorial service was held at St. John. Nearly one hundred of us packed into the sanctuary, including a film crew from a local news station. Emmala's pastor officiated and opened the service with song, then offered the podium to anyone who wished to share special memories of Ammie. I listened as her family and friends, including Emmala, Christy, and my mom, spoke, but I remained seated, fearing that if I got to the microphone, I wouldn't be able to do anything but sob.

Something pulled me to my feet, however, and compelled me to go to the microphone. Taking a deep breath, I said, "Please, y'all pray for me so I have the strength to say what I need to." I was embarrassed that my voice quavered a little, but I noticed heads nodding, and that gave me strength.

"As I sat listening to y'all, I thought back to when Ammie died. I consider myself blessed to have been one of the people in the room with her. When I walked in, there were people that I didn't know. There were a lot of people who didn't know each other, but even though Ammie was dying, she was still working."

Feeling stronger, I went on, "She was pulling us together. We were holding on to one another, crying together, supporting each other. We were young. We were old. We were black. We were white. Rich. Poor. It didn't matter. We were together, and it was because of Ammie. She's at work in this church now; just look around here." I gazed down upon the vast diversity of faces. "It's the same thing. Ammie's work continues."

And it does.

EPILOGUE

In the course of a year, hundreds of compelling people appear on *Oprah*. However, only a small number are selected to have their stories updated. In early December of 2000, Christy came on the show to talk about her mother's death and living legacy. The program was broadcast on January 14, 2001, in commemoration of Martin Luther King's birthday.

Seated next to Oprah, Christy recounted a conversation she and Ammie had during the cookout at Emmala's. "Do you see all those people out there?" Ammie said as the two of them peered into the den. It was fast filling up with people responding to the call for volunteers to care for Ammie during the week that Emmala and Christy had to be away. "Every one of them is there because of St. John."

It had been through St. John that most of us in the den, myself included, had met Ammie. But we grew to love her because of her courageous compassion and indomitable spirit. Her inspirational qualities were evident not only to those of us who knew her well, but also to those who had met her only once. Jack Mori, one of the producers for *Oprah,* told Christy that Ammie had been one of the most extraordinary people he had ever seen on the show.

While hospitalized, Ammie asked me to call him so that he, the rest of the staff, and Oprah would be aware of her serious illness. "They were so sweet and kind to me," I remembered her saying. "I want them to know what's going on."

I left the message concerning her condition on Jack's voice mail, although I didn't have the heart to tell Ammie that they probably treated all guests as nicely as they had her and chances were he wouldn't have the slightest memory of her. Little did I know that after getting the message, he and several others on the production staff gathered into a circle, held hands, and prayed for her.

I also didn't know that I would soon see Ammie every time I watched the program during that television season. Her joyous surprise as she embraced Pete "The Greek" Critsimilios was included in a medley of images shown during the introduction of each show.

Christy told Oprah that no significant vandalism had occurred at St. John since its rebuilding, and I am glad to report that, as of this date, that remains true. The congregation is still small. I can't remember a regular Sunday service with more than twenty-five people in attendance, but about half are school-age children or young adults, and their youthful presence holds promise that the church will live on into the future.

Most of the people in this book have successfully weathered the daunting challenges chronicled throughout these pages along with other tough times. Although he continues to be rail-thin, Matt regained his health and devotes much of his renewed energy to being a doting grandfather, dedicated church member, and occasional fisherman.

John O'Leary found that his position as director of the state's Criminal Justice Academy became much more tenuous after he campaigned for a Democratic gubernatorial candidate who ultimately lost to a Republican rival. He left the agency in 1988 and now has a thriving law practice.

Butch Spires scaled back his political activities, but he stays busy with his family, career, and numerous volunteer activities.

Jerry Bellune dutifully publishes the *Lexington County Chronicle* every week, and Tom and Judy Turnipseed continue fighting for social justice at every opportunity.

Despite others wanting him to pursue higher positions, such as director of the State Law Enforcement Division, Sheriff James Metts loves the job he has held for more than thirty years and has no interest in leaving it. James "Stick" Harris earned a promotion to the rank of major and has kept up the Halloween stakeouts at St. John. A heart attack forced Darryl "Bulldog" Yarborough to leave the department, but he works part-time as a real estate agent and does occasional investigative work for Solicitor Donnie Myers.

The church fires in Clarendon County cost Sheriff Collins his job. Many county residents pointed to the Klan rallies as being the foundation for the hate crimes, and Collins could not make them understand that the First Amendment prevented him from telling the Klan that they could not hold such events. He lost his bid for reelection but harbors no bitterness. He found a part-time job with a phone company and enjoys having less stress and more time for family.

Shortly after news of the lawsuit spread, Rev. Jonathan Mouzon discovered that he was scheduled to work every Sunday morning at his second job as a security guard supervisor. In all the years he had been with the company, he had not been asked to work Sundays because everyone knew of his church obligations. No one else's schedule had been changed.

He went to his supervisor. "I'll work any day and any time except Sunday morning. If I can't be there then, I won't be able to work here anymore."

His boss replied that he would see what he could do.

When the new schedule was posted, Reverend Mouzon saw he had to work the next eight Sunday mornings. He turned in his resignation. Fortunately, Macedonia had grown so much under his leadership that he is ministering there full-time.

Reverend Mackey was promoted to a larger AME church in Charleston, where he spearheaded the formation of the National Coalition for Burned Churches, an organization that provides prevention education, referral services, and political advocacy related to church arsons.

Jesse Young retired from the sheriff's department and bought a convenience store in Bloomville. Romeo is a frequent customer. His sentence was reduced to sixteen months because of his assistance to prosecutors. Arthur Haley, Herbert Rowell, Chris Cox, and Tim Welch remain in federal prisons.

Wanda Mitchum's life took a difficult turn a year and a half after Macedonia won its lawsuit. While trying to defend herself against her husband, Aaron, during one of their violent fights, the shotgun he wielded accidentally went off, blasting buckshot pellets into his chest. He died a few days later. Wanda has since struggled with grief and depression.

Although they continue to do volunteer labor for Habitat for Humanity and other charitable causes, Al and Linda Hoelscher closed down their roofing business. They decided that long-distance trucking offered more financial stability, so Al bought an eighteen-wheeler and crisscrosses the country. He delights us with a visit whenever he is in South Carolina.

Every so often, Barbara would call me or I would drop by her small rented house. Her valiant efforts to spruce it up didn't disguise that it was a dark, dingy place in a run-down neighborhood. Once she mentioned that while she had seen the outside of St. John since it had been rebuilt in 1998, she had never been inside.

That bothered me, and I told her so. "You're a big reason that the church is standing today. You and Ammie started it all.

I wish you could see it. It's beautiful and you would be welcomed. No one holds anything against you, especially Willie. He's only spoken well of you."

Her eyes grew wide. "You're kidding!"

"No, I'm not." Indeed, I think he would have been the first to greet her warmly.

"I'm going to go there one day, Sandra, but I won't say when. I'm not going to tell anybody. When I come, everybody will be real surprised."

She never did go, at least the way she expected to. She died February 28, 2001, less than seven months after Ammie. Doris Nelson called me with the news. It took several moments for the information to pierce through my shock. I had seen Barbara just the previous month. She mentioned that she had recently gotten over a bad case of the flu, but was feeling great and looked that way, too.

But shortly afterward, pneumonia hit her hard. She ended up in on life support in Lexington Medical Center's intensive care unit. In addition to her lungs, the infection ravaged her heart until it finally quit beating that winter's day. She had been only fifty-four years old.

Over one hundred of us packed into St. John for her funeral. I saw many people who had worked alongside her and Ammie from the earliest days: Matt, John O'Leary, Jerry Bellune, Rev. Isaac Heyward, and others. Willie did his best to comfort family and friends.

He joined us as we accompanied her out to the cemetery where she was buried not far from Deacon Sulton. The sun shone brightly and birds sang from amidst the pines as they lowered her into the earth. She had returned at last.

—Sandra E. Johnson
July 30, 2001

ACKNOWLEDGMENTS

I thank God for leading me to this story, and my deepest appreciation goes out to my family for their love and support, especially to my dad for his compassion, to my mom for her belief in the power of dreams, and to my sister, Helena, for her insightful feedback.

My editor, Alicia Brooks, has been a guiding light throughout writing *Standing on Holy Ground*, and had it not been for my wonderfully talented agent, Neeti Madan, this book never would have become a reality.

I will be forever indebted to Glenda Howard and Claudia Smith Brinson for opening doors of opportunity that I had not thought imaginable.

Thanks also to fellow members of the South Carolina Writers' Workshop, particularly Carrie Allen McCray, Carol Williams, Carol Guthrie Heilman, Betsy Taylor Thorne, and Carole Rothstein for their encouragement, and to Bonny C. Millard for listening to me talk on and on about the joys and occasional frustrations of being a writer.

The staff members at both the University of South Carolina's Caroliniana Library and the Richland County Public Library have shown me what true job dedication is all about. They went above and beyond the call of duty in assisting me in research, especially Debbie Bloom with the Richland County Public Library. After I had left the library and nearly drove away, she came running out of the building and down the street to tell me that she had finally found some crucial information that I had given up hope of obtaining.

I received tremendous support from the *Lexington County Chronicle* and *The State* newspapers and wish to extend special thanks to Kim Kim Foster with *The State*'s photography department. I am also grateful to Carol LeFebvre for providing court transcript of *Macedonia Baptist Church* v. *Christian Knights of the Ku Klux Klan, et al.*

My month's residency at Hambidge Center in Rabun Gap, Georgia, was invaluable. The serene solitude of my mountain cabin near the beginning (or end, depending on where you start) of the Appalachian Trail was exactly what I needed to have uninterrupted time to write.

I have been blessed by the spiritual nurturing from fellow members of Eastwood Baptist Church, notably the Young Women's Sunday School Class.

Words cannot adequately express my thankfulness to St. John Baptist Church for enveloping me with so much love that I consider St. John to be my other home church.

And finally, writing this book would not have been possible without the dozens of people who cumulatively spent hundreds of hours with me in interviews. Along with providing critical recollections, documents, and photographs, they opened their homes and hearts to me. May God bless each of them.